ADVANCE PRAISE FOR *THE CARROT AND THE STICK*

"This book is a must-read if you want to compete and win in the markets of today and tomorrow. Success requires understanding how to think in both win-lose and win-win ways. William Putsis lays out a rigorous framework with clever real-world examples to help understand how sustainable profits depend upon ownership of strategic points of control and win-win incentives along the value chain."

Ravi Dhar, Director, Yale Center for Customer Insights, George Rogers Clark Professor of Management and Marketing, Yale University

"After reading *The Carrot and the Stick*, you will start to look at everyday situations differently. William Putsis provides a compelling narrative across industries and time periods showing how considering strategic control points can swing business outcomes. William Putsis's role as a strategic advisor to many global brand-name corporations allows him to go beyond what would otherwise be theory and academic and connect it to the practitioner."

Michael Lohnert, Managing Director, Boeing HorizonX Ventures

"I especially appreciated that *The Carrot and the Stick* did not `talk at me' with a series of lessons, but through simple exercises guided me to explore and discover what will make our own unique businesses more valuable. Providing more than just the `what' and the 'why,' William Putsis most importantly lays out the `how' of executing a value creation strategy based on building critical importance to customers."

Terry Theodore, Partner, Center Rock Capital Partners

"In his first book, *Compete Smarter, Not Harder*, William Putsis presents a process to strategically prioritize market opportunities. In *The Carrot and the Stick*, he follows up on this by extending the concept of strategic control to multiple market opportunities. We have found his process to be instrumental to the success we have been having in growing our markets and to our move to adjacent market opportunities. Highly recommend the book to anyone interested in growing their business."

Keith E. Williams, President, Chief Executive Officer, and Trustee, Underwriters Laboratories Inc.

WILLIAM PUTSIS

The Carrot and the Stick

Leveraging Strategic Control for Growth

UNIVERSITY OF TORONTO PRESS
Toronto Buffalo London

© University of Toronto Press 2020
Rotman-UTP Publishing
University of Toronto Press
Toronto Buffalo London
utorontopress.com
Printed in Canada

ISBN 978-1-4875-0165-5 (cloth)   ISBN 978-1-4875-1369-6 (EPUB)
                                   ISBN 978-1-4875-1368-9 (PDF)

Library and Archives Canada Cataloguing in Publication

Title: The carrot and the stick : leveraging strategic control for growth /
    William Putsis.
Names: Putsis, William, 1959– author.
Description: Includes bibliographical references.
Identifiers: Canadiana 20190172886 | ISBN 9781487501655 (hardcover)
Subjects: LCSH: Strategic planning. | LCSH: Business planning.
Classification: LCC HD30.28 .P88 2019 | DDC 658.4/012—dc23

University of Toronto Press acknowledges the financial assistance to its
publishing program of the Canada Council for the Arts and the Ontario Arts
Council, an agency of the Government of Ontario.

Canada Council   Conseil des Arts
for the Arts   du Canada

ONTARIO ARTS COUNCIL
CONSEIL DES ARTS DE L'ONTARIO
an Ontario government agency
un organisme du gouvernement de l'Ontario

Funded by the   Financé par le
Government   gouvernement
of Canada   du Canada | Canadä

MIX
Paper from
responsible sources
FSC® C016245

In memory of my parents, who always taught me the importance of learning

Contents

Figures and Tables

Figures

Tables

Preface

We so often spend our time thinking about how we can move the pieces on the chessboard to our advantage when what we really need to be doing is moving the board . . .

A New Moment in History

This is arguably the most exciting time – ever – to be in business. We are experiencing sweeping changes worldwide that are affecting business today in ways that we have never seen before – and providing once-in-a-lifetime business opportunities. Furthermore, the speed and magnitude of the changes are unprecedented – the dissemination of information via the internet has fundamentally changed the way firms compete and win. To illustrate, contemplate the following:

In less than five years, RIM (now BlackBerry) went from having a higher market share of the smartphone market than Apple and Samsung combined to a market share of less than 1 percent.[1] Such rapid change is unprecedented.

---

1 It is also worth noting that the global market share of the RIM / Blackberry Operating System (OS) went from 20.6 percent in Q1 2009 to just 0.72 percent in Q4 2013. Sources for these statistics: IDC, "Global Market Share Held by Leading Smartphone Vendors from 4th Quarter 2009 to 4th Quarter 2018," *Statista – The Statistics*

The Renaissance and the Industrial Revolution.
Michelangelo, da Vinci, Vanderbilt, and Rockefeller

We look back on periods of expansion like the Renaissance or the Industrial Revolution and imagine them as exciting times with world-expanding possibilities wherein giants of culture and titans of industry changed our world. As Bill Gates once said, "We always overestimate the change that will occur in the next two years and underestimate the change that will occur in the next ten."[2] Today, the pace of change is so fast that it's hard to *overestimate*.

At some point in the future, people will look back on today and view this as the greatest period of expansion and opportunity in the history of the planet – and a time like no other in the world of business. To understand why, think back to the early days of the internet and the "dot.com" period of the late 1990s. The claim then was that the internet would transform our lives, and instant communication (e.g., email) would transform our productivity. However, while many have indeed worked harder with 24/7 connectivity, the impact on innovation, productivity, and opportunity often hasn't mirrored the hope and the hype.

Interconnectedness. Ubiquity. Always on. Mobility

One of the central reasons is that applications and users were often "stand alone." For example, when we used to create a Microsoft Word file and email it to a colleague, we often needed to do it while chained to an Ethernet-wired desk; similarly, while we may have

---

Portal, Statista: www.statista.com/statistics/271496/global-market-share-held-by-smartphone-vendors-since-4th-quarter-2009/, accessed 5 March 2019. For an article on Blackberry falling below 1 percent, see Carly Page, "Blackberry's Global Market Share Shrinks to Less than One Percent," *The Inquirer*, 31 July 2014: http://www.theinquirer.net/inquirer/news/2358108/blackberry-s-global-market-share-shrinks-to-less-than-one-percent.

2 Source: http://www.brainyquote.com/quotes/quotes/b/billgates404193.html.

calculated forecasts using an Excel spreadsheet or SAS® database, the data weren't linked to other parts of the production process. Thus, our work, at our desk, wasn't fully available in real time.

The combination of "interconnectedness," "ubiquity," "always on," and "mobility" today has brought multiple devices, forms of production, platforms, and huge data/analytical capabilities together to fundamentally transform business – in ways we have never seen before and probably will never see again in our lifetimes. This is a time when someone in a remote village can write an app that becomes a multimillion-dollar business, and a student writing code in a dorm room can become one of the richest people on the planet. The "industrial internet," sensors, interoperable devices in our homes and factories, advanced robotics, artificial intelligence, and 3D printers are just starting to transform the nature of production, distribution, finance, and business strategy. To illustrate, we are expected to have more than 50 billion connected devices in 2020,[3] and IDC forecasts that the worldwide market for "internet of things" (IoT) solutions will be $7.1 trillion in 2020. Cisco estimates that the economic value created by the "internet of things" will be $19 trillion in 2020.[4]

Jobs, Zuckerberg, Musk, Bezos, Brin, Schmidt, Gates

Google was once "just" a search engine; however, now it is poised to be dominant elsewhere – in internet advertising, mobile phones, television, internet provision, and maps, for example. We no longer exclusively book hotel rooms through the usual hotel brands but

---

3   Source: Vala Afshar, "Cisco: Enterprises Are Leading the Internet of Things Innovation," *Huffington Post*, 28 August 2017: https://www.huffingtonpost.com/entry/cisco-enterprises-are-leading-the-internet-of-things_us_59a41fcee4b0a62d0987b0c6.

4   Source: Gil Press, "Internet of Things by the Numbers: Market Estimates and Forecasts," *Forbes.com*, 22 August 2014: https://www.forbes.com/sites/gilpress/2014/08/22/internet-of-things-by-the-numbers-market-estimates-and-forecasts/#6a893772b919; see also McKinsey & Company, McKinsey Global Institute, "Digital America: A Tale of the Haves and Have-Mores," December 2015.

rent rooms or private apartments from Airbnb; we no longer hail taxis but "rent" rides from companies such as Uber or Lyft; and we increasingly rent cars as we need them, by the hour, through companies like Zipcar. Olli, an offering by Local Motors, will even pick you up (like Uber) in a driverless bus powered by IBM's Watson – and the list goes on. Just think about the fact that "Uber, the world's largest taxi company, owns no vehicles. Facebook, the world's most popular media owner, creates no content. Alibaba, the most valuable retailer, has no inventory. And Airbnb, the world's largest accommodations provider, owns no real estate."[5]

However, there is often a fine line between success and failure. Just think about the following:[6]

- There were more than 17,000 "YouTubes" before YouTube.
- There were 18 web search services before Google – some quite similar to Google.
- Net2Phone launched the year before Skype.
- Friendster (and many others) came before Facebook.

So, what's so different about today? And why do some succeed while others fail?

An Illustration of What's New about Today

Imagine being a manufacturer of "white goods" (i.e., washing machines, dryers, and refrigerators). For most of your career, you have competed on a combination of cost, distribution, sales, and features – the latter ranging from the "beautiful" avocado colors of the 1970s to the more recent stainless-steel finishes. You may segment your market and have a range of offerings, lines, and prices to match

---

5 Source: Tom Goodwin writing for Tech Crunch: https://techcrunch.com/2015/03/03/in-the-age-of-disintermediation-the-battle-is-all-for-the-customer-interface/.
6 Source: http://thenextweb.com/boris/2013/10/28/17000-youtubes-youtube/#gref.

differing budgets and preferences. Your entire career may have been spent on competing in the value chain, working the production system (to gain advantage on the cost side), and working the sales teams (to compete in a consolidating retail environment) – all in an attempt to squeeze margin inside an intensely competitive industry.

However, in the early 2000s, white goods manufacturers were salivating over the prospect of charging huge margins on "internet-enabled" devices (i.e., refrigerators and other similar devices that would be connected to the internet via touchscreens on the devices). This connection could, for example, enable users to control the devices while away from home – and order food items to complete recipes. However, although manufacturers could potentially extract huge margins for these new internet-enabled devices, they ran into at least a couple of major obstacles. First, customers didn't flock to the devices when they were introduced. There simply wasn't enough benefit – smartphones didn't have a huge penetration yet, so connecting to the appliances remotely was difficult. Besides, what exactly would you do with your refrigerator when away from home anyway? Second, once smartphones and tablets began to pervade the market, any functionality offered by your internet-enabled fridge could be replicated – with a great deal of additional functionality and mobility. So, why in the world would anyone need an internet-enabled refrigerator?

Fast forward to 2020.

Imagine a world where the objects around us can talk to each other.[7] The baby is crying? Soothing music plays in response. A storm is coming or the ground is sufficiently moist? The irrigation system automatically shuts off. You drive your car out of the garage? Your lights turn off, heating or cooling adjusts, your alarm and motion sensors are automatically turned on, and your doors automatically lock. Your coffeemaker coordinates with your clock so that it turns on five minutes before your alarm goes off – or your local Starbucks senses your

---

7 The ideas for many of these examples were taken from *Wired*, June 2013, "Wired Awake," Bill Wasik, pages 142–7.

approach and begins preparing your usual order. The tag on your dog's collar sends you a text message in the event that Fido leaves the yard. The heating system in your swimming pool coordinates with your Outlook calendar, and your basketball court automatically tracks your shot percentage. Well, maybe *all* of this isn't such a good idea!

However, this isn't the plot from some new movie, but rather a reality that is feasible today – and it's becoming commonplace. Each individual part has generally been feasible for some time now, but it is the interconnected and ubiquitous nature of the information that has transformed the merely feasible into business opportunities and modern-day realities.

Another play might be in the home, interconnecting all of this information. Indeed, Microsoft's Microsoft HomeOS is an attempt to develop "The Operating System for the home" – interconnecting the home's nervous system, so to speak.[8] While this may, at first glance, sound attractive, imagine choosing between this offering – one that stops working when you walk out the door and can only be accessed via the app you have on your mobile device – and an offering that seamlessly tells you that the subway line is down, gives you an alternative route, finds a nearby Uber, and can find an item on the shelf in a store while cross-referencing prices. Associated future devices will need to work in the home, on the streets, and at work and connect key information, devices, and schedules. Seamless integration will win, since it provides multiple benefits with ease of interaction to each and every customer.

Think: Ecosystems Not Platforms – and Platforms Not Products

Now, back to the white goods example. Imagine a smart refrigerator that can determine the expiration date on a carton of milk in your fridge and cross-reference its contents with what is available

8 http://research.microsoft.com/en-us/projects/homeos/.

in your pantry to confirm your choice of recipe on a Friday night. You no longer need the touchscreen on the front of the refrigerator as originally envisioned – you can do all of that with your smartphone or tablet. However, what if the refrigerator could automatically order – and have delivered to your door – a new carton of milk to replace the one you used up the night before?[9] Are you interested *now* in the premium that the manufacturer will charge? There is a whole host of evidence, from Wi-Fi-enabled smart televisions to home "assistants," that suggests that consumers are willing to pay more for the devices themselves when they are internet-enabled. Thus, there may be opportunities for companies that can interconnect it all seamlessly – in and out of the home. At present, Alphabet (Google) is the company poised to do just this – particularly with their $3.2 billion purchase of Nest back in January 2014. Time will tell if they win out. However, our lesson is that this is exactly the right play today; Nest is a perfect fit for them – inside the home.

The World Is Changing at Light Speed. Use Change to Your Advantage

Much of this book is about technology and transition – be it in the technology space, in old-line manufacturing industries, in services, even in small local businesses. Business is changing at speeds we have never seen before; furthermore, we are interconnected in ways we have never been before. Even the "futuristic" technologies discussed

---

9 Note that, at the time of the writing of this book, Samsung had introduced an "internet-enabled" fridge with a camera inside and a touchscreen on the outside that connects to your smartphone. The Samsung fridge plays out a slightly different approach: its camera enables you to see inside, so you know what you need when you are at the grocery store. Also, it has a tablet on the front that plays music, mirrors a connected Samsung TV, has a calendar for the family, can let kids draw on it, displays photos, and connects to phones.

in this book are old before they take off – for example, Google's Glass is giving way to images projected onto "augmented reality" contact lenses produced by Sony, Google, Alcon, Samsung, and others.[10] The research and processes presented in this book highlight very specific strategies that can be used for modern-day success. In today's business environment, one that is characterized by ubiquitous, always-on, and interconnected information, our research suggests that a very specific "Carrot and Stick" approach – utilizing the concepts of *vertical incentive alignment* (the "Carrot") and *strategic control points* (the "Stick") – leads to substantive and lasting strategic advantages.

In order to drive home the point, it is interesting to note that the battle fought from 2005 to 2011 between Google and Apple set the stage for what we see today. In an interesting book about Google and Apple, Fred Vogelstein tells the story well:[11]

> Both companies [Apple and Google] see themselves as becoming new kinds of content distribution engines – twenty-first-century TV networks, if you will. They won't make content as the TV networks do today; but their control of huge global audiences, and their enormous balance sheets, will enable them to have a big impact on what gets made and who sees it.
>
> Together they controlled $200 billion in cash alone by mid-2013 [author's note: this figure is over $500 billion in 2019]. That's not only

---

10 See Scott Stump, "Sony Applies for Patent on Contact Lens Camera That Shoots Photos in a Blink," *CNBC*, 3 May 2016: https://www.cnbc.com/2016/05/03/sony-applies-for-patent-on-contact-lens-camera-that-shoots-photos-in-a-blink.html; and *CBS Market Watch*, "Smart Contact Lenses Market 2018 to 2023 Outlook," 14 August 2018: https://www.marketwatch.com/press-release/smart-contact-lenses-market-2018-to-2023-outlook-samsung-sony-alcon-google-sensimed-sa-etc-players-counting-72-bn-in-terms-of-revenue-2018-08-14. Note that, at the time of the writing of this book, some of these projects have been put on hold. See Abrar Al-Heeti, "Google Sister Company Puts Glucose-sensing Contact Lenses on Hold," *CNET*, 16 November 2018: https://www.cnet.com/news/google-sister-company-puts-glucose-sensing-contact-lens-project-on-hold/.

11 Fred Vogelstein, *Dogfight: How Apple and Google Went to War and Started a Revolution* (New York: Farrar, Straus and Giroux, 2013), 10–11.

enough to buy and/or finance an unlimited amount of content for their audience; it's actually enough to buy most of Hollywood. The market capitalizations of News Corp., Time Warner, Viacom, and CBS total that much combined. Although most people don't think of Apple and Google as entertainment giants, Apple through iTunes controls roughly 25 percent of all music purchased and 6 to 10 percent of the $18 billion home video market.

But despite the power of Facebook, Amazon, Netflix, and Microsoft, at the moment they all still have to largely go through two companies – Apple and Google – to get to the increasingly massive audiences using smartphones and tablets for their news, entertainment, and communications.

This passage broadly hits at the heart of what it takes to win in business today. When every bit of key content is largely going through two players, they can squeeze at every turn. Back in 2005, Google founders Sergey Brin and Larry Page, Apple's Steve Jobs, and a handful of others knew that it was *strategic control points* that mattered, and they built empires around them – much as Vanderbilt did with railroads, Rockefeller did with oil, and Morgan did with financing many years ago.

The "Carrot and Stick" Approach to Strategy

Thus, the key premise of this book is that in today's environment, effective and long-lasting strategies must take a "Carrot and Stick" approach, based on the principles of *strategic control points* and *vertically aligned incentives*. Companies that not only realize this, but execute around it, are the ones that dominate the competitive landscape today. This book is about what we can learn from this understanding and how you can utilize these principles for your business.

Acknowledgments

The acknowledgments are many, from the companies that I have worked with and learned from to the generosity of thought shared by those cited and footnoted throughout. The Kenan-Flagler Summer Research Fund at the University of North Carolina at Chapel Hill and their generous donors supported much of the time devoted to this research. The Yale faculty, particularly Jeff Sonnenfeld and his uniquely Jeff Yale CEO Summits, have inspired me to *think* over the years. Most importantly, none of this could have happened were it not for my family, who indulged my long trips and far too many ramblings on strategic control!

Introduction

After a recent talk at the Yale CEO LATAM Forum in Miami, the CEO of one of the largest insurance companies in Latin America came up to me and said, "I hate Google." I responded by saying, "That sounds pretty harsh," and asked why he felt so strongly. His response was both simple and telling. He said that Google was "extorting much of my profits." He said that in his home country, via mobile phones, Google now has the ability to show that Driver A has a heavy foot on the gas, Driver B doesn't leave enough space between his car and the one in front, while Driver C respects all traffic rules – including speed limits. Therefore, armed with such data from Google, insurance companies can now better match risk-rate profiles of their customers and charge premiums for drivers who are high risk. However, according to this insurance executive, Google wants a significant "cut" of the resulting profits.[1] Indeed, according to this CEO, if he didn't "pay up," Google threatened to sell similar

---

[1] In the United States, companies like Progressive are trying to do this in the automobile insurance market with products like Snapshot® (see https://blog.joemanna.com/progressive-snapshot-review/). However, these can be implemented only via a limited set of customers (i.e., only Progressive's customers) and only for a subset of these customers who are willing to put a device in their cars; indeed, fewer than 25 percent of their customers have agreed to install it. In fact, it is ironic that only a small subset of Progressive's customers opt in to allow Snapshot® to track their driving habits when Google and others are already doing it.

information to his competitors; thus, nonpayers are at a significant disadvantage vis-à-vis their rivals. In sum, Google owns a key *strategic control point* in this industry – data on drivers' locations and speeds – and is demanding a cut of the insurer's margin as a result.

There are many things that Google must have in place in order to exert such margin pressure. Primarily, of course, they need to be able to access the data. In the example above, Google is accessing data via its Android operating system and a location-based app (Google Maps). According to the insurance executive, over 90 percent of the phones in his home market use one or the other. This gives Google access to movement data for over 90 percent of drivers on the road. In addition, Google needs digital mapping and navigation software (Google Maps, Waze). So, Google has slowly been building the infrastructure to gather and own the data that they need to extract margins from this insurance executive's company.[2]

Perhaps even more importantly, through various internet transmission methods (Fiber, balloons, and satellites) as well as Google Nest Hub (formerly Home Hub), Google Wifi (formerly OnHub), and Nest thermostats, Google may know not only our driving habits but also a myriad of other details about us: what we buy, whether we're home, how often we move, how many steps we take, what size clothing we wear, and where we shop. Furthermore, they can leverage such information well beyond insurance and into stores, health care, and advertising. Google can do this because they are building an infrastructure around information vis-à-vis internet access that can be leveraged not just to insurance but also across an entire *ecosystem* of industries. This is what good companies do today: they find and access points of strategic control in one industry (e.g.,

---

2   Worldwide, the Android OS commands approximately 88 percent of the smartphone installed base. Source: Gartner, "Global Mobile OS Market Share in Sales to End Users from 1st Quarter 2009 to 2nd Quarter 2018." *Statista - The Statistics Portal*, Statista: www.statista.com/statistics/266136/global-market-share-held-by-smartphone-operating-systems/, accessed 6 March 2019.

access to data via the Android operating system or via internet provision) that can be leveraged across multiple, interconnected value
chains – something we will refer to as an *ecosystem*.

The basic premise of this book is that today's successful companies are those that are able to exert strategic control (i.e., "the Stick")
and align incentives (i.e., "the Carrot"):

1 *The "Stick" (strategic control points)*: A *strategic control point* is a
  part of a market that, if controlled by one party, can be leveraged
  for superior margins; this can be in the supply chain, a related
  business, or even an unrelated market, such as patented intellectual property (IP) or the supply of critical inputs for production.
  By controlling a critical input, for example, a firm can often leverage this to earn superior margins throughout its value chain.

  Many successful companies find points of strategic control and
  develop unique capabilities in core markets; however, companies
  that have long-term success in today's business environment are
  those that are able to leverage strengths across multiple (versus
  singular) markets – something that will be referred to throughout
  this book as the *"competitive ecosystem."* No longer will successful businesses be able to focus solely on their primary industries:
  for instance, (i) Google's entry into internet provision (i.e., via its
  Fiber, Loon, and other related projects) will enable it to succeed
  via diverse offerings (e.g., mobile phones, searches, maps, insurance, and the provision of television content);[3] (ii) Amazon now
  leverages an online platform – Amazon Marketplace – to take
  a cut of transactions in just about every legal industry in North

---

3 In August 2015, Google, headquartered in Mountain View, California, reorganized
   under the parent Alphabet, trading under the symbols GOOG and GOOGL. Alphabet was created as the parent of Google (and several other companies previously
   owned by Google). Subsidiaries include Google, Calico, Verily, GV, Google Capital,
   X, and Google Fiber. For ease of exposition, we will refer to Alphabet as "Google"
   throughout, fully recognizing the set of companies under the parent, Alphabet.

America; (iii) Amazon's Blue Origin, Airbus's Zephyr and One-Web constellation of satellites, and Elon Musk's SpaceX threaten Boeing's satellite and space business; (iv) smaller, nimbler cyber security firms threaten Lockheed Martin's defense business; (v) mobile payments (e.g., Apple Pay, Samsung Pay, Google Pay, Venmo) threaten to undermine traditional players. And the list goes on.

Business success will always be about "competing in the right space." If you compete well but in the "wrong" part of a market (e.g., where the margins are thin or where you are squeezed by someone else who exerts power on your core market), you will not be successful – regardless of how well or vigorously you compete. This book suggests that today's markets are different and that the competitive game can reverberate not only throughout an industry's value chain but also across markets.

One of the central tenets of this book is that the competitive game being played across firms and across markets plays a crucial role in the success of any organization. We've learned a great deal from the game theory[4] literature over the past decade; for example, while the competitive interactions across firms in one part of a market are important, competition and the game being played in other markets (or other parts of a firm's supply chain) can exert influence and have a significant impact on a firm's core business. Thus, today's competitive environment is no longer about simply being successful in an isolated part of the market – the new game is one of competition across *different* markets.

The primary objective of this book is to present a process that enables firms to (i) locate key areas of strategic control,

---

4 Game theory, originally developed by John von Neumann in the 1940s, utilizes mathematical models of conflict and cooperation to address interactions across agents (e.g., across firms). Over the past two decades, a new branch of empirical game theory has been developed that helps provide intuition and prescriptive guidelines on how to compete effectively against rivals – intuition that is incorporated throughout this book.

(ii) obtain capabilities in these areas, and (iii) utilize competitive tactics to not only extract margins in this part of the market but also leverage this through to other markets.

2 *The "Carrot" (vertical incentive alignment)*: Contrasting with the "Stick" of strategic control is the "Carrot" of incentive alignment. *Vertical incentive alignment* refers to the concept of aligning upstream and downstream incentives (i.e., those of suppliers and customers) to be compatible with your own: setting up your entire value chain and customer-incentive structure so that it is in *suppliers' and customers'* best interests to do what's in your best interest.

Often, the key for aligning incentives is joint investments. We will refer to this as "asset specificity," assets specific to the relationship that align the incentives of all parties involved – something like a joint investment. However, "asset specificity" is just one tool that is now being utilized to align incentives both internally and externally. The overarching lesson is that the control and influence of incentives are essential to managing and running businesses today.

The utilization of a "Carrot" and a "Stick" together is central to successful, modern-day strategy. Later in the book, we show why this matters: the use of strategic control and vertically aligned incentives together is material to the financial performance of firms. For example, a detailed statistical analysis of the financial performance of firms in the S&P 500 over an eight-year period revealed that when firms did an exceptional job of utilizing strategic control points and aligning vertical incentives, their earnings before interest, taxes, and amortization (EBITA) more than doubled during that period (with almost 70 percent share price appreciation). Conversely, those that performed poorly on both the "Carrot" and the "Stick" actually had EBITA decline over this period – and appreciably worse share price performance.

Thus, this book argues that the key strategic principles necessary for winning in today's hypercompetitive business environment are *strategic control points* (i.e., the "Stick") and *vertical incentive alignment* (i.e., the "Carrot"). The utilization of these concepts – in concert – can provide unique competitive advantages for you and your organization. Furthermore, we will utilize market-wide perspectives to focus on the *net response* of the market to a company's offering – incorporating both *"coopetition"* (cooperating with suppliers and competitors alike) and *competition* throughout the scope of a firm's operations.[5] In fact, this is a competitive advantage that this book can provide – a way of approaching markets that is practical, feasible, and groundbreaking in modern-day managerial strategic thinking.

The book is divided into three parts. Part I addresses strategic control (the "Stick") in a single-industry setting with the primary objective of detailing the fundamental principles of strategic control. In addition to explaining the concept of strategic control points, it presents a process for spotting strategic control points in your markets. Part II extends strategic control to multiple industries, noting that the internet and associated platforms now enable dominant firms in one industry to extend this dominance to multiple industries. In addition, we discuss what to do when someone else owns a point of strategic control and what can go wrong if you own one. Finally, Part III discusses how to combine strategic control with the concept of vertical incentive alignment (the "Carrot") to develop a strategic approach and thereby attain competitive advantages in today's markets. We show that, financially, firms that utilize these two key principles outperform firms that do not. We also discuss the role that game theory plays in helping firms stay one step ahead of the competition when utilizing the tools and approaches presented in this book.

---

5 Adam M. Brandenburger and Barry J. Nalebuff, *Co-Opetition: A Revolution Mindset That Combines Competition and Cooperation: The Game Theory Strategy That's Changing the Game of Business* (New York: Doubleday Business, 1996).

Finally, it is important to note that many of the concepts, tools, and methodologies discussed in this book have only been developed in the academic literature in the last ten years or so and have only been integrated on a piecemeal basis in business books and in the business press over the last few years. Hence, this book provides new insights, tools, methodologies, and strategic thinking to enable firms to uniquely compete (via strategic advantages) in today's market environments. Its main and most important benefit, however, is in integrating these concepts and extending them from products to ecosystems.

Use it to your advantage.

PART I

STRATEGIC CONTROL
IN A SINGLE MARKET CONTEXT

Understanding Strategic Control Points ("The Stick")

The Story of Cornelius Vanderbilt's Hudson River Bridge

Jack Welch once said about Vanderbilt and all great executives: "They have the ability to see around corners." At the start of the Civil War, Vanderbilt realized that a transcontinental railroad could slash coast-to-coast travel times by a matter of months. As a result of this vision, he sold virtually all of his shipping interests in order to invest in railroads. By the end of the war, his vision had resulted in a railroad empire that was worth the equivalent of $75 billion today.

However, he was soon challenged for being "soft" when he was pushed by rival rail companies during tough negotiations. He fought back, looking for a key *strategic control point* to leverage against his rivals. Since he owned the only rail bridge in and out of New York City (the Hudson River Bridge, pictured in figure 1.1), he owned the gateway to the country's largest port. Without access to the bridge, every other railroad would be effectively shut out of New York City.[1]

---

1 This story is taken from the opening episode (1) of the History Channel's *The Men Who Built America*. See also https://competesmarternotharder.wordpress.com/2013/10/03/the-story-of-vanderbilts-hudson-river-bridge/.

Figure 1.1 The Hudson River Bridge[2]

Vanderbilt, like many after him, realized that he owned a crucial *strategic control point*, one where all rail traffic flowed between a crucial port in New York City and the rest of the country. The Hudson River Bridge was that *strategic control point*.

Accordingly, after Vanderbilt's rivals failed to give him the deal he wanted, he cut off the bridge to them and then famously asserted, "We're going to watch them bleed ..." Vanderbilt single-handedly created a blockade around the nation's busiest port and the rest of the country (long before many of today's antitrust laws were created). When a rival railroad, New York Central, started to "bleed" and shares fell precipitously on the New York Stock Exchange, Vanderbilt bought up every share he could and, in just a few days, took control

---

2   Image source: Originally published in *Harper's Weekly*, 17 March 1866, p. 164. Digital file courtesy of the Catskill Archive, http://catskillarchive.com/rrextra/albbrdg.Html.

of the rival railroad. He eventually went on to own 40 percent of the nation's rail lines and built Grand Central Depot (now Grand Central Station, the largest building in New York at the time) to bring together his three new lines: the Harlem, Hudson, and NY Central.

A few decades later, John D. Rockefeller knew that he needed leverage when he was faced with a coordinated effort to raise passage rates for shipping oil out of Standard Oil refineries in and around Cleveland; the railroad companies owned the lines (a classic *strategic control point*) and he needed to transport his oil. Consequently, he decided he needed an alternative and thus built a network of oil pipelines to circumvent the need to transport via rail. Rockefeller knew that he would be squeezed for higher rates by the railroads that owned the only viable way to transport oil – unless he could break this control point. His pipeline enabled him to work around an existing point of strategic control – although it took him years to construct it.

DEFINITION: STRATEGIC CONTROL POINT

A *strategic control point* is a part of a market that, if controlled by one party, can be used to leverage power elsewhere; this can be throughout the supply chain, in a related business, or even in an unrelated market. A classic example might include patented intellectual property or the supply of a critical input in the supply chain. By controlling the supply of a critical input, for example, a firm may be able to extract extraordinary margins in other parts of the supply chain or across other industries as a result.

We will see that a common theme of successful companies today (e.g., Alphabet, Apple, Amazon, Alibaba) is not just that they exert the power derived from owning a point of strategic control but that they have *the foresight to own the point of strategic control in the first place*. This affords them the ability to exert pressure on an as-needed basis later on – much as Vanderbilt did during the Industrial Revolution. Remember this as we work through the book. You will discover that a plan to leverage strategic control, through various methods, is one of the key components of successful strategies in today's environment.

Sources of Strategic Control

We will develop the concept more fully throughout the book; as we proceed, you will find that there are many different potential sources of strategic control. We divide them into six main sources:[3]

1 Distribution/Access
2 Information
    a. Hardware/Software
    b. Information More Generally
3 Production/Capacity
4 Raw Material and Input Factors of Production
5 Intellectual Property and Regulatory-based Market Access
6 Key Manufacturing Components

In this chapter, we delve into the details of how to spot, access, and utilize *points of strategic control*. In order to illustrate how this plays out in practice, we will begin by presenting examples of each of these six main sources of strategic control.

---

3 An original source dates back to Adrian J. Slywotzky's and David J. Morrison's *The Profit Zone: How Strategic Business Design Will Lead You to Tomorrow's Profits* (New York: Crown Business Press, 1997). They cover this in a mere three pages, but it is an important concept that is extended beyond a single market here. The key is to leverage points of strategic control *across* markets. For an excellent and prophetic look at strategic control in the context of investment in information across the extended enterprise, see Benn Konsynski, "Strategic Control in the Extended Enterprise," *IBM Systems Journal*, 32 (1), January 1993, 111–42.

Source 1. Distribution/Access

Locking up Distribution Effectively Keeps Competitors at Bay

Distribution is perhaps one of the most common sources of strategic control; lock up distribution and it can be exceedingly difficult for someone else to gain access to the market.

The story of Vanderbilt – and how the Hudson River Bridge afforded him a stranglehold on the transport of goods during the Industrial Revolution – is a classic example of how distribution and market access can be used as a strategic control point. The ownership of the bridge out of Manhattan enabled Vanderbilt to control the terms of shipping in and out of the nation's busiest port because *access* to New York went across *his* bridge.

Some more recent examples include eyewear, men's razors, taxi cabs, and shelf space at DIY (Do It Yourself) retail, each of which is being or has been disrupted in recent years (the stories of how each of these industries is being disrupted today are told later in the book):

- **The market for eyewear**. One major supplier of eyeglasses and sunglasses controls multiple brand names and owns most retail distribution outlets throughout much of the world. Prior to a 2017 merger that brought the two largest players together, Milan-based Luxottica owned more than 8,000 retail locations in over 150 countries and had a dominant 50 percent market share in sunglasses. French company Essilor owned 45 percent of the prescription lenses market and 15 percent of the sunglasses market in 2015. In January 2017, the two companies announced that they were merging (the merger was approved by U.S. and EU regulators in March of 2018). The combined entity now owns over 50 percent of the prescription eyewear and over 65 percent of the sunglasses market. Add in the only other significant player, Safilo, with a 14 percent market share in sunglasses and a 3.7 percent market share in prescription lenses, and the two companies own a staggering percentage of the retail eyewear market with tight retail distribution control. Significant new competitive entry through retail distribution would be exceedingly difficult and certainly fought tooth-and-nail.[4]

- **Men's razors**. Gillette's and Schick's traditional dominance of the men's shaver market is another classic example. Gillette alone had over a 70 percent market share as recently as 2010, and they routinely introduced relatively minor product variants to occupy most of the available retail shelf space.[5] Entering the market with a new razor with an additional blade and pushing behemoth Gillette off pre-existing allocated shelf space has been exceedingly difficult for any potential new entrant over the years. Who truly *needs* the fifth, sixth, or seventh blade anyway?

- **Taxi cabs**. The monopoly traditionally afforded to taxi cabs by local municipalities vis-à-vis the medallion program (a system whereby a vehicle needs a "medallion," often posted on the vehicle itself, in order to legally operate a taxi cab under local jurisdiction) is yet another example. In cities like New York and San Francisco, the right to own and operate a taxi cab has been historically tightly regulated by local governments. For example, in New York, the medallion program began in 1937 when the supply of taxi cabs was significantly greater than demand. Medallions in New York were selling for $2,500 in 1947 and peaked in 2013 at a hefty price tag of $1.3 million. A limited number of medallions were approved by the City of New York, and competition – at least prior to

---

4   Source: *Coresight Research*, "Quick Take: Disruption Eyewear," 3 January 2018: https://coresight.com/research/quick-take-disruption-in-eyewear/; also see Statista, *Luxury Report 2018 – Luxury Eyewear, Statista Consumer Market Outlook*, August 2018, accessed 12 March 2019. Also see Dennis Green, "2 Companies Control Most of the Sunglasses Bought in the US," *Nordic Business Insider*, 25 August 2017: https://nordic.businessinsider.com/companies-dominate-sunglass-market-luxottica-safilo-2017-8/.

5   Source: Sharon Terlep, "Gillette, Bleeding Market Share, Cuts Prices of Razors," *Wall Street Journal*, online edition, 12 March 2019: https://www.wsj.com/articles/gillette-bleeding-market-share-cuts-prices-of-razors-1491303601.

ride-sharing companies such as Uber and Lyft – was prohibited. This was obviously a very strong point of strategic control.[6]

- **Windows, faucets**. In DIY (Do It Yourself) "big box" retail (e.g., Lowe's, Home Depot, Menards), Anderson and Pella dominate windows, while Kohler, Moen, and Delta dominate faucet shelf space. Combined, Kohler, Moen, Delta, and American Standard own a 78 percent market share in the United States in the construction market.[7] In retail, shelf space allocation is almost everything, and manufacturers routinely pay "slotting allowances" (paying to get on the shelf) and are required to guarantee sales performance (known as "failure fees").

The list of companies that have successfully locked up distribution and precluded entry by rivals is long and varied. Examples ranging from Microsoft's inclusion of Internet Explorer as a feature "tied" to its Windows operating system to Vanderbilt's bridge have been covered in depth in antitrust-law classes and business school MBA classes. The use of distribution as a "stick" (under the advice of legal counsel) for excluding competition via distribution can be viewed with admiration (in some business classes) or as a risky and potentially illegal strategy (in some antitrust-law classes).

We can summarize distribution-based strategic control points as follows:

- Distribution is an area where companies can gain strategic advantage (e.g., Luxottica, Moen, or Delta) or be strategically disadvantaged, but it is also an area ripe for disruption.

---

6 Source: Matthew W. Daus, "The Real Story of Taxi Medallions," *Crain's New York Business*, 12 July 2017: http://www.crainsnewyork.com/article/20170712/OPINION/170709938/the-real-story-of-taxi-medallions.

7 The most recent year for which data are available is 2015. Source: Hanley Wood, "Faucets Used the Most by Construction Firms in the United States in 2015," *Statista – The Statistics Portal*, Statista, www.statista.com/statistics/307423/most-used-faucets-brands-in-the-us/. Accessed 12 March 2019.

- Later in the book, we will discuss strategies for dislodging distribution-based sources of strategic control.
- The identification of strategies for overcoming a rival's distribution-based point of strategic control can often be the difference between success and failure in many industries today.

Source 2a. Information: Hardware/Software (Today's Version of Give Away the Razor to Sell the Razor Blades)

Information as a Source of Strategic Control: The Battle for Data – in the Wind and the Cloud

Windmill technology has dramatically improved over the past few decades. For example, GE has developed blades and rotors that sense the wind direction and adjust a windmill's tilt/shift in order to optimize its ability to catch the wind. In addition, many windmill "farms" (i.e., groups of windmills in close proximity) optimize the way they work together, since one windmill's direction and tilt affects the downwind performance of the other windmills. Thus, a group of windmills, operating together, is more efficient than individual windmills operating separately; as a result, when one windmill fails, the efficiency of the entire farm can be adversely affected.

Industry leaders (e.g., GE and Siemens) have developed their own optimization and monitoring services that use the data coming off the windmills to send performance data to the cloud and, using this data, remotely monitor performance and proactively do repairs to maximize windmill uptime. However, the market for windmills is fragmented, with a few large players and a series of smaller players – many of whom are lower-cost manufacturers from Asia who do not have the scale and/or capabilities to develop and maintain such services.

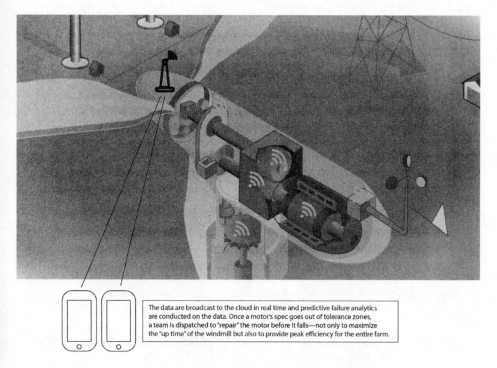

The data are broadcast to the cloud in real time and predictive failure analytics are conducted on the data. Once a motor's spec goes out of tolerance zones, a team is dispatched to "repair" the motor before it fails—not only to maximize the "up time" of the windmill but also to provide peak efficiency for the entire farm.

Figure 1.2 A typical windmill sensor structure[8]

In response to GE's and Siemens's control of this space, a few ingenious companies are in the process of installing – for free – sensors in both new and existing (i.e., retrofitted) windmills. These sensors (see figure 1.2) monitor motor vibration and temperature so that they can predict motor failure before it happens. The data are broadcast to the cloud in real time, and predictive failure analytics are conducted on the data. Once a motor's spec goes out of tolerance zones, a team is dispatched to "repair" the motor before it fails – not only to maximize the "up time" of the windmill but also to provide peak efficiency for the entire farm (see figure 1.3).

---

8 Figure 1.2 courtesy of the U.S. Department of Energy: https://www.energy.gov/eere/wind/how-do-wind-turbines-work.

This can enable the smaller players to compete effectively with the larger firms; for example, for smaller Chinese manufacturers trying to compete with GE and Siemens, being able to provide this service is often the difference between making the sale and losing it.[9]

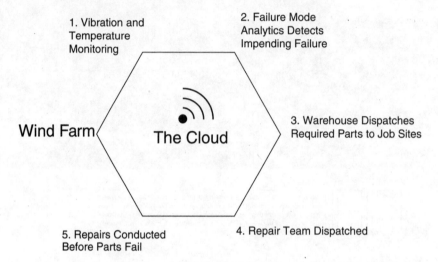

Figure 1.3 A windmill sensors ecosystem. Information is continuously sent to a "cloud data storage facility" where (1) real-time automatic monitoring takes place, (2) failure mode analysis is performed to sense and predict when a motor is out of temperature and/or vibration tolerances (to predict an impending failure), which can trigger (3) warehouse parts disbursement, (4) the dispatch of a repair team, and (5) the "repair" of a motor before it fails – resulting in near 100 percent uptime for the windmills.[10]

---

9 See, for example, the following: for an excellent general article on wind turbines, Sandi Horvat, "Predictive Maintenance in Utilities – Wind Turbine Use Case," *Comtrade Digital Services*, 25 September 2017: http://blog.comtradedigital.com/blog/predictive-maintenance-in-utilities-wind-turbine-use-case (companies in this space include Lufthansa Industry Solutions, Envision, HBM, Oros, and others); and Mike Kavis, "Envision Energy Leverages IOT Technologies to Optimize Renewable Energy," *Forbes.com*, 13 February 2015: https://www.forbes.com/sites/mikekavis/2015/02/13/envision-energy-leverages-iot-technologies-to-optimize-renewable-energy/#5ed98de2745e.

10 Source: author. Unless otherwise noted figures have been provided by the author, throughout.

So, how do you make money by installing sensors for free? The key is to own exclusive access to the data generated via the sensors and leverage it by selling higher-margin maintenance contracts back to windmill manufacturers (for newly built windmills) and to farm owners (for retrofitted, existing windmills). In order to understand how and why this works, note that the smaller players are more than willing to allow the sensors to be installed, to grant access to the data, and to pay for higher margin maintenance, since they can't efficiently do this themselves (due to their size and scale). Further, they gain the ability to compete with the GEs and Siemenses of the world on services, while simultaneously maintaining their cost advantages. In doing so, they can eliminate downtime to at or near zero by offloading this to the sensor supplier. Therefore, it's a win-win arrangement for all parties.

DEFINITIONS: IOT, INTEROPERABILITY, AND THE CLOUD
In this example, it is worth noting that the ability to remotely monitor a device and allow different parts of the value chain to "interoperate" (here, sensors that allow remote monitoring to make all windmills on a farm collectively more efficient) is often referred to as IoT (internet of things) interoperability. This is just a fancy term for enabling parts of a firm's supply or value chain to work together by connecting different parts via the internet. We use the term "IoT interoperability" here, but note that this simply means that a device (e.g., a windmill) is connected to the internet (e.g., via sensors on a windmill) and sends data to a central data facility (i.e., the cloud).

This is the modern-day equivalent of the "give away the razor to sell the razor blades" story. Today, the razor equivalent (the sensors) is of value because of the (i) ability to monitor motor performance remotely via the cloud, (ii) ability of the system ("the farm") to interoperate, and (iii) ability of failure mode analysis to predict failure before it happens. Indeed, in today's world, it is often beneficial to give away the hardware but own the data. Data is the new currency and often the point of strategic control in many industries.

Source 2b. Information More Generally (Ownership of / Access to Information, and Privacy Concerns)

Wearables and the Internet Access Wars: Why the Battle for the Last Foot between You and Your Internet Is So Valuable

There is a battle raging that most of us don't know about: the battle to "own" our internet connections. Whatever company owns the data coming off a device (e.g., a smartphone, router, or interconnected machines on a factory floor) will own a huge point of strategic control in future competitive value chains – within and across industries.

In order to illustrate this point, think back to the story of Google and the Latin American insurance executive (in the introduction). What enabled Google to "extort" (according to the executive) margins from the insurance company? Google controlled information on driver position, speed, and acceleration via a device and internet connection associated with each of the insurer's insured drivers. Thus, by owning the connection *and* the key app (i.e., Google Maps and the Android OS), Google has access to all of the information generated via the vast majority of smartphones in this region: with 88 percent of the worldwide smartphone operating system installed base in calendar year 2018, the Android operating system provides a treasure trove of data for Google to leverage.[11]

---

11   Source: Gartner, "Global Mobile OS Market Share in Sales to End Users from 1st Quarter 2009 to 2nd Quarter 2018." *Statista – The Statistics Portal*, Statista, www.statista.com/statistics/266136/global-market-share-held-by-smartphone-operating-systems/. Accessed 6 March 2019.

In today's interconnected world, the control of information is often an important point of strategic control. Hence, there is an enormous global battle for ownership of the connections of internet users; this is why Google is in the router business with its Google Wifi (formerly OnHub) system and is launching balloons and satellites (via its Skybox acquisition).[12] Google, AT&T, and Nokia are focused on fiber-optic cables and "5G" terrestrial high-speed transmission methods; and Airbus and OneWeb have a joint venture to build a high-capacity satellite factory to churn out as many as fifteen low earth orbit (LEO) satellites a week. Google doesn't want to be in the router business, and Airbus isn't looking to be in the satellite business; however, they realize that the company that "owns" your connection also owns and/or has access to the information coming from you, such as where you are, how you drive, what you buy, what you say (e.g., political and social views), what you do, and how often you move. The possibilities for leveraging this information via relationships with insurance companies, healthcare providers, plumbers, service technicians, and so on, are almost limitless.

Now, in order to understand why this is so important – and why the CEOs of Microsoft and Alphabet have both commented recently on the importance of "seamless" interactions with the information we need – let's examine the future consumer world.

The next big technology, the Internet of Things, will embed sensors in our appliances, electronic devices, and our clothing. These will be connected to the Internet via Wi-Fi, Bluetooth, or mobile-phone technology. They will gather extensive data about us and upload it to central storage facilities managed by technology companies. Google's

---

12 Source: Aditya Tiwari, "Google Plans to Cover Our Earth with 1,000 Satellites and Beam Internet," *Fossbytes*, 20 January 2017: https://fossbytes.com/google-satellite-constellation-patent/.

Nest home thermostat already monitors our daily movements to optimize the temperature in our homes. In the process, Google learns all about our lifestyles and habits. Our smart TV's will watch us to see if we want to change channels – and learn which shows we like and how attentively we watch them. Our refrigerator will keep track of what we eat so it can order more food – and know our dietary weaknesses.[13]

There is one thing in particular that any of these IoT-enabled (always-on connectivity to the internet) "wearable" technologies (e.g., the capabilities of our phones built into a pair of glasses, contact lenses, a watch, or on our sleeves)[14] will need to work: seamless, ultra-high-speed broadband internet connection. Thus, our internet devices will need to work in our homes, on the street, in stores, on rooftops – all seamlessly and without disruption from wireless source to wireless source. Much like the insurance executive in Latin America, key players today realize that if they have access to all of the information coming off always-on, ubiquitous, internet connections, their ability to leverage this information throughout multiple value chains is enormous. Indeed, if I were to own all of the available information about you (e.g., what you do, buy, and think), I could use this to extract margins from banking, insurance, video content, telecommunications, advertising, and so on.

In the internet space, there are multiple forms of provision – and multiple companies vying to win the war for your information. In 2018, Google, Apple, Cisco, Oracle, and Microsoft were collectively

---

13   Source: Vivek Wadhwa, "When Your Scale Talks to Your Refrigerator: The Internet of Things," 14 March 2016: http://wadhwa.com/articles/, accessed on 18 March 2019, and used by permission of Vivek Wadhwa.
14   See Tuan C. Nguyen, "Will These Augmented-Reality Contact Lenses Replace Your Smartphone?" *Smithsonian.com*, 13 January 2014: http://www.smithsonianmag.com/innovation/will-these-augmented-reality-contact-lenses-replace-your-smartphone-180949342/; and Todd Bishop, "Google's New 'Smart Contact Lens' Program Began at UW, with Help from Microsoft," *Geek Wire*, 17 January 2014: http://www.geekwire.com/2014/googles-new-smart-contact-lens-project-began-uw-help-microsoft/.

Table 1.1 Key players in internet provision, late 2019

Terrestrial	Non-Terrestrial	Key Players
Fiber interlaced with Wi-Fi		Google, AT&T, Verizon
	Satellite	SpaceX
		OneWeb Satellites
		Blue Origin
5G (chips)		Intel, Qualcomm, Huawei
5G (network)		Nokia, AT&T, Verizon
		Google
	Drones	Airbus
	LEO Balloons	Google
Tier 1 "backbone" providers	Traditional	CenturyLink, Cogent, GTT,
	Tier 1 ISP	Telia, NTT, Tata, T1 Sparkle

sitting on almost three-quarters of a trillion U.S. dollars in cash, and the battle thus involves significant war chests (to wage and win the war). Table 1.1 summarizes the key players in internet provision as of late 2019.[15]

If one entity (e.g., Google) were to dominate the ISP space, incorporate internet access into wearable devices (e.g., for Google this is now their Pixel offering, but this will eventually be new devices such as glasses, watches, contact lenses, or virtual reality devices), and bundle it with a current suite of offerings, the bundled suite would be exceedingly difficult to compete against.[16] The primary reason is the fact that the ISP, phone, or wearable unit does not have to be profitable in its own right, since the real money is in what the data (e.g., locations) will allow us to do, most of this generated via devices and various apps. Much like the old "give away the razor to sell the razor

---

15 See Brian Sozzi, "Apple, Microsoft and Google are Sitting on Stupid Amounts of Cash," *The Street*, 7 March, 2018: https://www.thestreet.com/story/14513643/1/apple-microsoft-google-are-sitting-on-crazy-amounts-of-cash.html.

16 In principle, this act of tying is one that Microsoft faced with the U.S. and EU action vis-à-vis its Internet Explorer. Legal issues are discussed later in this book.

blades" strategy, the primary ISP providers can subsidize internet provision and the wearable device to sell and/or use the data.

There are countless companies that would pay dearly to understand every move we make. In principle, if you provide internet access and devices to consumers at substantially discounted prices, you then have access to the full set of information generated via the consumers' devices (e.g., you know how much they move, where they are, and what they buy). You then have the ability to sell services (e.g., targeted advertising) based on this information about customers at supra-normal profits. Conversely, potential competitors who provide only a subset of the offerings generally do not have the ability to cross-subsidize their offerings with margins from services based on the data.[17] Thus, they are at a key competitive disadvantage.

Think through all of the offerings that Google has put together over the years (e.g., Gmail, Google Maps [indoor as well as outdoor], the Android operating system, Chrome, and Google television [i.e., YouTube TV]). They haven't simply been amassing a set of disparate offerings; they have been covering the entire range of offerings that connect to the central node (i.e., the internet connection). Think of it this way – with this connection and all of the offerings, you may not need your ISP, wireless cellphone carrier, cable or satellite provider, or even your bank anymore – in the latter case, thanks to Google Wallet.

In short, the key to the next generation of communication and information devices is the internet connection that is combined with the services; this is the *strategic control point*, Vanderbilt's Hudson River Bridge in today's business environment.

This last point illustrates what is truly different about the business environment of today – and what is discussed throughout this

---

17 A recent U.S. law, signed into effect on 3 April 2017, allows ISPs to resell data – a policy that varies widely from country to country across the globe. See Alex Johnson, "Trump Signs Measure to Let ISPs Sell Your Data without Your Consent," *NBC News*, 3 April 2017: https://www.nbcnews.com/news/us-news/trump-signs-measure-let-isps-sell-your-data-without-consent-n742316.

book. In the past, points of strategic control were leveraged within an industry and across that industry's value chain (again, as with Vanderbilt's Hudson River Bridge). Today, industries are often interconnected in ways we have never seen before. For example, Google, a search engine company, can leverage internet provision advantages into strengths in multiple, diverse markets, from television and movie content provision to mobile phones and mapping. Also, Amazon's infrastructure enables it to leverage its initial forays (into publishing and book selling) into Amazon Marketplace, data services, cloud computing, and local services. Thus, companies that succeed today recognize that strategic advantage is no longer about leveraging *across an industry* but about leveraging *across industries*.

Privacy and Winning Business Models in the Future: Now, I can imagine that many are reading this and thinking: What about privacy? What about the public outcry after Facebook's Cambridge Analytica scandal? What about recent regulations to restrict what companies can do with our data such as GDPR (the General Data Protection Regulation 2016/679 – a regulation in EU law on data protection and privacy for all individuals in the EU, but which effectively extends to most large multinational corporations)?

These are all fair concerns, and outright selling of data – or a lack of transparency in how your data are used – is just bad business. Selling of data is most likely going to be a subject of debate and further restrictions. Any business model that is based on selling of data is one likely to be in peril as privacy debates move ahead around the globe.

This is, however, exactly the central point of many of the examples in this book. Models where the use of advanced analytics provides a "better mousetrap" will likely win. Giving away sensors on windmills to provide more efficient maintenance; helping insurance companies pare risks by identifying risky drivers; providing targeted and more effective ads without being "creepy" – these are examples of strategies that benefit all parties.

The Profit Motive: One should always keep in mind that companies are in the business of making money – in fact, they have a fiduciary responsibility to their shareholders to do so. This leads to a logical question: Would you be willing to pay $29.99 a month for Facebook? Or Instagram? No? How about $8.99? If these companies weren't able to monetize the data, you would need to be charged for the service they provide. You can't have it both ways – you don't want them to use your data, but you don't want to pay for the service. The real question is how much of your privacy are you willing to give up to get something for free? Companies use your data to provide a service and make money on that (not sell your data to third parties) or you have to pay for the service.[18]

Moving forward, we are currently in the "wild west" of data ownership – a situation that will have repercussions for many years to come. Contracts must be written now with foresight. For example, monetizing owning the temperature and vibration data that come off windmills requires that contracts written for sensor installation *today* grant exclusive access to data rights for many years into the future. In fact, that's all that's needed. Think of it this way – in the windmill sensor example, no agreement for maintenance services needed to be written into the contract for sensor installation. Service agreements often involve contentious negotiations focusing on low cost and, for a provider of the services, should be avoided at all cost. By having the *only* stipulation for no-cost sensor installation be that the sensor installer owns all the data coming off the sensors (on the face of it, quite reasonable), the installer sets up a market where they are *the*

---

18 Alternatively, some have argued, that since Facebook (for example) earns $34.86 a month in revenue for each user in the United States and Canada, you should be paid for using Facebook. The argument is an interesting one, with merit. Source: Statista, "Facebook's Average Revenue per User as of 4th Quarter 2018, by Region (in U.S. dollars)." In *Statista - The Statistics Portal*. Retrieved 29 June 2019, from: https://www.statista.com/statistics/251328/facebooks-average-revenue-per-user-by-region/.

preferred maintenance provider for the length of the contract, since they can keep the windmills operating more efficiently at lower cost. This is accomplished at no cost to the windmill owner/operator – and usually with little resistance, since it is costless to them. Brilliant.

The type of business model that will prevail moving forward is clear. Choose one where you collect data and then sell the data and you will face significant headwinds through GDPR and analogous initiatives. However, choose one where you build a better mousetrap by using the data to provide a better service, and you will win nearly every time.

The Potential Role of "Net Neutrality" as a Point of Strategic Control: Finally, relevant to this discussion is the concept of "Net Neutrality," an Obama-era rule that states that all internet traffic should be treated equally. This essentially means that a company like AT&T, which bought Time Warner, can't favor their own content over competitors' content. The Trump administration overturned this rule in June 2018, but the overturn has not been in effect as of the time of the writing of this book. Many suits are currently challenging the Obama-era rule, but the U.S. Supreme Court has recently announced that it would not take up challenges to it. If the Net Neutrality rule goes away, the idea that "if you control the internet, you control the content delivered to the customers" will be even more powerful. The fight is still ongoing, with many suits hanging in court while individual states are starting to create their own rules. It is important to note, however, that the absence of Net Neutrality rules will make all that is suggested here even more relevant.

We can summarize information-based strategic control points as follows:

- Just as Vanderbilt recognized that all rail traffic went through the Hudson River Bridge in New York after the Civil War, Google recognizes that all of your activities run through whatever hardware or software you have that allows you to access the internet from wherever you are located.

- This hub (i.e., your internet provider) is the strategic control point that connects multiple industries, can yield substantial competitive advantages, and lets Google and/or others leverage the data coming off that connection.
- Similarly, by placing sensors on devices such as windmills, other companies are able to own a key point of strategic control – data – and leverage it for strategic advantage.
- In the wake of privacy concerns raised by events like the Facebook Cambridge Analytica scandal and in the wake of regulations such as GDPR, how the data are used and the opportunities to utilize potential points of strategic control will look much more like the windmill example than like the outright sale of the data (as with Cambridge Analytica).
- Business models that entail monetizing data need to have foresight. Just like Vanderbilt, who needed to have the foresight to own the bridge in the first place in order to utilize it as a strategic control point, companies need to have the foresight to build data-exclusive arrangements into future contracts.

Source 3. Production/Capacity

All the World's a Stage: The "Hostage" Problem

The use of strategic control is by no means limited to high-technology markets. In fact, it tends to be even more prevalent in old-line industries such as manufacturing, building, and construction. There are numerous examples of this, of course, but one classic and recent example involves production capacity and how it can create short- to intermediate-run control points.

I recently worked with a firm selling a line of popular household goods that had a difficult problem to solve. The company – call them

"Cornell," after my alma mater – sold a high-end line of consumer products in China.[19] The products had huge margins; they were also somewhat difficult to manufacture to a high standard, and worldwide production was limited. Their contract producer, let's call them "Ace," incorporated in France, produced about 80 percent of their world's supply.

In late 2017, Cornell realized that they had a problem. Ace had just been bought out in a private equity deal. The timeline for a typical private equity acquisition is for the private equity firm that buys a company to sell it within three to five years at a profit after growing the business a multiple of at least three to five times current earnings. Hence, the new owners had to grow – and grow fast. Moreover, Ace was supplying 80 percent of Cornell's key product line for the lucrative, high-end market in China. This constituted 50 percent of Ace's production capacity; the other 50 percent was dedicated to their own production – a rival but somewhat lower-quality product that was also being sold to the Chinese market.

If you feel something tickle at the back of your neck, a warning of something disconcerting, it is well founded – if you were Cornell, this *should* be extraordinarily disconcerting. Having your sole supplier be a key (lower-priced) competitor in a highly profitable market is most definitely *not* a situation you would want to create for yourself. Worse yet, Cornell had few alternative supply options: it had shut down its U.S. plant a number of years ago, and companies in Japan (7 percent) and Korea (13 percent) made up the rest of its supply. However, these suppliers had little ability to expand output; even if they could, they could not consistently produce the level of quality needed to meet the high-end Chinese market demands. Worse yet, a "Made in France" label carries much more weight in China than do "Made in Japan," "Made in Korea," and "Made in China" labels.

---

19 The names of the companies, the industry, and the numbers have been changed to disguise the industry and firms involved.

So, in summary, Cornell had no credible alternative supply (at least in sufficient quality and quantity), and their contract producer (Ace) had a competing product in an expanding Chinese market. Further, the supplier had just recently been purchased by a private equity shop that had a mandate to grow significantly within a three-to-five-year time horizon. It didn't take a rocket scientist to figure out that Ace would take advantage of their unique production capability in this area, their unique strategic control point. If Ace were to cut off Cornell's supply, it would take a minimum of two to three years for Cornell to develop alternative supply capabilities or build its own plant. Therefore, a credible strategy for Ace would be to:

1 cut off Cornell's supply (although there is a contract in place, enforcing the contract in French and international courts would be exceedingly difficult, expensive, time-consuming, and distracting), and/or
2 raise the production prices they charge to Cornell substantially, and/or
3 flood the market in China with Ace's own brand – decimating Cornell's lucrative business in China.

Worse yet, Cornell would have few alternatives available. As with Vanderbilt's bridge, Ace owned a key strategic control point, namely production capacity and – vis-à-vis the private equity acquisition – the newfound imperative to *use* the *strategic control point* (production capacity) in this market. Indeed, because of Ace's ability to sell its production capacity in China, cutting off supply to Cornell would be not only a feasible but also a credible threat.

So, what did Ace do? It threatened to pull production entirely and demanded more favorable terms; specifically, if Cornell didn't make it worth their while to continue producing for them, they would decimate their market. Thus, Ace was exerting its *power* inside this point of strategic control to increase prices significantly – much like when Vanderbilt closed the bridge to Manhattan.

In a later chapter, we will discuss how game theory can be successfully employed to address this difficult dilemma. This will illustrate how it can be possible to free yourself from a *strategic control point* that is owned by someone else. For now, however, it is simply important to understand how production capacity, in this industry, was the point of strategic control and how Ace was able to exert control in the value chain to significantly increase margin – much as Google did to the Latin American insurance executive and Vanderbilt did many years ago in New York!

We can summarize production/capacity-based strategic control points as follows:

- Having the foresight to own a point of control is crucial (Ace).
- Thinking ahead far enough is crucial – indeed, think ahead so that you (like Cornell) are not in the position to be squeezed by someone else who owns a key point of strategic control.
- Strategic control points are not limited to high-tech markets – production capacity, patents, process IP, and related tools can be used just as effectively in "traditional" and "low-tech" industries.

Source 4. Raw Materials and Input Factors of Production

Avoiding the "Hostage" Problem: Owens Corning and Granules

Sometimes, firms need to be concerned about defensive moves, such as what would happen if part of a market is – or could be – controlled by others. For example, Owens Corning is a Fortune 500 company that develops, manufactures, and markets insulation, roofing, and fiberglass composites. Based in Toledo, Ohio, Owens Corning posted 2018 sales of $7.1 billion and employs about 19,000 people in thirty-seven countries.[20] They manufacture various lines of building-related products that use glass fiber as a base, ranging from composites (e.g., tubing used in outdoor furniture, fiberglass pipe, etc.) to asphalt roofing shingles to insulation. They are a leading manufacturer of roofing shingles, competing against a couple of other large manufacturers, including one owned by Berkshire Hathaway's Johns Manville.

During the process of manufacturing asphalt shingles, a fiberglass mat forms a base (and adds weather protection and fire resistance); asphalt holds the granules on the shingle (and protects the roof from water); and colorful mineral granules (made of crushed stone and/ or recycled glass granules) help reflect the sun's rays and add a bit of style to the roof. At the end of the process, a heat-activated adhesive strip bonds the shingles into a single, watertight unit. A few years ago, after walking through a Competitive and Capabilities Map exercise (to be discussed in detail later in this book), Owens Corning became concerned that the granules on the shingles (a key ingredient in roofing shingles) were largely controlled by a third party – and it was the only major roofing manufacturer not vertically integrated into granules. This, of course, set them up to be frozen out of shingles if the granule supply was restricted in some way, which raised a number of red flags – especially since one of the major granules suppliers was a competitor (Johns Manville). Strategically, Johns Manville had the potential to exert its capabilities in an area of strategic control by significantly raising prices on granules – or freezing Owens Corning out entirely.

This led Owens Corning to integrate and develop granule-production capabilities as a purely defensive play – and a smart one at that. This anecdote illustrates how an analysis of *strategic control points* can reveal potential areas where strategic control by *someone*

---

20   Source: *CNN Business*: https://money.cnn.com/quote/financials/financials. html?symb=OC; and Owens Corning company website: https://www.owenscorning. com/corporate/sustainability/about-us/our-story.

else can have negative consequences for your firm; therefore, paying attention to potential areas of "negative strategic control" is prudent. Sometimes this can mean the difference between continuing to compete and succeed in a market – and being frozen out.

We can summarize input-based strategic control points as follows:

- Remain aware of potential competitor ownership of key strategic control points.
- The ability to think ahead far enough is crucial; make sure that you don't put yourself in a position to be squeezed by someone else's ownership of a key point of strategic control.
- Strategic control points are not limited to high-tech markets – also, certain strategic control points (e.g., production capacity, patents, and process IP) can be used just as effectively in "traditional" and "low-tech" industries.

Source 5. Intellectual Property and Regulatory-Based Market Access

Fintech, Traditional Banking, Blockchain, Bitcoin, and the Role of Coopetition

Imagine two scenarios. First, imagine that you have always dreamed of (and recently saved for) a shiny new car. You are at the dealer's and have agreed upon a great price. You shake the salesperson's hand and are passed off to the finance manager to finalize the deal, "do the paperwork," and arrange financing. We've all been there. Of course, in the meantime, various transactions, checks, and processing activities are going on behind the scenes. Second, imagine a friend is stranded in Europe and you are trying to get cash to her quickly; however, through the traditional banking system, you have limited options. Wiring money would be quickest, but this could take a day or more and is expensive (banks need to "talk" to each other, confirm available funds, and transfer and reconcile accounts across banking intermediaries). The transfer of funds involves a variety of ledger checks, transaction fees, and processing rigidities built into a complex international banking and regulatory system.

Banking transactions have involved similar systems for more than a century. Traditional banks have built a platform based primarily upon their vast number of customers, the trust that exists in the banking system (due largely to regulations), and the ability of the banks to deal with the federal government in compliance areas. Indeed, the fundamental foundation of our banking system is trust. This trust (between banks and their customers) took centuries to build and is supported by stringent banking regulations and, in the United States, $250,000 in federal deposit insurance (FDIC), as well as the full backing of the U.S. government and the Federal Reserve.

This trust is also built upon a complex reconciliation process. For example, banks keep their records in proprietary systems. So, how do we know that the records with one bank are consistent with those of another bank? These records are checked and reconciled by multiple, trusted third parties. Traditionally, if I wanted to send money to someone in another country, the following would need to be done: (i) I would go to my bank (and inform someone at the bank of my intention); (ii) the bank would send the request to the country's central bank; (iii) the central bank would talk to the associated European country's central bank, which would communicate with the associated local bank; and (iv) the friend could then pick up his money. The whole process could take from days to weeks.

Traditional banks effectively utilize the regulatory system (vis-à-vis the FDIC) as well as related trust as a strategic control point. You and I can't simply open a bank; doing so involves following a specific and well-regulated process. However, let's consider today's new and innovative environment. Banks and financial services firms are being pressured by financial technology start-ups (i.e., "Fintech") on technology initiatives such as the following:

1 "Peer-to-peer" (P2P) money transfer that is instantaneous, done over an app on your phone, and much easier than having to hand over cash or write a check (e.g., I can transfer money to you directly through organizations like Lending Club or Venmo). Non-bank institutions have successfully been making inroads in P2P lending via new technologies that have made P2P fund transactions quick and easy.
2 Beyond P2P lending, Fintech start-ups have been developing "distributed ledger" or "blockchain" technology in an attempt to "open up" the banking system to non-banks. Blockchain is an open (or public time-stamped) ledger that, because of its specific time sequencing, can be accessed quickly, securely, and at exceedingly low cost. Transfers can be processed and verified almost instantly, without risk of fraud, because each transaction is verified (or denied) based on unique time sequencing, which is presented across an openly available ledger. The main benefits are its quick processing (a transaction that used to take days or weeks can be verified and enacted in seconds), its low (near-zero) cost, and, in theory, its ability to eliminate fraudulent transactions. Traditional banks are quite concerned, since many Fintech start-ups seek to eliminate the fees that are the revenue streams for banks.

Thus, Fintech start-ups have been making progress in P2P lending; however, they face regulatory hurdles due to their utilization of the "distributed ledger" blockchain technology to lower transaction costs and speed transaction clearing times. If you were a large "traditional" bank, what might you do to leverage your *strategic control points* and keep Fintech competitors at bay? Banks are indeed smart; accordingly, there are two very different yet parallel paths that they are taking; their choice of one versus the other depends on how

vulnerable they are and how tightly they can exert existing points
of strategic control:

Path 1 (Utilizing Coopetition): Traditional banks have typically been
losing ground to start-ups in peer-to-peer (P2P) lending; hence, in
this domain, they are cooperating by "opening up" their systems
and data to competitors (i.e., Fintech start-ups). One way that big
banks are leveraging the power of Silicon Valley is by sharing
application programming interface (API) protocols with start-ups
and thus allowing access to their proprietary data and leveraging the innovations of Fintech start-ups. By offering open APIs,
banks have become back-end platforms; furthermore, third-party
developers are creating innovative apps for customers (to access
the bank data). Apps are increasingly important to banks because
of the prevalence of mobile phones and mobile banking and commerce needs. Therefore, banks are opening APIs to Fintech start-
ups in order to "cooperate" in areas where (i) barriers are low and
(ii) Fintech start-ups are already making inroads.

Path 2 (Leveraging Strategic Control): On the other hand, banks have
advantages that the Fintech start-ups do not: well-established trust
and government backing (e.g., via FDIC guarantees). Accordingly,
they are vigorously protecting traditional banking operations
(e.g., traditional accounts and commercial and mortgage lending)
outside of P2P settings. For example, in the area of blockchain,
Bank of America filed fifteen patent applications just last year
(and intends to file twenty more); Goldman Sachs is developing
SETLCoin, its own blockchain-based currency for post-trade set-
tlements; and banks are also creating their own digital currencies
(e.g., Citibank with its CitiCoin and Bank of New York Mellon
with its BKoins) – all while vigorously protecting their core assets.

Further, banks have a history of working together: indeed, fifty
of the world's leading banks have joined a consortium that is

spearheading the application of distributed ledger technology and "smart contracts." For example, R3CEV is leading this consortium with the mission to save money, decrease transactional errors, and significantly increase settlement speeds. In terms of scalability, Visa, Citibank, and the NASDAQ-backed chain.com can process tens of thousands of transactions per second, an impressive feat – especially when compared to Visa's capacity of 65,000 transactions per second.

One thing is certain: all banking products will be digitized before long. However, this is an industry that is still based on trust. Thus, all else being equal, the brand equity of incumbent banks will win. Furthermore, traditional banks have a long history of protecting their core assets vis-à-vis key points of strategic control: trust and the regulatory backing of the government.

We can summarize IP and Regulatory Market Access-based strategic control points as follows:

- The ownership of strategic control points by incumbent banks includes the regulatory process, which results in confidence and trust.
- Fintech start-ups have made inroads in P2P lending; as a result, banks have been cooperating by opening their APIs to technology start-ups.
- Since banks notably make money via transactions, they will use Fintech start-ups to develop the back end of new systems; however, they will fiercely protect the part of the business that utilizes their competencies in existing areas of strategic control points – namely through trust via federal FDIC protection.
- Key strategic lessons for incumbent banks (and other industries) include the following:
  1. Leverage existing capabilities by cooperating with potential competitors in the areas where you are most vulnerable (e.g., P2P).

2. Fiercely protect key margin areas when you have points of strategic control that are sustainable (e.g., traditional banking versus start-up, blockchain-based initiatives), while simultaneously developing your own capabilities in these areas.

Source 6. Key Manufacturing Component

William Sheppard, Minnetonka, Crème Soap on Tap, and the Story of the Pumps

Perhaps the best – and most dramatic – example of a *strategic control point* is that of Softsoap®, the liquid hand soap that we use to wash our hands. William Sheppard of New York was granted a patent for "Improved Liquid Soap" in 1865. His invention was a good one and had many practical uses;[21] however, it did not make its way into people's homes until much later (like many inventions). In 1980, the Minnetonka Corporation started offering "Crème Soap on Tap" through boutique distributors. The product was a success, and the corporation decided to follow up with a similar product for mass retail sale. There was a decision during the launch to package the product in a distinctive-looking pump bottle; however, retailing is intensely competitive, with requirements to get on the shelves ("slotting allowance") and performance guarantees ("failure fees") once on the shelves – both tough barriers to overcome for a small manufacturer that could potentially face overwhelming competition. For example, industry giants such as P&G, Johnson & Johnson, and Unilever could easily attempt to imitate its success. However, Minnetonka believed that if it had a ten- to twelve-month head

---

21 Originally discussed in William Putsis, *Compete Smarter, Not Harder* (Hoboken, NJ: John Wiley and Sons, 2014), pp. 67–8, 163. See also: Steven Greenhouse, "Minnetonka's Struggle to Stay One Step Ahead," *The New York Times*, 28 December 1986, p. 3008, available as archive post https://www.nytimes.com/1986/12/28/business/minnetonka-s-struggle-to-stay-one-step-ahead.html. See also http://www.chestnuthillconsulting.com/Bookexcerpt1.htm.

start, it could build up enough brand presence and shelf-space allocation that it would be able to maintain at least a one-third market share – even after the "big boys" entered. So, how could it do this? The answer again is via *strategic control points*.

In this instance, Minnetonka decided to *buy up the world's supply of plastic pumps*! Consequently, if any of the major manufacturers wanted to enter the liquid soap market, they would have to wait until the supply built up again – or build their own factories to make the pumps. This process would take close to a year – roughly the amount of time that Minnetonka needed to build distribution, shelf allocation, and a brand presence! In this instance, pump manufacturing was a classic *strategic control point* (i.e., a part of the supply chain that, if controlled, could enable Softsoap® to gain a differential competitive advantage in the key part of the market – retail – that it was pursuing). Note that there may or may not be a profitable business in pump manufacturing; however, controlling that part of the supply chain was key in this circumstance. And, as they say, the rest is history – just as with Vanderbilt and the Hudson River Bridge.

We can summarize key manufacturing component-based strategic control points as follows:

- Look beyond your immediate industry for strategic control. Minnetonka and Softsoap® was not in the pump business; however, the pump was a necessary component and in short supply at the time. Often, a point of strategic control involves building capabilities in unrelated markets.
- The ownership of points of strategic control is often temporary. Today, markets move at light speed; therefore, the key to owning points of strategic control is often keeping rivals at bay while you develop your next strategic move and/or market opportunity.

Based on all of these potential sources of strategic control, there are a few fundamental points to keep in mind as you read through this book and as you think through your own industries and applications. These points are crucial to understanding how to use the "Stick" part of the "Carrot and the Stick."

Strategic Control 101 – Fundamentals

1 *Strategic control points are not binary.* There is a continuum – from being a commodity on one end to exercising complete control (e.g., you own a patent) on the other. Think of strategic control as being weak or strong (versus simply existing or not existing).
2 *Strategic control points are market- and industry-based; competencies are firm-based.* This is one of the points that companies confuse the most. Points of control exist because of a unique aspect in a market; thus, they are market-driven. For example, a raw material or form of data may be scarce and can thus only be accessed by one entity at a time. In this circumstance, a firm should strive to have unique competencies in an area of a market with a *strategic control point.* For example, if satellite transmission is important to an offering because it enables real-time updating of data (which is pivotal to the success of an offering) and there is limited satellite bandwidth for transmission, this could create a type of *strategic control point* because of the lack of satellite transmission bandwidth. If you are the only one with competencies in this area (i.e., you are the only one with access to the satellite capabilities), then you should be able to extract supernormal margins. Thus, this strategic control point is created by a lack of satellite transmission capabilities in the market. In sum, you should ideally strive to have unique, essential capabilities in underserved areas of markets (where a component is in short supply). This will be a key part of the analysis when the Competitive and Capabilities Maps are developed and discussed later in this book.

3 *Strategic control points can only be implemented in contexts that generate something of value to the customer.* If something isn't important to the customer, there is no extra margin to be leveraged if
no one is willing to pay for it; it must be important to the customer. Nevertheless, customer demand is not the sole criterion.
For example, salt may be important to customers; however, it is
not in short supply and is generally thought to be a commodity
with no point of strategic control.

4 *Strategic control points must be rivalrous in nature.* If my owning a
point of strategic control doesn't preclude you from also owning
it, how can it be a point of control?

5 *If everything is a point of strategic control, nothing is; if everyone has
competencies in an area of strategic control, it is not a point of strategic control.* This should be self-evident; a strategic control point
involves a limited supply and/or capability. If everyone has capabilities in a certain area, there is no unique capability (i.e., for
extracting margins).

6 *Employing points of strategic control can (and should) be used in
conjunction with other strategic approaches.* In *The End of Competitive Advantage*, Rita McGrath wrote that modern-day competitive advantages are "transient" since markets move so quickly.
She argued that the transient nature of competitive advantage
means that we need to move faster to stay ahead of competition. Since markets do move much more quickly today, finding
and leveraging *strategic control points* can help firms hold onto
competitive advantages that much longer; indeed, while competitors fight to break the stranglehold you have on the market,
you can be moving onto the next market opportunity correlated with your current strategic control point – hoping to be
one step ahead of the competition. Further, unique agreements
with suppliers and others, as Adam Brandenburger and Barry
Nalebuff argue, can potentially provide you with capabilities
that are in short supply in an area of strategic control. Find these

opportunities and you're firing on all cylinders – and creating a network for long-term success.[22]

7 *Today's applications are all about the broader ecosystem ("Think platforms, not products; ecosystems, not platforms").* Along these same lines, companies that succeed over time are able to leverage strategic control points in one market and apply them to other markets and other market opportunities. Amazon has been a master at this via leveraging their platform to generate Amazon Marketplace, cloud services, and Amazon Web Services (Amazon AWS).

Is This "Unfair"? Should We Breakup "Big Tech"?

The issues at the heart of this book shed important light on current conversations about breaking up big technology companies such as Facebook, Alphabet, Amazon, and others, many of whom have successfully employed the strategies presented in this book. The use of strategic control points and the competitive dynamics between those that hold points of strategic control and those that attempt to disrupt them go to the heart of this debate. This book makes no value judgments on technology firms – or any others, for that matter. What the book does address are (i) the strategies that lead to market dominance today – whether for Amazon and Alphabet or a smaller firm competing for its survival, and (ii) strategies that can be employed to fight back when someone else owns key points of strategic control. Knowing how to develop dominant strategies as you build your business across multiple, interconnected markets

---

22 Rita Gunther McGrath, *The End of Competitive Advantage: How to Keep Your Strategy Moving as Fast as Your Business* (Boston: Harvard Business School Press, 2013); Adam M. Brandenburger and Barry J. Nalebuff, *Co-opetition: A Revolution Mindset That Combines Competition and Cooperation: The Game Theory Strategy That's Changing the Game of Business* (New York: Doubleday Business, 1996).

and knowing how to disrupt those that dominate is often *the* key to success in today's environment. It is also the key to rational, intelligent debates about the role of antitrust policy today.[23]

Choosing When NOT to Compete: Find Parts of the Value Chain with Profit and/or Margin Opportunities ("Pools") and Points of Strategic Control – or Exit as Quickly as Possible

When I work with companies, I find that it is important, early on, to map out the relevant industry value chains associated with the company. We look for profit or margin opportunities (sometimes referred to as "pools") arising in the value chain (e.g., due to things like a lack of competition or entry barriers at one stage of the value chain), and points of strategic control, and we often discuss ways to align incentives. These conversations can result in concrete and constructive conversations about the company's relative position in the market. However, occasionally, when we work through a detailed value chain, we don't find a margin opportunity or a point of strategic control, which inevitably leads me to ask: *"Why are you in this business?"* Three times in the last couple of years, it has led to a divestiture – one in solar, one in windows, and one in the chemical space. You need to ask the tough questions and then make the tough calls.

In closing, it is important to note that finding points of strategic control is rarely as "easy" and simple as was the case in the Softsoap® or Vanderbilt Hudson River Bridge examples. Indeed, finding points of control is usually considerably subtler and more complex. Further, it is important to note that it can (i) involve owning the entire value chain (back to front) and leveraging this

---

23 For an interesting and rigorous, albeit controversial, take on this question, see Lina M. Khan, "Amazon's Antitrust Paradox," *Yale Law Journal*, 126 (3) (2016): 709–805. Available at: https://digitalcommons.law.yale.edu/ylj/vol126/iss3/3.

across industries (as Amazon has done); (ii) lead you to conclude that there are no points of strategic control in your market at all; and/or (iii) sometimes warn you of impending danger from those already holding points of strategic control. This book is about how to find the important *strategic control points* and what to do if you don't have them or another firm has them – and how to leverage them across multiple industries (which is often the key to success in today's markets).

To be clear, the basic concept of a *strategic control point* is not new; indeed, the concept was clearly recognized by Vanderbilt and others. However, a detailed treatment of how, why, and when the use of *strategic control points* can be advantageous doesn't exist (e.g., for one of the rare discussions, see the three-page coverage in Slywotzky and Morrison's *The Profit Zone*, cited in note 3 above). More importantly, there has been no recognition of what is unique about today's business environment and, particularly, the fact that *strategic control points* can be leveraged across industries, at light speed, and in ways we have never seen before.

Chapter 1: Key Foundations and Business Principles

- The business of a *strategic control point* may or may not be profitable in its own right. Don't require it to be its own profit center. For example, buying up the world's supply of pumps in the Softsoap® example wasn't profitable on its own, but it enabled the Minnetonka corporation to build its Softsoap® business.
- Gaining control over the part of the value chain with strategic control enables greater value extraction at other points in the value chain.
- A *strategic control point* provides the basis for a sustainable competitive advantage; thus, it should not be temporary or fleeting unless the objective is short term in nature (as in the Softsoap® example).
- There can be more than one *strategic control point*. Alternatively, there may not be any.
- *Strategic control points* are not binary (i.e., there is a continuum from low to high).
- Strategic control is market- or industry-based, not firm based. You try to have unique capabilities in one area of the market that, if controlled, allows for disproportionate margin attainment.
- *Strategic control points* must be "rivalrous" in nature; if everyone has capabilities in an area of strategic control, it isn't a *strategic control point.*
- A *strategic control point* must result in something that is important to the customer. After all, if a *strategic control point* doesn't help generate something that the customer truly needs or wants, who cares?
- Nevertheless, it can't *just* be about this. For example, salt is important to the customer; however, it is just a commodity, since many can produce and deliver salt to the market.
- Often, a valuable question to ask is: "If one of my competitors gained control of this *strategic control point,* what would this do to my business?" If the impact would be negative, it may be important to form a defensive strategy.
- Is the investment commensurate with the rate of return? Sometimes, the investment in the *strategic control point* can be prohibitively expensive, and hence it may not make sense to compete in this market. Decisions of this sort are crucial to success.

How to Spot Strategic Control Points: A Process for Identifying Them in Your Market

Buy a Whiteboard, Sketch It Out, Follow the Money: Sherpaa

As Walter Isaacson, the biographer of Steve Jobs, commented in a CBS *Sixty Minutes* interview, "Only a complete control freak like Steve Jobs could obsessively control the value chain from back to front like Apple has."[1] Like Vanderbilt, who recognized that the railroads would dominate after shipping and knew that oil would be next; or like Rockefeller, who knew that oil distribution was the key to dominating the U.S. market for kerosene; or like Carnegie, who knew that dominating steel production would be the key to future infrastructure growth, great leaders can "see around corners," as Jack Welch once said.[2] Good leaders today – as Steve Jobs was in his day – see where those corners are. However, not everyone can instinctively "see around corners." So, this chapter works through a process for identifying *strategic control points* – how to find them, how to leverage them, what to do once you own one, and what to do in the event that they simply don't exist in the market where you are competing.

---

1 CBS *60 Minutes*, "Revelations from a Tech Giant." Interview with Walter Isaacson. Original air date 23 October 2011.
2 From the opening episode (1) of the History Channel's *The Men Who Built America*.

Before we do this, however, it may be helpful to learn from Jay Parkinson, co-founder of a company called Sherpaa. In making a compelling case for change in health care, he notes that:

- In the United States, 75 percent of all doctors are now specialists, with an average age of fifty-six.
- Our projected health insurance premiums this year, in 2020, will be $29,000 (split with our employers).
- The mean wait time to see a primary care physician (PCP) in the United States is more than twenty days.

Jay founded Sherpaa as a medical intermediary – a sort of telemedicine/concierge service that lets you talk to a doctor in fifteen minutes or less to *see if* you need further help.[3] Over 80 percent of PCP visits are unnecessary; we often go to our doctors to see *if* we need to go to the doctor.[4]

I asked Jay to share some advice with other new start-ups. His answer? Sketch it out; buy a whiteboard. For Sherpaa, he and his partners sketched out the flow of money in the industry and simply "followed the money." In this value chain, they found that the real money was with employers, since they typically pay the bulk of the premiums for employees. So, Jay and his team simply "followed the money" and approached the employers with information on how to save money on their health insurance – and help them have more productive, healthier employees.

We will follow this approach (i.e., "sketch it out") throughout the book by drawing the relevant value chains – something that we will

---

3   For an interesting twist on venture capital (VC) funding, see Jay Parkinson's posting: "It's been a year since Sherpaa went from VC-funded to Independent: aka how to be a sustainable digital health company," 20 July 2017: https://www.linkedin.com/pulse/its-been-year-since-sherpaa-went-from-vc-funded-aka-how-jay-parkinson/.

4   Facts and figures are from a talk by Jay Parkinson to the *UnleashWD* conference, October 2014, and personal conversations.

refer to as a *"Visual Value Map"* – because perhaps the best advice anyone can give you is to buy a whiteboard and "sketch" out any industry you are working in!

My Father's Beloved Indian Motorcycle and the Queen of England – from "Old School" to "It Changes Everything" in Just Fifty Years

My father was "old school." He grew up in the Bronx, New York, joined the Navy at the age of seventeen, served in World War II, and joined the New York Police Department when he returned from service. He proceeded to walk a "street beat" in the toughest neighborhoods of New York, back when cops walked patrol by themselves. He eventually worked his way up to become a motorcycle cop and would chase speeders in the Bronx.

He was also an interesting character (to say the least), complete with handlebar mustache and New York attitude. He often spoke fondly of his old "Indian," the brand of motorcycle (figure 2.1) he rode on the streets of New York and while escorting such dignitaries as President Kennedy, President Truman, Fidel Castro, and the Queen of England.

Stories. He never lacked for stories. My dad had "escorted" (the police term for the motorcycle riders or "escorts" in a motorcade) President Truman, for example, on multiple occasions. On one occasion, he stood at President Truman's side after the President had left office and asked him, "Mr. President, now that you are out of office, how should I address you?" President Truman characteristically responded, "Just call me Harry." My dad also "escorted" the Queen of England when she was in New York; while visiting Buckingham Palace many years later, he struck up a conversation with one of the palace guards, mentioning to him that he had "once escorted the queen." He didn't realize that the comment probably was ill-advised until later when he saw two guards pointing at him and snickering. It

Figure 2.1 Indian Motorcycle storefront, Paris

turns out that "escorting" the Queen means something very different in England – they thought he was claiming to have escorted her to a ball or palace event! Of course, they didn't know that snickering at a rough-and-tumble ex-New York cop might also have been ill-advised!

One day, while chasing a speeder at more than ninety miles per hour on his beloved Indian, his bike went one way and he the other. Not a good thing to do while traveling at ninety-plus miles an hour on a motorcycle. Fortunately, he survived a broken neck and lived a mostly healthy life until he passed away – still ornery – at eighty years of age.

Jay Rogers is also an interesting guy. His grandfather *owned* the Indian Motorcycle Company. Jay eventually went from Princeton University to a start-up in China and then to the U.S. Marine Corps. During his nine years of service in the U.S. Marine Corps, he applied to Stanford University, got accepted, and did something very few do – he turned Stanford down. Indeed, he felt that he had more service to give to his country and that to do so was more important than getting his business degree. However, he eventually finished his tour and "settled" on that "other" business school, the Harvard Business School (as Yale faculty, to me Harvard will always be the "other school"), where he earned his MBA. His time at Harvard was often spent working on his dream, which was not only to start his own automobile company but also to revolutionize the entire automobile industry, a lofty goal to be sure.

DEFINITION: ADDITIVE MANUFACTURING (AM), ALSO KNOWN AS 3D PRINTING

"3D printing," also known as "additive manufacturing," or just AM for short, refers to the process of creating objects via software-controlled industrial robots or "printers," by forming successive layers (with various types of material) to create a desired shape or object. Although early applications were limited to thermoplastics, they have advanced considerably and now involve metals, edible materials, rubbers, modeling clay, metal alloy, powdered polymers, and plaster at near production speed; they have even been used to produce human organs.[5]

It turns out that this goal was even loftier than you might think. Jay has already done something else that no one else had done before; his company, Local Motors, has "3D-printed" a car. The important point of this story, however, is not the impact of "additive

---

5 For a comprehensive and detailed treatise on additive manufacturing and advanced manufacturing in general, a must read is Richard D'Aveni's, *The Pan-Industrial Revolution: How New Manufacturing Titans Will Transform the World* (New York: Houghton Mifflin Harcourt, 2018).

manufacturing" (3D printing) on the automobile industry, but rather the reverberations throughout every aspect of manufacturing.

> Think of walking into a store, the likes of which you have never seen before, order a car of which there are five new models every month, and you can order it and take delivery that afternoon ... Then, if you get into a crash and the materials for that car only cost $2,000, you take the components that work off it – there are, after all only fifty parts – and print a new car. You had four seats to begin with, what about five seats this time?[6]

Local Motors was founded in 2007 with the vision of designing, building, and delivering vehicles differently. The concept is relatively simple: use the collective brainpower of the crowd by having innovative people from all over the world design the car, a process known as "crowdsourcing." Then, use this design – which can easily be modified by any buyer for uniqueness – to build it in local "micro factories" that produce vehicles locally, faster, with far fewer parts (50 versus 25,000-plus parts in a traditional mass-produced automobile). For example, Local Motors brought their Strati vehicle to production in a quarter of the time it took Tesla to bring its first model to production and used one one-hundredth of the capital that Chevrolet used to develop its Volt electric vehicle. They can do this in part because they "crowdsource" both interior and exterior design from community users. For the Strati, the global crowdsource contest winner was an Italian, Michele Anoe, who came to the United States from Italy with tears in his eyes saying, "This is a country that put a man on the moon and now I'm helping in this country 3D print a car." He didn't even have a passport, and Local Motors had to move mountains to get him over to the United States quickly. It truly is a different world in which we live today.

---

6 Jay Rogers, Local Motors founder, talk to *UnleashWD* conference, October 2014. Details in this section come from his talk at this conference, personal conversations, and emails with him and Local Motors executives, as well as his talk at the Yale School of Management on 22 July 2017.

Local Motors have plans to build 100 "micro factories" over the next ten years with initial locations in Phoenix, Arizona; Knoxville, Tennessee; and National Harbor, Maryland, just outside of Washington, D.C.

Perhaps most importantly, under traditional automobile manufacturing (with 500 to 1,500 suppliers delivering 25,000 parts), you can't change quickly. However, in just four weeks, Local Motors used crowdsourcing to design a car, the Strati, with fewer than 50 parts. They are thus able to control all aspects of production (i.e., back to front in the value chain); they can control and earn margins every step of the way and have learned that owning the chain – right down to the retail level – enables them to leverage their platform and community of engineers and designers in ways that few others can imitate. According to Jay,

> Car companies have killed each other on the retail end because they sell the same product to a ton of different retailers – dealers – and then they all compete for the razor-thin margin of price. We won't do that in our business because we control the chain. And you've heard of Tesla fighting to distribute products differently to the world, and they are being fought tooth and nail by the dealers of the world, and we have to stop that because it's stifling innovation.[7]

Indeed, via its ability to leverage strength in one industry to another (i.e., one of the key principles of this book), Local Motors has expanded beyond its ability to design, build, and deliver vehicles to work with GE's microwaves (before the business line was acquired by Haier) on microwave ovens and rapid design testing, Domino's Pizza and BMW on parts, and Airbus on crowdsourcing the design of its drones. Thus, Local Motors has taken ownership of the value chain back to front in one industry and leveraged it to other industries – much as Amazon has done.

---

7 Jay Rogers, Local Motors founder, in a talk to *UnleashWD* conference, October 2014.

Contrast this with the strategy of Hewlett-Packard (HP). Back in early 2016, HP introduced a line of 3D printers (used now by BMW, Nike, and Johnson & Johnson) that cost between $130,000 and $155,000 and can print at high speeds. BMW plans to integrate HP's printing system into the future production of parts and personal customization, according to Jens Ertel, head of BMW Group Additive Manufacturing Center. Nike has been using 3D printing for what it calls "performance innovations" in footwear for several years, according to Tom Clarke, president of innovation at Nike.[8] HP could come to own a disproportionate share of the value chain across all industries utilizing additive manufacturing in a number of ways: it could design and build high-speed printers in a way that few (or no) others can (and thus stay ahead of the hardware arms race); it could lock up top design and/or coding talent; or it could patent a key part of this technology. However, these alternatives are expensive and would be exceedingly difficult to control. Alternatively, HP could own the value chain in a portion of an industry, like Local Motors, and then expand to other industries. Thus, companies are confronting these kinds of strategic choices today in ways that we have not seen before, and these choices are often key to their successes or failures in the rapidly changing markets of today.

The Value Chain Concept

A basic foundational concept for today's markets is the notion of an industry's value chain. The concept of an industry value chain was developed decades ago; indeed, its origins go all the way back to Wassily Leontief's input-output tables from the 1950s (for which,

---

8   See Jon Swartz, "HP's New 3-D System to Print Nikes, BMW Parts," *USA Today*, 19 May 2016: https://www.usatoday.com/story/tech/news/2016/05/17/h-ps-new-3-d-system-print-nikes-bmw-parts/84247506/.

in part, the Nobel Prize in Economics was awarded to Leontief in 1973). In its simplest form, the industry value chain is a physical representation of the flow of various processes that are involved in producing goods and services. As such, it is a representation of the process flow from raw materials on through to delivery, service, and support of the final offering in the market; each, in turn, adds value that is ultimately captured by sales in the market.

While inherently "silo" in design, as well as process-oriented, a value chain can provide a very useful sense of where value is created within the supply chain in a given industry; this understanding can help a firm see where additional gains may be achieved in terms of efficiency or margin extraction. For example, if a firm is selling a physical product with merely decent margins and sees that there is little competition in distribution (or for a key raw material input), it may decide that it makes sense to move into distribution or acquire raw material production capabilities in order to extract the additional margins available in that part of the industry.

However, such a view of a firm's activities overlooks much of what is interesting about today's interconnected, fast-paced markets: since so many parts of multiple industries are "interconnected," industry-level views of value chains can be misleading in terms of future opportunities for the associated firms. Consequently, we will make important distinctions between what happens at the (i) firm level (and firm-level competencies inside the relevant value chain), (ii) industry or market level (e.g., the market for smartphones), (iii) platform level (e.g., Apple's iOS), (iv) "ecosystem" level (e.g., within and across all the interconnected parts of an industry), and (v) "cross-ecosystem" level (e.g., the potential for interconnected parts within one industry or "ecosystem" to be leveraged to other, entirely different industry ecosystems). For now, as a building block, we will begin with the most basic "industry value chain" and then build to a more complicated "ecosystem" later in the book.

A Process for Building and Developing a Value Chain Analysis for Your Industry

While all of this may be interesting, fully understanding and utilizing value chains and the concept of *strategic control points* requires a bit of homework. Fortunately, such analysis for any market opportunity isn't that difficult if you build it one step at a time:

Step 1: Map out the value chain in your industry: Let's begin with an example. Imagine drawing a high-level "industry" value chain for electronic maps, such as Google Maps, Apple Maps (in the mobile environment), or MapQuest (online). Imagine you were trying to do this in the early days (i.e., before Google Maps or Apple Maps). What process would an organization, operating in this space, need to follow? What are each of the steps? How do they fit together in a way that ultimately creates value for the end user?

First, (1) raw data would need to be collected (e.g., on streets, towns, and locations of buildings). Google collected this by sending cameras, affixed to cars, around every street in the country and throughout the world; indeed, there have even been pictures posted from Google cameras atop camels in the Middle East. Future data may be collected automatically via satellite, drones, and/or advanced balloons in low-earth orbit. Next, (2) the data collected by cameras must be digitized (and put into electronic form); (3) the digital maps themselves must be created; (4) a graphical user interface (GUI) must be created; (5) the data must be fused into the interface (an app) so that customers can access the maps in user-friendly fashion and interact with them (e.g., to find things, map out locations, and get directions) and distributed to end users (e.g., via iPhones, internet web pages, automobile navigation systems, handheld GPS devices, or Android devices). After the offering has been launched, (6) the physical infrastructure to maintain the maps must be established. Then, (7) the data, interface, and software must be updated/maintained, and (8) customer service and support needs to be put in place (e.g., for technical issues, billing questions, and other customer-related issues). Each stage of the process requires labor and/or capital, returning profits in some fashion. This value chain is depicted diagrammatically in figure 2.2.

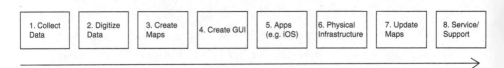

Figure 2.2 A high-level industry value chain for electronic maps

For your industry, the steps will of course be different – you will need to customize the steps in your industry's value chain to the unique ways in which value is created as you bring an offering to market. Often, the best way to do this is to imagine you were starting from scratch – what steps would you need to take in order to create an offering and bring it to market?

Step 2: Identify potential areas for strategic control in your industry's value chain. Are there areas that, if controlled, would enable someone to extract higher margins?: Once a high-level "map" (something we refer to as a "level one" value chain) like the one just described is created, it is important to note that each stage of the level one value chain is likely to have its own respective value chain. Thus, we could drill down deeper into any of the "level one" steps in order to create a "level two" value chain. For example, one step in the level one value chain presented above, collecting data, may involve its own steps: obtaining a camera and car equipment, hiring drivers, contracting for labor, purchasing fuel and computer equipment to record the data, and so on. These days, this might even entail launching a drone or utilizing autonomous vehicles to collect data more efficiently.

As we explore the level two value chains, we again look for areas that may be in short supply or controlled (e.g., the pumps in the Softsoap® example). For example, if we can control access to autonomous vehicles or a network of drones – or simply collect data in a way that is much more efficient and cost-effective than before – then we could control a key input associated with delivering these maps to the market. Within both the "level one" and "level two" value chains, if we can find any area in short supply or where competition is low or barriers to entry are high, we may be able to exploit these for superior margins. A *strategic control point* provides leverage to extract greater margins in any portion of either a level one or a level two value chain (as with Vanderbilt's Hudson River Bridge, Minnetonka's pumps, and sensors on windmills).

As discussed earlier, there can be many sources of strategic control. Sometimes customer relationships, feature advantages, and/or customer-offering advantages are discussed as sources of strategic control; however, it will be argued throughout this book that these should be viewed only as advantages that are temporary in nature, as they are usually not enduring points of strategic control. By contrast, patents can be. For example, Amazon's patent on its "Buy now with 1-click" button on Amazon.com, a method known as the "method and system for placing a purchase order via a communications network," a patent issued to Amazon in 1999, has withstood both U.S. and international court challenges.[9] Although this feature alone does not give Amazon strict strategic control, it does give Amazon a strategic advantage and allows them not only to gain licensing revenue from others that use a "one-click" system but also fits in with their overall strategic control of the value chain, back to front.

Now, think back to the value chain for digital maps. Are there areas which, if exclusively owned/controlled, would give someone

---

9 Fred Vogelstein, *Dogfight: How Apple and Google Went to War and Started a Revolution* (New York: Farrar, Straus and Giroux, 2013), 175–6.

an important source of strategic control (e.g., the sensors on wind-mills)? The way we often capture this is through the use of "Harvey Balls," as shown in figure 2.3:

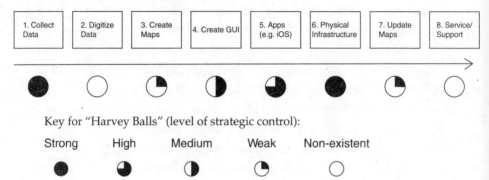

Figure 2.3 Value chain with Harvey Balls

For example, collecting data may be difficult and capital intensive. It requires fixing cameras on top of cars, driving them across every road, compiling and storing the images, and so on. Once one firm has collected the data, it may be less attractive or even impossible for another firm to also collect such data; for example, there have been various patents issued for Google Maps. Thus, data collection might be a three-quarter or full Harvey Ball (represented as a full Harvey Ball in figure 2.3) since it appears to be a relatively strong point of strategic control. Conversely, armed with the data, many firms may be able to digitize the video footage, and so stage 2, digitizing the data, might be represented by an empty Harvey Ball – there is nothing proprietary about digitizing video footage. Similarly, given access to the maps, anyone can provide service and support and so this would again be represented by an empty Harvey Ball. Alternatively, building the physical infrastructure to transmit those maps may be more difficult to do; therefore, this stage might be a three-quarters or a full Harvey Ball (represented as a full Harvey Ball in figure 2.3) since it too may be an important source of strategic control.

As you may have noted from this example, it is important that we take the stages independently, one at a time. So, if stage 2 is digitizing the data, we take stage 1 (collecting the data via cameras mounted on cars for example) as given and ask the question, "If many firms had access to the data, is there any reason why any one of these firms might have unique capabilities for digitizing the data that was collected?" Perhaps one firm had a patent on digitization of image data collected from cameras or had a near monopoly on computer scientists who could write the appropriate computer code. Note that having a competitive advantage in this stage (i.e., one firm can do this stage better than rivals) is not enough; there needs to be something that prevents others from doing so (see the concept of "rivalry" discussed below). While there is an element of subjectivity here, you can always research the key components further once you have identified where they may be in a value chain.

As you draw your Harvey Balls, contemplate two questions: If you had capabilities in this area, would it prevent someone else from doing it? Also, if someone else had capabilities in this area, would it stop you from competing effectively in this market? If the answer to one or both of these questions is no, it probably is not a strong point of strategic control. Once again, think of the Softsoap® example – the key to the company's success was buying up the world's supply of pumps. If they had simply secured pump-manufacturing capacity but competitors could also make pumps inside the aforementioned critical ten-to-twelve-month time horizon, then it wouldn't have been an effective strategic control point. Thus, we look for situations where when one firm controls certain capabilities, it prevents others from competing (or makes it difficult for them to do so). Ideally, buyers should have no other effective option; this enables the procurement of higher margins. An example noted earlier was Amazon's network; indeed, by establishing their distribution network (along with features like Amazon Prime and "one-click" shopping), they can extract margins throughout the value chain in ways that others cannot match.

Note that *strategic control points* are not "binary"; there is a continuum of degrees of control. On a scale of one to ten wherein one is *no control* and ten is *complete control* (i.e., the equivalent of Vanderbilt's Hudson River Bridge), various industries fall along the continuum, as originally noted in Slywotzky and Morrison's *The Profit Zone*.[10] For example, a firm that owns a key, unbreakable patent in an industry (e.g., a pharmaceutical or biotechnology firm) may be a ten. Some examples of firms along this continuum include the following:

10 Owns the patent (e.g., a patent-protected pharmaceutical); thus, entry is restricted

 9 Owns "the standard" (e.g., Jeppesen in aviation charts)

 8 Dominates the standard

 7 Leads the standard (e.g., Google in search and Amazon in books) or dominates market position (e.g., Coke and Intel)

 6 Has significant and material brand, distribution, and/or product differentiation

 5 Has important product or brand advantages only (e.g., Apple and Samsung)

 4 Has moderate product or brand advantages

 3 Has a small position or cost advantage (e.g., Sony and Nucor Steel)

 2 Has virtually no position or cost advantage (numerous)

 1 Has a commodity or contestable market, no source of strategic control (numerous)

The Concept of Rivalry

In economics, a distinction is sometimes made between rivalrous and non-rivalrous goods. The example often given of a non-rivalrous good is national defense or even a streetlamp: my standing under

---

10 Adrian J. Slywotzky and David J. Morrison, *The Profit Zone: How Strategic Business Design Will Lead You to Tomorrow's Profits* (New York: Crown Business Press, 1997).

a streetlamp doesn't preclude you from standing under it as well and also enjoying the light. Alternatively, a steak is "rivalrous": my consumption of a particular steak means that you can't consume the same steak; you may be able to consume a different steak, but not the same steak I just ate.

For a part of the value chain to be a strong point of strategic control, it must be rivalrous in nature; that is, if one entity owns it, this prevents others from doing the same in a certain time horizon (much like the Softsoap® and Hudson River Bridge examples).

Step 3: Identify strategic control points where your firm has unique capabilities. In your industry, where would your firm be positioned on the chart above? Is there a point of strategic control where only your firm possesses the requisite capabilities?: Let's take the example above and extend it to an analogous market. For example, imagine trying to build a business that consists of digitally mapping the world's ports for large commercial shippers (e.g., Maersk, Exxon-Mobil) and interconnecting these digital charts with route-optimization software to save fuel on shipping routes (e.g., as the company Jeppesen has done). Let's also examine a few distinct phases across the larger value chain in this opportunity space. In order to put together such a business, you would need to (1) access data across all of the world's ports and oceans, (2) digitize the data (and fuse it into a single data set) and create the software to make it useful to users on board the ship (including the graphical user interface), and (3) distribute your electronic maps onto the bridge of a ship.

These three distinct phases can be utilized to illustrate the concept of rivalry in strategic control (using digital charting in the marine industry as an example):

1 *Data access may be rivalrous.* If your vision of the crew on the bridge of a ship is of a "salty sea captain" complete with captain's hat,

·your vision isn't that far off reality; interestingly, much of the navigation on large ships is still primarily done via paper charts. Unlike in aviation, where there is an international agreement across nations to share public runway approach data, maritime charts and data on ports and approaches to harbors are owned by individual country "hydrographic" offices (HO) and are tightly held (territorial waters are often fiercely protected in the interest of national security). However, the U.K. Hydrographic Office (UKHO) has compiled over 80 percent of the world's marine data (the Brits have been sailing the high seas almost forever after all). If, in an attempt to move paper maps to the digital age, a company could secure the exclusive rights to the UKHO data, they would own a key *rivalrous strategic control point*. The key would be the exclusivity (i.e., *exclusive* access to the UKHO data would preclude another firm from creating maps with the same data, since the UKHO owns the data). If you could secure *exclusive* access to the UKHO data, any future competitor would need to go to each individual country's hydrographic office and, one by one, obtain access to the individual country's port and approach data, and then compile a database that the UKHO has amassed over centuries (a near impossibility). Even if competitors were able to do this, the time it would take to secure consent from even most of the hydrographic offices in the world would give the first entrant (i.e., the one with the UKHO data) a tremendous first-mover advantage and a huge head start. Thus, access to the UKHO data could be rivalrous if data access were exclusive – and non-rivalrous if it were not.

2 *Software, graphical user interfaces (GUI), and data fusion are non-rivalrous.* My writing software code and creating a digital navigation program doesn't preclude you from doing the same – as long as we both have access to the data. A company may or may not be relatively good at producing software and graphical user interfaces, but in principle, any company that has access to the data can do so; hence, this

isn't a *strategic control point*. It also highlights the difference between a *competitive advantage* and a *point of strategic control*: data access can be rivalrous and hence can be a strong point of strategic control; however, programming (and the utilization of that data) is non-rivalrous and hence not a point of strategic control. It may be a competitive advantage for you because you do it better than others, but it is not a point of strategic control.

3 *Access to the bridge of the ship is rivalrous.* Once a firm has compiled the data and written the code, gaining access to the bridge of the ship can be rivalrous. Since data and programs would need to be embedded into the onboard systems of large ships to impact navigation, it would be impractical (if not impossible) to have more than one software charting program on board and integrated into the ship's systems. Thus, the "real estate" on board large ships is rivalrous in nature: one program's presence on board the bridge would essentially preclude another from being on board as well.

Note that the application of these concepts is very much contextual. Indeed, while it may be impractical to have more than one charting software program integrated into the bridge of a ship, it is not impractical to have more than one mapping program on an iPhone – hence, many of us will have Google Maps *and* Apple Maps on our phones. Thus, in this example, the real estate on a smartphone (versus the bridge of a large ship) is non-rivalrous (e.g., my putting my map on your phone doesn't preclude someone else from also putting their map on your phone).

In short, a non-rivalrous part of the value chain can generate strategic advantages if customers value what you bring to the table and if you have a competitive advantage in its delivery; however, it can't be a *strategic control point*. Conversely, a rivalrous part of the value chain can be a source of strategic control and represent a huge strategic advantage in the market. This distinction is crucial: competitive advantages often result in an "arms race" where you need to continuously work to stay one step ahead of the competition, whereas a point of strategic control is often enduring and hence considerably more powerful than a non-rivalrous advantage.

There are innumerable examples of rivalrous *strategic control points*; the obvious, aforementioned ones include Minnetonka's pumps and Vanderbilt's Hudson River Bridge. Other examples include pharmaceuticals with patents (e.g., Viagra when it first came to market, which provided a huge financial windfall to Pfizer). Even social networking sites can produce rivalrous control points (e.g., once Facebook or LinkedIn gains critical mass, there is little or no room for another, similar offering). Note that while the mere existence of Facebook and LinkedIn doesn't preclude other firms from developing similar apps, the sheer scale of the existing networks makes it practically impossible to do so effectively and makes the networks rivalrous in nature.

Now, try this for your firm and your industry, building on the value chain you created earlier. Is there a point of strategic control where *only your firm* possesses the requisite capabilities?

Step 4: Draw out a "Competitive and Capabilities Map" in order to identify rivalrous strategic control points where your firm may have unique capabilities. In your answer to the questions for Step 3 above, what are the rivalrous sources of strategic control? What are your capabilities in these areas relative to competition?: In answering the questions above, be sure not to define your competition too narrowly. Often, this is an opportunity to spot potential future competitors. Furthermore, the examination of rivalrous *strategic control points* can provide opportunities for companies within disparate industries; indeed, the concept of rivalry in capabilities can be a key to determining cross-market opportunities.

A "Competitive and Capabilities Map" entails an honest, candid comparison of the capabilities across all relevant firms (e.g., competitors and suppliers) in this area. Building on the preceding example of electronic maps, we can add an objective assessment of each firm's capabilities across all areas of the value chain (denoted by capabilities in capital or lower case letters in figure 2.4):

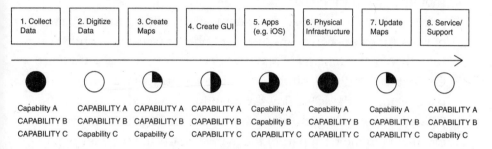

Figure 2.4 Value chain with capabilities

In figure 2.4, imagine, in this hypothetical example, that there are three firms (A, B, and C) in this industry. Imagine that you are firm A. Further, imagine that CAPITAL LETTERS mean that the firm has world-class capabilities in that part of the value chain and lower case letters mean that they have no capabilities. In the simple made-up example represented in figure 2.4, it highlights some serious areas of concern: in the two areas of high-strategic control in the market, data and infrastructure, you have no capabilities. Worse yet, there is at least one competitor in each of these two areas that possesses significant capabilities (firms B and C have world-class capabilities in both data and infrastructure). This suggests that you have three choices: (1) develop these capabilities in-house organically, (2) acquire them inorganically through an acquisition or joint venture, or (3) decide not to compete in this market at all (the market position of such a company is simply not sustainable). Analysis of this sort is pivotal at the strategic end of mergers and acquisitions (M&A) decisions.

In principle, you would like to compete in the areas that have the greatest potential for capturing margin – and stay away from areas that are commodities in nature, with little potential margin capture. More generally, the objective is to find areas in the Competitive and Capabilities Map where there are areas of high *strategic control and only one firm possesses capabilities in this area*. If the one firm is yours, great; if not, acquisition, partnering, or even exiting the industry should all be considered.

While the process is relatively simple, it can require a fair amount of work (often done in teams over a number of weeks or months) to actually plot it out in detail and dive deep into each area within the Competitive and Capabilities Map. The result can be a fairly complete picture of the value flows in an industry and, accordingly, can provide a useful diagnostic tool to address whether or not a firm is competing in the right part of the market space and/or if an acquisition is needed to compete in the "right" parts of what we call the Competitive and Capabilities Map.

Figure 2.5 is a complete yet simple example of what a Competitive and Capabilities Map in the provision of marine charts might look like.

In figure 2.5, there are four main components:

1 *Value Chain.* As discussed above, the first row(s) are the high "level one" or more detailed "level two" value chain (from left to right).
2 *Strategic Control.* The next main row is the level of strategic control for that part of the value chain. You can use the aforementioned "Harvey Balls," "stoplight" (red/yellow/green) color codes, or some other visual that you may prefer.
3 *Capabilities Required.* A list of the key capabilities required for each part (or column) of the value chain.
4 *List of Competitors and Competencies.* The remainder of the first column should contain a list of all of the key current and

○ ◔ ◑ ◕ ●

Value Chain	Data		Application		Distribution			
Value Chain (Details)	Source Data	Mine Data	Fusion (Application)	Software Code	Paper Distribution	Network Distribution	Access (Hardware)	Product Interface
Level of Strat. Control	High	Low	Low	Low	Low	Med	High	Med
Capabilities Required	Relationship with data owners	Data mining and cataloging software	Algorithm	Software development expertise	Printing Packaging Shipping	Distribution network, hardwarwe access, certification authority (SOLAS)		
Jeppesen Marine	○	◕	●	●	●	◑	○	◕
UK Hydrographic, NOAA/NGA,etc.	●	●	○	○	●	○	○	○
C-Map (Recreational)	●	●	○	○	◕	◕	●	●
Navonics (Rec./Coastal)	●	●	○	○	◕	◕	●	●
IIC	○	○	●	●	◑	●	◑	◑
Seven C's	○	○	●	●	◕	◕	●	◕

Figure 2.5 Competitive and Capabilities Map for digital marine services in the marine navigation market

potential competitors (e.g., UKHO to Seven Cs in the table) and/or relevant suppliers across the value chain – followed by an *objective* measure of their competencies and capabilities in each area of the value chain. For example, in the table, Seven Cs has high capabilities on the application side (Fusion/Software Code), weak or inconsistent capabilities in network distribution, and no access to the data at current. As with the Strategic Control portion above, you can use the aforementioned "Harvey Balls," the "stoplight" (red/yellow/green) color codes, or some other visual that you may prefer.

The table should be created using *today's* capabilities. In some applications, you may want to create a map of where you are today versus where you want to be in the future (i.e., current versus goal), which can help you think carefully about how you plan to obtain the necessary competencies to get from where you are today to your end-goal. You can acquire the competencies organically (if there is time) or via a merger or joint venture (inorganically).

As a general rule, an M&A is preferred if a competitor/supplier listed on the Competitive and Capabilities Map has ownership of a key capability in an area of strategic control but you have few competencies to add to their capabilities in other potential areas of strategic control. Conversely, a joint venture (JV) or partnership is generally preferred when each firm can offer something (i.e., key points of strategic control) to the other firm in the value chain. Think of it this way: when both parties are filling critical needs for one another (i.e., in areas that cannot generally be obtained elsewhere), there is little incentive for the parties to deviate from the partnership. In short, they have a need for each other – an important ingredient in sustainable joint ventures.

The single most common mistake firms make when applying these concepts – and the one point that seems to be the most difficult to grasp – is that the presence (or absence) of a *strategic control point* is industry-based, whereas capabilities are firm-based. A "dream" scenario is when there are points along the value chain that are rivalrous in nature and are significant *strategic control points* while your firm is the only one with capabilities in this area and your capabilities would be exceedingly difficult (or impossible) to imitate. Conversely, the "nightmare" scenario could occur when *strategic control points* exist in the value chain and competitors have capabilities in this area that you do not.

Resist the urge to say "our points of strategic control" since it is not possible for you to own them. Instead, they exist (or do not exist) in the market. You may own competencies in key areas of strategic control. This is not just a nuance; it is an important distinction.

> **Key Takeaway**: Strategic control points are industry-based, whereas competencies are firm-based. We look to obtain difficult (or impossible to imitate) competencies in areas of strategic control that exist in our markets. Avoid confusing the two.

So, what should we do when we've completed all of these steps? Sometimes this is the hardest part:

Step 5: Plot out a course of action for your firm. As you answer the questions above, you should contemplate whether there are rivalrous sources of strategic control – and if there are, how you plan to acquire unique capabilities in these areas. If there are none, are there areas of sustainable, high margins due to entry barriers and cost advantages? If not, perhaps you should consider exiting, doing something else for a living, and competing in another market space: In my book *Compete Smarter, Not Harder*,[11] I detailed the story of MP3.com, an early entrant in the market for digital music distribution, which was started by Thomas Robertson in the late 1990s. In response, the big record labels began suing digital start-ups like MP3.com and Napster. Obviously, suing each start-up that distributed music digitally in the year 2000 wasn't going to stop the tide of digital distribution of music over the internet; it was inevitable. Like the Dutch boy putting his finger in the dike to stop water from flowing through the crumbling dam, they might have stopped one firm by suing but then another would pop up – like a game of

---

11   William Putsis, *Compete Smarter, Not Harder* (Hoboken, NJ: John Wiley and Sons, 2014), pp. 48–9.

whack-a-mole. Unless it's done as part of a sand fence or roadblock strategy (see the definitions below), such a tactic is doomed to fail.

Even business geniuses and legends sometimes adopt futile strategies. Once upon a time, John D. Rockefeller desperately tried to stop Edison and Tesla's electricity from becoming mainstream because it threatened Standard Oil Company, his kerosene business. Fortunately for Rockefeller, a man named Ford saved his refineries by creating an alternative need for crude oil: gasoline (which is a byproduct of kerosene production).

DEFINITIONS: SAND FENCE AND ROADBLOCK STRATEGIES
Firms can use legal maneuvers to slow ("sand fence") or temporarily stop ("roadblock") rival firms from entering their markets. For example, these techniques are often utilized when legal drugs or chemicals come off patent and generics work their way into the market at substantially reduced prices. Sand fence (slowing) or roadblock (trying to stop) strategies can be effective in slowing competitive entry (e.g., via lawsuits) while companies simultaneously build their own entries to beat potential rivals to market. Consider the old adage that "I'd rather cannibalize my own sales than have a competitor do it." While such strategies may buy you time (i.e., to develop your own strategic response to a new entrant or technology), they never work indefinitely by themselves. For example, no one could have prevented the internet from pervading our lives by suing to stop it!

Application to Today – History Repeats Itself

Recall the old George Santayana adage, "Those who cannot remember the past are condemned to repeat it." Well, history is repeating itself again today.

There is a battle going on for the right to deliver content and entertainment directly into our homes. The old model (i.e., boxes atop our television sets, supplying content via a cable or satellite provider, and network broadcasters – such as CBS, NBC, ABC, and PBS – on fixed schedules) is dead. No matter how hard a network, cable, or satellite company might try to do so, it can't stop the inevitable from happening. For example, a local internet provider in Kansas tried to prevent Google Fiber from extending its installation outside of Kansas City. Kansas Senate Bill 304 (SB 304), commonly known as the "Municipal Communications Network and Private Telecommunications Investments Safeguard Act," proposed to restrict a firm's ability to "provide one or more subscribers video, telecommunications or broadband service" "except with regard to un-served areas." SB 304 died in committee on 4 May 2018. It's amazing how little we learn from history.

The future of home entertainment is one of convergence; the delivery mechanism (e.g., fiber optic cable, satellites, drones, balloons, or terrestrial 5G) will be the key to enduring competitive advantage in the future. In order to envision this, think about one interface for all of your content (e.g., television shows, movies, news, and YouTube). You pick the shows that you want to watch (and when you want to watch them); however, you don't stop watching your favorite episode of *Game of Thrones* when you leave the living room; you take it with you on your iPad, smartphone, or glasses. In this environment, the programming flows and follows you seamlessly. The interface and choices are the same no matter what device you are using.

Of course, such a world has already begun. Satellite providers (e.g., Dish) and cable companies (e.g., Comcast and Verizon) already offer the ability to watch content on the go; however, these "content providers" are already facing a different problem – namely, relevance. What if I don't need my cable or satellite television at all anymore? What if I can get my connection from a satellite or UAV overhead? What if my choice of content is on Hulu.com (a content aggregator with shows available on the go) or on demand from Netflix or Amazon Prime (as opposed to on network television at the same time every week)?

In the past, the "big three" networks were a viewer's gateway to content; however, in the future, access will be controlled by the company that can put it all together, offering both content and universal connectivity. In an increasingly streamed environment, the gateway between someone else's content (e.g., movies and television shows) and the end user is most definitively non-rivalrous. Generally, content providers (e.g., Netflix) do not have exclusive distribution rights over the content that is developed by someone else. Indeed, the ability of Netflix to stream a new movie doesn't prevent Amazon from doing the same; however, if they can create in-demand content that is unique, for instance, to Netflix (e.g., *House of Cards* or *Black Mirror*), this can indeed be a form of rivalrous content provision; specifically, when Netflix pays for rights to develop a show exclusive to and for Netflix, this means that you can *only* get it from Netflix. Indeed, like HBO, Netflix has decided that it can create its own control point: original content. To this end, Netflix and Amazon spent almost $11 billion on content in 2017 (only ESPN at $7 billion spent more than either company), ballooning to $13 billion for Netflix in 2018.[12] Of course, the success of such a strategy will depend upon the demand that, for example, Netflix can create for its unique-to-Netflix content.

What may be most important to note is the difference between two very different strategies: (1) an "over the top" or OTT strategy

---

12 See Jeff Dunn, "Netflix and Amazon Are Estimated to Spend a Combined $10.5 Billion on Video This Year," *Business Insider*, 10 April 2017: https://www.businessinsider.com/netflix-vs-amazon-prime-video-content-spend-estimate-chart-2017-4; and Jenna Marotta, "Netflix's Content Budget for 2018 Balloons to $13 Billion," *IndieWire*, 6 July 2018: https://www.indiewire.com/2018/07/netflix-original-content-spending-13-billion-1201981599/.

(typified by Verizon and aggregators such as Hulu) versus (2) an "own the data" or OTD strategy (typified by Google and Facebook):

1 An OTT strategy involves content provision over someone else's network. In the past, this meant that the major networks competed for the hit shows; today, it might be HBO competing with Showtime for the next *Game of Thrones*. While this can certainly be a profitable business model, long-term success requires staying one step ahead with the next hit show. However, this is both expensive and difficult to sustain over time.

2 An OTD strategy enables a Google or Facebook (or a Verizon or a Nokia, for that matter) to leverage the ownership of data not only on who is viewing what show but also on a myriad of other details (e.g., what they are doing, where they are, what they're buying, and where they are going), across virtually every industry in existence.

Which would you rather have – a significant stake in one market that requires continuous and significant ongoing investment to stay one step ahead of rivals (i.e., an OTT strategy) or an investment (as in the OTD strategy) that you can leverage across many industries, taking a cut of each because you own the data critical to every company in that industry (e.g., as Google does in relation to certain insurers in Latin America)? The big picture is, of course, more complicated than this; however, where would you place your bets? Indeed, it is no wonder that the fight for internet provision and location access (i.e., from the "hub" in your house – Google Home Hub, for example – to Fiber on the ground to the satellite, balloon, or a mesh system of drones in the sky) has been intense and led by the companies with the greatest ability to do so.

Finally, it is worth noting that the strategy doesn't have to be either/or. Companies such as Netflix and Amazon have been quite adept at attempting to do a bit of both. For example, while Netflix and Amazon are building their own content, Netflix has decided to pay Comcast for direct access to its network, and Amazon has explored every aspect of an OTD strategy (from Jeff Bezos's Blue Origin venture to its cloud business).

Final Note: On the Importance of Criticality

One important final note relates to the concept of "Criticality," a concept created by Terry Theodore.[13] "Criticality" exists when the failure to perform can result in catastrophic consequences to the offering. An example might be a small seven-cent fastener used in traditional manufacturing. While the value of the part itself is quite small, a fastener that fails may result in significant liability and/or injury or death. Hence, the "criticality" of the fastener is high; however, its cost is quite low. Thus, if a firm producing a fastener has a new and improved process that dramatically reduces the probability of failure, it could potentially earn extraordinarily high margins if it owns the technology that can help reduce the probability of this type of catastrophic event. The key is that the firm must recognize that the part has "criticality" and also have a sustainable advantage in reducing the likelihood of failure.

---

13 Credit goes to Terry Theodore, partner and executive vice-president at Center Rock Capital Partners, for this concept, something he termed "Elements of Strategic Gravity." It is a principle he created and has extended to 42 measurables, employing it effectively as a tool to assess the franchise value of businesses across multiple industries. It can be another effective way of finding and exerting strategic control.

Chapter 2: Key Foundations and Business Principles

- Utilize a process for spotting and identifying points of strategic control:
    - Step 1: Map out the value chain in your industry.
    - Step 2: Identify potential areas for strategic control in your industry's value chain.
    - Step 3: Identify strategic control points that may be controlled by your firm.
    - Step 4: Complete a "Competitive and Capabilities Map."
    - Step 5: Plot out a course of action for your firm.
- The elements in these steps are as follows:
    - Draw out a "level one" value chain for your industry – expand each level by one box in order to build a "level two" value chain. Are there areas of potential strategic control?
    - Expand on the value chain (that you drew above) on a whiteboard. For each portion of the value chain, use your judgment as you add "Harvey Balls" to each step of the value chain.
    - Expand on the value chain you drew above on the whiteboard and create a Competitive and Capabilities Map (as described above). Be sure to include all key competitors (i.e., current and potential) as well as potential suppliers inside the value chain.
- Carefully consider the concept of "rivalry" (i.e., when one firm owns a point of strategic control, it prevents another firm from owning it).
- Identify a *strategic control point* (some key questions to answer):
    1. Does your offering have patent or unbreakable IP protection?

2. Are there rivalrous portions of the value chain?
   a. Can you secure these portions?
3. Do you own (or control) a key portion of the value chain?
4. Can this be leveraged across the value chain?
5. Do you have a key, installed base advantage with switching costs?
6. Do you have a substantial cost advantage (defined by industry/product)?
7. Is there a supply constraint in this sector that you control (e.g., key inputs, capacity constraints on the finished product)?

If you have points of strategic control inside the value chain to leverage:

8. Can these be leveraged to other value chains for other products, in other sectors, in other industries?
9. If yes, how big is the opportunity?
10. Are there advantages that you can leverage simultaneously across different value chains?

PART II

EXTENDING STRATEGIC CONTROL TO MULTIPLE MARKETS

The Competitive Ecosystem and the Visual Value Map

The Internet Connected Coke Machine (1982) – the Internet of Things and the Competitive Ecosystem Are Born

Michael Kazar, former Carnegie Mellon graduate student: There was a Coke machine on the third floor of this eight-story building, and people didn't like the fact that they would go down all the way to the third floor and discover that the Coke machine was empty. Someone said, "Hey, why don't we set it all up so the Coke machine was on the Internet."

David Nichols, fellow graduate student: I was in my office one day and I was thinking I really want a Coke. I can wander all the way down, a five-minute walk, but it might be out. And I thought, I don't need to do this.

Kazar: The way the thing was structured is you had the Coke machine and then a serial line connecting the Coke machine to some terminal concentrator that it just so happened we had control over the source code. It could check 10 times a second. No one really regarded it as the vanguard of things to come or anything. I remember people start talking about when your toaster was on the Internet – but it was always a joke thing and not anything serious.[1]

In many ways, this early "prototype" illustrates what the internet of things (IoT) is all about; in principle, the Coke machine could automatically reorder supply when stock was running low or dynamically change prices, depending upon stock or demand. Coke suppliers would know ahead of time that the syrup supply to the bottlers needed to be increased because the demand at vending machines was increasing. The interconnected vending machine had the potential to impact bottlers, distribution (for firms supplying vending machines), repair and maintenance companies that serviced the vending machines (who could now tell that a machine was out of order or out of stock), even the demand for coffee in the building's cafeteria that might benefit from vending-machine stock-outs. And the list goes on.

One simple idea, connecting vending machines to the internet, had the potential to affect multiple industries. This type of interconnected ecosystem makes today's economy unique. One action affects multiple value chains across multiple high- and low-tech industries alike.

From Internet-Enabled Vending Machines in 1982 to Traffic Lights in 2020

In December 2017, I was at a gathering of about 200 of the world's leading CEOs in New York. One of the people at the summit was Larry Page, the cofounder of Google and CEO of Google's parent company, Alphabet. The moderator, Jeff Sonnenfeld of the Yale

---

1   Source: Danny Vinik, "The Internet of Things: An Oral History," *Politico*, 29 June 2015: https://www.politico.com/agenda/story/2015/06/history-of-internet-of-things-000104.

School of Management, was leading the discussion on the impact of the soon-to-be-passed Tax Cuts and Jobs Act of 2017. In front of this group, Larry Page was asked what he would do with the $86 billion in cash that Alphabet had at the time (mostly overseas) when tax policy changed so that he was able to bring that money back to the United States with more favorable tax treatment. One might think he would respond with "invest in artificial intelligence or blockchain or virtual reality" or some hot new technology. His answer: "traffic lights." In fact, twice more in the next ten minutes, he was asked about topics that had absolutely nothing to do with traffic lights, and his answer each time was "traffic lights." This answer was surprising yet telling. He went on to explain that he sits at his desk in Mountain View, California, most mornings and watches his employees sitting at a traffic light, waiting to come to work. Oftentimes no traffic is moving in any direction; his people are just sitting there waiting for the light to change. He sees this as a waste of time that reduces productivity and impacts the environment (from engines idling for minutes at a time).

However, when he answered "traffic lights," he wasn't talking about traffic lights. He was thinking many steps ahead. He looks into the future and sees that when cars are automated and start talking to each other, we won't need traffic lights at all. Cars will slow, not stop, for other cars automatically, and thus accidents will be avoided and traffic flow will be smooth and unimpeded. In order for this to happen, however, an ecosystem must be built (e.g., cars need to be increasingly autonomous, and inter-vehicle communications must be predictable and secure). Thus, it's not about the traffic lights; the elimination of traffic lights would be the *result* of successful interconnected vehicles, not the *objective* of interconnecting them. Furthermore, it's about building all of the components of the ecosystem so that we won't need traffic lights.

In order to fully understand the ramifications, think of the demands on our infrastructure. There are constant and never-ending calls for more roads to alleviate congestion in urban and suburban areas. However, in a world where most traffic is autonomous and interconnected, we would actually have an *over-abundance* of roads. We just use them inefficiently today. Hence, the impact of autonomous, interconnected vehicles extends well beyond automobile (and related) production to impact road construction-related firms and industries (from asphalt and paving companies to heavy equipment to laborers) as well as local municipal and federal highway budgets.

All of this requires thinking many steps ahead. Larry Page and Sergey Brin, the cofounders of Google, are the only two individuals I have ever heard publicly talk about strategic control points in interconnected markets. They clearly "get it."

"Competitive Diffraction" and the "Competitive Ecosystem"

"Competitive Diffraction"

In previous chapters we addressed various notions of *strategic control points* within an industry. This chapter will expand this notion to include a key element that is unique about today's interconnected world: the impact of a *strategic control point* in one industry on another industry. Indeed, this is how the interconnected nature of today's markets makes the world truly different from that of Vanderbilt, Rockefeller, and Minnetonka.

Often, controlling one part of the market (e.g., a critical component or raw material) can reverberate across other parts of the industry (i.e., away from a core business) – and to other industries as well. Like a sound or light wave that expands once it passes through a small opening (a process called *diffraction* in physics), the impact of owning a *strategic control point* can expand across industry supply chains and multiple and disparate industries via a process we call *"competitive diffraction"* (from the term used in physics). The associated impact can be as close as the next step in the supply chain and as far away as an entirely different market.

DEFINITION: COMPETITIVE DIFFRACTION

In physics, "diffraction" is a term used to describe the spreading out of waves beyond small openings. After a wave passes through a small opening, it has the potential to spread out throughout a large area (e.g., small openings in speakers or a flashlight pointing through a pinhole can spread sound or light throughout an entire room).[2]

"Competitive diffraction" is the process by which one action – often vis-à-vis a point of strategic control – spreads out to and has influence on other industries, much in the way a beam of light spreads beyond an initial small opening.

Analogously, the domination of one small part of an industry vis-à-vis a *strategic control point* can have a significant impact throughout other markets as well. Thus, this chapter addresses the crucial building blocks for competing in the right space today: we should choose market opportunities that can be easily and effectively leveraged into other adjacent markets. In short, before we can decide *how* to compete, we need to decide *where* to compete. Good companies today choose to compete in areas where competencies in

---

2 The same phenomenon that causes waves to bend around obstacles causes them to spread out past small openings. This aspect of diffraction has many implications – for example, this has consequences when you are trying to soundproof a room. Good soundproofing requires that a room be sealed, because any openings will allow sound from the outside to spread out in the room.

areas of strategic control in one market can be leveraged into other adjacent market opportunities.[3]

"The Competitive Ecosystem"

In reality, competition happens not only at each stage of the industry's value chain but also across multiple layers of an entire ecosystem of connected market opportunities via a competitive game being played across markets. While the concept of a value chain is often inward looking based on processes, the concept of a competitive ecosystem is market facing, including both internal processes and market-based effects – most notably competitive interactions across markets. The basic premise is that good companies today are able to leverage competitive strengths in one market for strategic advantage and margin extraction in another. Some examples include the following:

- Apple's strength across its core products enables it to extract greater margins on associated products (e.g., accessories).
- Amazon has leveraged its publishing and supply chain strengths to extract margins for unrelated categories in its marketplace – often to the tune of 20 percent.
- Google leverages strength via its core sponsored search and advertising businesses to support a bevy of other seemingly unrelated businesses (e.g., insurance).
- The sheer scope and volume of Walmart's core business enables it to leverage strength throughout its supply chain.

Thus, an understanding of the notion of a complete market "ecosystem" requires an understanding of the competitive game being

---

3 Indeed, too many companies focus on how well they are competing in their existing markets when this may not even be relevant – such as when firms compete in a part of the market where margins are low or someone else has ownership of critical *strategic control points*. Doing a great job in a bad market is still bad business and will always be a bad business proposition.

played across firms (i.e., at every stage and across stages) and of the *chain reaction* of competitive interactions that occurs. Think of a dynamic *"competitive ecosystem"* where one part of the ecosystem can have a substantial impact on another part.

The Amazing Story of Kudzu[4]

A classic example of the need to anticipate the impact on other parts of an ecosystem is that of the plant kudzu. If you have ever driven in the eastern portion of the United States (particularly in the south), you have seen it. Kudzu has taken over. This plant grows so voraciously that it quickly takes over trees and other plants (choking off their roots). It has become such a problem that study after study and proposal after proposal have been undertaken with the objective of finding a solution to keep its growth and expansion in check; still, it continues to expand and thrive – leaving plant and tree devastation in its wake.

Ironically, kudzu was introduced to the United States *intentionally*. In 1876, at the Centennial Exposition in Philadelphia, countries were invited to build exhibits to celebrate the 100th birthday of the United States. The Japanese government constructed a beautiful garden filled with plants from their country. Kudzu's large leaves and sweet-smelling blooms captured the imagination of U.S. gardeners, who began to use the plant for ornamental purposes. During the Great Depression, the Soil Conservation Service then promoted kudzu for erosion control. Hundreds of young men were hired to plant kudzu via the Civilian Conservation Corps. Farmers were paid as much as $8 an acre as an incentive to plant fields of the vines in the 1940s.

---

4 Source: Excerpts and quotations taken from Max Shores, "The Amazing Story of Kudzu": http://maxshores.com/the-amazing-story-of-kudzu/; accessed 19 March 2019. Original poem, "Kudzu," by James Dickey, *The New Yorker*, 18 May 1963, p. 44: see https://www.newyorker.com/magazine/1963/05/18/kudzu.

"Cotton isn't king in the South anymore. Kudzu is king!"

Channing Cope

"In Georgia, the legend says ... that you must close your windows at night to keep it out of the house."

James Dickey

Since then, kudzu's growth has stretched from Rhode Island to Texas.

While the devastation that kudzu has left in its wake is the subject of much debate,[5] this story illustrates a principle that we see in markets all the time today; had at least some of the consequences of kudzu's devastation been anticipated, it seems unlikely that it would have been allowed to be imported into the United States in the first place. In business, the same principles apply. All too often, we think we're being "sophisticated" by concentrating on supply chain efficiencies – or even thinking about competition inside the supply chain – and finding solutions that work in this narrow frame. Unfortunately, this is often analogous to importing kudzu. Unless we think about all of the unanticipated effects from *outside* this supply chain – or worse yet, fail to consider an effect that one of our competitors *does* anticipate – we run the risk of being the metaphorical plant or tree (depending upon the size of the firm) and being suffocated by kudzu.

In short, the importers of kudzu concentrated only on the reason that it was being imported and ignored the consequences for the associated ecosystem. Similarly, in business, we need to recognize that our core business exists inside of an entire ecosystem; however, ignoring the rest of the ecosystem is what most firms do. This is as bad as ignoring the consequences for the eastern U.S. horticultural ecosystem of importing kudzu.

---

5   Source: Bill Finch, "The True Story of Kudzu, the Vine That Never Truly Ate the South," *Smithsonian*, September 2015: https://www.smithsonianmag.com/science-nature/true-story-kudzu-vine-ate-south-180956325/.

For the business implications, we need look no further than to Samuel Brannon, one of the few to consistently make money from the "Gold Rush" in California in the 1840s, becoming its first millionaire. Yet, Sam Brannon never panned for gold (most of those who went west in search of gold never found it and ended up penniless). Sam Brannon sold pickaxes, overpriced supplies, food, and beer to those who would eventually lose their shirts. In business today, it is rarely very different: the real business opportunities often lie in the wake of the technology.

Nowhere is this more evident than in manufacturing, where advanced robotics, artificial intelligence (AI), IoT interoperability, and integrated supply chains have had impacts far and wide across numerous industries. Indeed, a new generation of robotics (e.g., from companies such as Rethink Robotics of Boston, ABB of Switzerland, and Universal Robotics of Switzerland) costs less than $40,000 and operates for as little as $1 an hour – fully "loaded," they cost approximately $2 an hour.[6] In fact, they can do routinized inline assembly in complex settings better than humans – with more consistency, less downtime, and more reliability.

The implications of this development span multiple industries; indeed, any company that outsources production to another part of the world may now be operating at a *disadvantage*. I recently asked five CEOs of small to mid-size manufacturing firms ($2b to $4b US) the following question: "In the wake of advanced robotics, IoT interoperability efficiencies, additive manufacturing, and the like, have you thought about bringing production back to the United States?" Every single one interrupted me before I finished and said, "We have already started to." In fact, the impact of advanced robotics reverberates across multiple industries, will impact global trade and manufacturing, and will affect industries ranging from automobile manufacturing to

6 Source: Vivek Wadhwa, "Trump's Demand That Apple Must Make iPhones in the U.S. Isn't Actually That Crazy": http://wadhwa.com/articles/; accessed on 18 March 2019, and used by permission of Vivek Wadhwa.

electronics to farming. For an interesting study, look no further than the automated farm equipment produced by the Dutch company Lely (www.lely.com). They automate dairy farming in a way that it has been suggested will help the family dairy farm. However, the impact of the capital required to automate to scale will likely put local family farms – those that are still around – out of business entirely. The "action" often happens behind ("in the wake of") the technology itself.

Similarly, manufacturing operations that are linked to customers "upstream" and suppliers "downstream" through "smart" manufacturing devices will be more efficient than those that are not; indeed, as with the aforementioned Coke vending machine, they can connect to the internet and communicate when additional supply needs to be ordered, thereby helping customers predict demand. Firms that have figured out how to do this efficiently can compete effectively across multiple and diverse industries; for instance, Local Motors has figured this out via crowdsourcing and additive manufacturing (e.g., in vehicles, drones, and microwave ovens), and Amazon has figured this out across a bevy of industries. It is truly a new world.

The consistent utilization of these concepts – in concert – can generate competitive advantages that only a handful of leading companies utilize today. We sometimes refer to this as a "holistic" approach; when we consider a complete view of a market, a holistic approach is the contemplation of every facet of the market affecting the *net response* of the market to a company's offering *before* the company makes any strategic move. This includes looking at things like:

- vertical (up and down the supply chain) and horizontal (across firms selling similar, substitute goods) competition;
- "coopetition"[7] and competition, throughout the scope of a firm's operations; and

---

7   Adam M. Brandenburger and Barry J. Nalebuff, *Co-opetition: A Revolution Mindset That Combines Competition and Cooperation: The Game Theory Strategy That's Changing the Game of Business* (New York: Doubleday Business, 1996).

- demand response net of competitive response (i.e., "residual" demand in the academic literature), which is discussed later in this book.

Assessing, measuring, identifying, and, most importantly, *influencing* all of these factors is an important part of gaining a competitive advantage today.

Extending the Single-Industry Value Chain

Conceptualizing an industry's value chain as we've discussed thus far is inherently incomplete. Competitive interaction across stages of a single industry's value chain, as well as competition across markets, will be crucial to the success or failure of any firm operating today. Fortunately, we can use prior work in economics and empirical analyses of competitive interactions to provide a more functionally useful map of the market. Specifically, research in the field of "empirical industrial organization" provides some direction, suggesting that we need to look at this across multiple dimensions – beyond a traditional single-industry value chain.[8] Competition can reverberate throughout a single value chain in at least a couple of ways: 1) within-stage (or silo), or 2) cross-stage. We begin by exploring each in turn. Building on this, we then detail how to build in and

---

8   There has been much work in economics on the issue of measuring and assessing vertical versus horizontal competitive interactions. See, e.g., R. Tyagi, "A Characterization of Retailer Response to Manufacturer Trade Deals," *Journal of Marketing Research*, 36 (4) (November 1999): 510–16; K. Sudhir, "Structural Analysis of Manufacturer Pricing in the Presence of a Strategic Retailer," *Marketing Science*, 20 (3) (August 2001): 244–64; D. Besanko, J-P Dubé, and S. Gupta, "Own-brand and Cross-brand Retail Pass-through," *Marketing Science*, 24 (1), (2005): 123–37; Ronald W. Cotterill and William P. Putsis, Jr, "Do Models of Vertical Strategic Interaction for National and Store Brands Meet the Market Test?" *Journal of Retailing*, 77 (1) (Spring 2001): 83–109. As a result of this body of work, the ideas set out here are not just conceptual but can be assessed empirically.

anticipate cross-market competitive effects in order to find adjacent market opportunities, the primary objective of this chapter.

1. Within-Stage (or Silo) Competition

Some recent work in the academic literature has focused on the nature and importance of competition across firms. Firms seeking to incorporate some of these best practices should first examine the competitive interactions between firms at each stage within their supply chains (e.g., the cost structures, competitive structures, and how firms interact and/or compete within each stage of the industry value chain). Imagine producing asphalt shingles for roofs (which fuse raw materials – such as asphalt and granulized glass – with fiberglass mats) and then packaging and shipping. A simple "level one" value chain might look like this (figure 3.1):

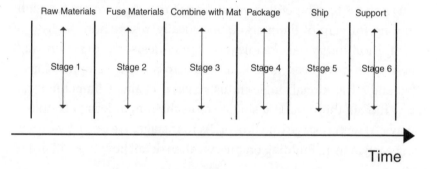

Figure 3.1 Level one value chain with silo competition

The arrows represent competitive analyses and the nature of competitive interactions (e.g., intensity of competition and level of cooperation) at *each* stage of the value chain. In its simplest form, competition takes place only within each stage (e.g., raw material producers compete with other raw material producers; 3D-printer manufacturers compete with each other, etc.); however, within each stage, we know that the form, structure, and intensity of competitive interaction can vary widely from category to category.[9]

So, while you may be a tough competitor in phase 3 above (combining the fused raw materials to the mat forming the base of the shingle), if someone else owns a unique competency in an area of *strategic control* (e.g., asphalt production) and exerts that control competitively upstream by squeezing the margins of the mat manufacturers, then it really doesn't matter how well you compete in phase 3 of the "mat" business (and how efficiently you run your supply chain) – all, or nearly all, potential margins will be squeezed by the asphalt manufacturer, who exerts leverage via any associated *strategic control points* upstream. The notion of "competitive diffraction" suggests that a small opening can create a much bigger wave, such as a reverberation of competitive control throughout the supply chain.

2. Cross-Stage Competitive Interaction

Indeed, we know that each stage does not exist in isolation; the Softsoap® story is just one example of this. In fact, a firm's ability to extract margins throughout the supply chain is correlated with its ability to utilize the power of one stage to extract (sometimes extort) value from another stage. For instance, the power of Apple or Amazon, at various stages of this process, enables them to extract superior margins throughout; Walmart's power, as a retailer, enables them to extract value in even early stages of the supply chain; Intel's power, on the input side, enables it to extract value through to the retail level.

Individuals who are concerned with only a traditional, single-industry value chain are playing the metaphorical equivalent of checkers when a version of three-dimensional chess is the actual game being played.

---

9 See, for example, Cotterill and Putsis, "Do Models of Vertical Strategic Interaction Meet the Market Test?"; and Jan-Benedict Steenkamp, E.M. Vincent, R. Nijs, Dominique Hanssens, and Marnik Dekimpe, "Competitive Reactions to Advertising and Promotion Attacks," *Marketing Science*, 24 (1) (Winter 2005): 35–54.

In short, a simple look at the traditional industry value chain (as presented earlier) is naive at best. The game being played is multidimensional: within stages, across stages, and over time. Further, it may be a competitive game in one part and a cooperative game (as in Brandenburger and Nalebuff's *Co-opetition*) in another. Competitive advantage today can be gained up, down, forward, and backward. Recognizing this can be *the* source of sustainable competitive advantage in a market and hence is a central theme throughout this book.

In the value chain illustrated in figure 3.2, the horizontal arrows represent the transmission of power via competitive interaction *across* stages within the industry's value chain.

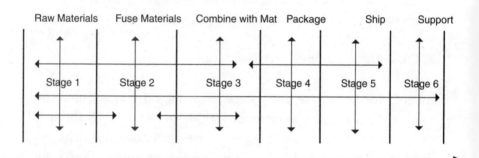

Figure 3.2 Value chain with competitive interaction

The winners in today's networked and information-empowered world will be those that recognize and take advantage of the multidimensional nature of competition – at every stage of what would be thought of as a competitive ecosystem. Today, successful companies (e.g., Google, Walmart, P&G, Apple, Amazon) recognize that transmissions of power – and the ability to extract margins across these stages – ultimately determine success in their businesses.

Building In and Anticipating Cross-Market Competitive Effects in Order to Find Adjacent Market Opportunities in the Competitive Ecosystem

Let's begin by considering the Competitive and Capabilities Map from the previous chapter; this time, let's imagine a series of them – each representing the key factors that influence success or failure in one part of the market. Imagine that we've completed a Competitive and Capabilities Map exercise not just for our core market but also for a number of connected markets – perhaps those at each stage of our core market's value chain as well as other potential adjacent market opportunities. Imagine further that we've printed each Competitive and Capabilities Map on paper and taped them all to a large whiteboard (think of the "Buy a Whiteboard" advice given by Jay Parkinson discussed earlier in the book). Armed with this, we can begin to think about and visualize how a competency in an area of strategic control in our core market may – or may not – translate to other market opportunities.

As an example, think of Apple and several of its core product lines (e.g., computers, iPhones, iPads, and accessories); we can draw a Competitive and Capabilities Map for each of them. Now think about the Competitive and Capabilities Map for televisions – a seemingly unrelated space. The key is finding competitive connections across these disparate industries (e.g., are there ways that Apple can leverage strength in one of its core businesses to exert influence and extract superior margins in the television market)?

We can illustrate this via the diagram capturing each respective Competitive and Capabilities Map (see figure 3.3).

In this final step, firms should examine how cross-market influence may be exerted (think back to the kudzu story from earlier). Indeed, capabilities in one market can often be leveraged into adjacent (or even unrelated) markets. For example, Amazon has taken its supply-chain expertise into multiple markets, and Local Motors is

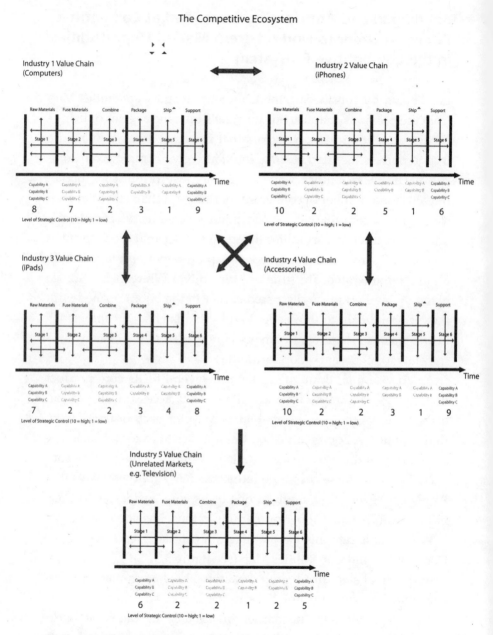

Figure 3.3 The competitive ecosystem

producing 3D-printed microwave ovens for GE and helping Airbus create revolutionary local parts-supply networks. The identification of these opportunities is the key to success in the interconnected environment of today and represents the difference between success and failure, disintermediation and dominance.

To illustrate, for Apple, in figure 3.3, the four core products may or may not give it a key advantage in an "unrelated" market (e.g., one that focuses on the manufacturing of televisions). The competitive advantage in iPhones and what this does to help Apple's position in the iPad value chain may be obvious; however, the interactions *across* each of the four product value chains and televisions may be less so. The key to success, in this example, isn't how well Apple can compete in the television business in its own right; the key will be how well it is able to leverage the strengths in a core business (e.g., iPhones and iPads) for strategic advantage and superior margins in this new market (televisions). Indeed, for years now, Apple has been leveraging these types of relationships within disparate industry value chains and thus creating and building a competitive ecosystem. More generally, the key in today's markets is how you can use these interconnected value chains to find competencies in areas of strategic control in one market and leverage them into other value chains.

As an illustration based on a recent consulting project, imagine that you have unique and proprietary intellectual property (IP) in your core market that is in a key area of strategic control (the "core market" value chain in figure 3.4). This IP enables you to collect data (labeled "Collection" in the value chains in figure 3.4) in a unique way that no other competitor can. Imagine further that you are considering entering one of two adjacent markets, let's call them "Market A" and "Market B," which have value chains as shown in figure 3.4 (recall that a full "Harvey Ball" denotes an area of the market that is a *strategic control point* while, on the other end of the spectrum, an empty Harvey Ball means that there is no *strategic control point*).

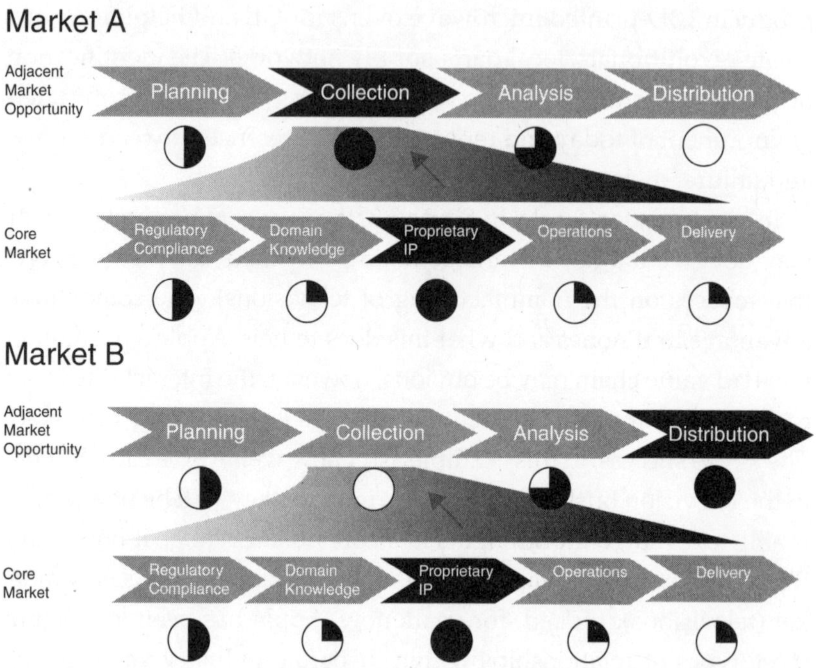

Market A

Market B

Figure 3.4 Adjacent market opportunities A and B: Harvey Ball comparison

In this hypothetical example, data collection is a key *strategic control point* in market A, whereas distribution is the key *strategic control point* in market B.

So, which market would you enter, A or B?

The clear choice is market A. The unique and proprietary IP that enables your firm to collect data more efficiently than all of your competitors gives you unique competencies in an area that is a *strategic control point* in market A but buys you nothing in market B (where distribution is a *strategic control point*).

This is what we look for in the interconnected world of today – a direct connection between unique capabilities that we have – a *strategic control point* – in one market (here, in our core market) and a critical *strategic control point* in another (here in Market "A"). Doing detailed analysis like this enables us to see connections across value chains that can drive long-term success.

The Importance of "Platforms" in an Ecosystem

In today's interconnected environment, we look for a series of interconnected value chains that enable us to leverage strength from one market to another. The reason for this is simple. What would you rather have – a unique capability in an area of strategic control in one part of a market that ends there or a unique capability that can be leveraged into strategic advantage (vis-à-vis a single strategic control point) across multiple markets? This is a lesson that the CEOs of good companies today recognize, from Elon Musk (Tesla) to Jack Ma (Alibaba) to Tim Cook (Apple) and Larry Page and Sergey Brin (Alphabet).

A "platform" is any offering that enables you to connect a competency in one market to multiple value chains. This platform doesn't have to be physical; it is any offering that enables us to leverage our strengths into multiple opportunities. For example, Amazon's cloud service (AWS) and Marketplace enable them to leverage these offerings into multiple markets; Google's Maps app and Android OS enable them to leverage this into numerous markets. An "ecosystem" comprises all of the interconnected value chains. Think of Apple's Mac OS and iOS as the platforms that allow all of the devices to interconnect. The individual devices (iPhone, iPad, Apple TV, Mac computers, etc.), together with the Mac OX and iOS, make up the ecosystem. It's that simple.

To illustrate, we build on the hypothetical market diagram in figure 3.4 presented earlier.

In this example, the proprietary IP that enabled us to own a strategic control point in our core market also gives us unique capabilities in key points of strategic control in adjacent markets (see figure 3.5). This is precisely what we look for in trying to spot new market opportunities.

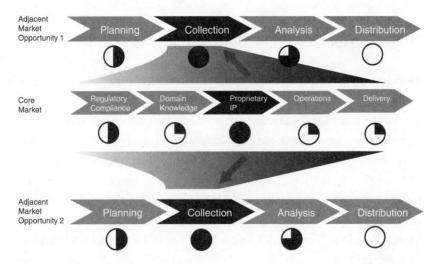

Figure 3.5 Adjacent market expansion: Building ecosystems by leveraging strategic control across markets

> **DEFINITIONS: PLATFORMS AND ECOSYSTEMS**
> The "platform" is the offering in our core market that can be connected or leveraged to other markets. The "ecosystem" consists of all the interconnected markets linked by market-based strategic control points.

Recognizing this often enables you to find multiple opportunities that can take a single competency to a whole set of markets and is a key to competing effectively today in our interconnected world. Once we have identified the core competencies that we can leverage across one or more adjacent value chains vis-à-vis points of strategic control, we can begin to set our strategy. As you begin to do this, consider whether there are any rivalrous sources of strategic control and how you plan to acquire or own them. If not, should we be in this market at all? Are there areas of sustainable and high margins (e.g., due to entry barriers and cost advantages)? If not, perhaps you should consider doing something else, such as competing in another market space.

Example: Lincoln Industries

Lincoln Industries is not typically a household name, but we all have seen their work. They are the largest privately held finishing company in the United States, based in, you guessed it, Lincoln, Nebraska. They are known for their world-class fabricating and plating, doing finishing for companies like Harley-Davidson and Peterbilt Trucks. Those shiny chrome exhausts on a Peterbilt truck or a Harley motorcycle are uniquely Lincoln, as they provide world-class finishes that shine for effect and don't pit. The shiny chrome is important to both Harley and Peterbilt customers, providing Lincoln with a unique capability in an area that is pivotal to these key customers. Further, they have been astute enough to move up Harley's value chain to manage their supply chain, something that provides superior margins.

However, in 2017, Lincoln Industries faced growth challenges and looked to leverage existing strategic control points to new adjacent markets. How could they find the "right" industries to expand to, those industries that would enable them to have unique competitive advantages that would afford them superior margins?

Wisely, they looked to the type of analysis addressed here – they developed Competitive and Capabilities Maps for each of their core lines of business, identifying key capabilities in areas of strategic control (e.g., high-end fabricating and finishing that were not easily imitated). From this, they developed a list of adjacent market opportunities that they *thought* these might fit well with and provide sustainable competitive advantages.

Using this list of potential opportunities, they produced a series of Competitive and Capabilities Maps (see figure 3.6), each concentrating

on areas of potential expansion. In figure 3.6 (where the details are concealed to protect confidentiality), imagine that this was your industry and try to use this example to bring it back to your particular situation (circles and arrows depict the parts of the industry value chains that are connected by the firm's core capabilities):

Industry 1: Lincoln's core industry
Industry 2: Potential market opportunity in an unrelated one-step
    adjacent market

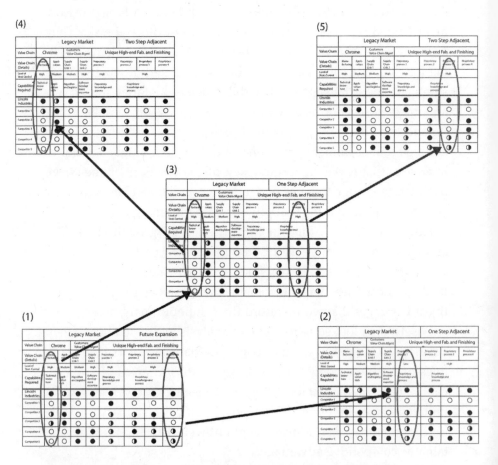

Figure 3.6 Competitive and Capabilities Maps for Lincoln Industries

Industry 3: Potential market opportunity in an unrelated one-step
   adjacent market
Industry 4: Potential market opportunity in an unrelated two-step
   adjacent market
Industry 5: Potential market opportunity in an unrelated two-step
   adjacent market

For industry 1, they developed a detailed Competitive and
Capabilities Map for motorcycles, focusing on what they do for
Harley-Davidson in terms of chrome plating, precision fabrication,
and supply chain. Industries 2 and 3 were entirely different markets
into which they had been contemplating expanding for years. The
analysis revealed that while, on face value, industry 2 seemed like
a logical adjacent market extension, their capabilities in their core
market afforded them no unique capabilities in areas of strategic
control in this market. Further, there were no unique capabilities in
industry 2 that could be expanded upon further. By contrast, industry 1 not only gave them a unique capability in industry 3 in a potential area of strategic control (two circles in industry 3 above) but
also gave them unique capabilities in markets adjacent to industry
3, namely industries 4 and 5. In figure 3.6, the circles in industries 4
and 5 indicate the capabilities in industry 3 that could be leveraged
to provide a competitive advantage in industries 4 and 5.
   That's what we look for today: an ecosystem of competitive advantage and avenues for growth into adjacent markets that take advantage of key core competencies. In figure 3.6, industries 1, 3, 4, and 5
would constitute an ecosystem in that an advantage in industry 1
provides leveraged advantages in industries 3, 4, and 5. By contrast,
industry 2 is a separate, stand-alone industry. While you may or may
not have sustainable competitive advantages in industry 2, they do
not constitute an ecosystem in that they do not build on and comple-
ment each other (since the industry two's competitive advantages
provide no unique advantages in another market opportunity).

We can begin extending the single-industry context to the world of Local Motors, the company mentioned earlier that additively manufactures (i.e., 3D prints) automobiles. We do this by sketching out a visual map (i.e., an illustration) of the major players in the immediate ecosystem; this way, you can begin to see what a "Visual Value Map" might look like. We begin with this example.

In order to additively manufacture something (i.e., via 3D printing), we need a number of tools. Of course, we need a "printer," which adds successive layers, cumulatively, to create a 3D version of an object, which is designed via computer source code; thus, we need to develop the source code and the material (e.g., plastics and composites) that will be used to manufacture our product and the printer itself. We might often also need to finish, assemble, pack, ship, and distribute the final printed product. Hence, we can outline a simple level-one industry value chain roughly as follows: (1) develop code (open or closed source, proprietary, or "crowd sourced"); (2) input code to the algorithm and printer; (3) distribute raw materials to the printing site; (4) develop and deliver the printer to the manufacturing site; (5) prepare tooling and set up; (6) process code ("printing process"); (7) implement tooling and final assembly; (8) complete final finishing; (9) carry out distribution; and (10) provide for sales, service, and support. Additionally, each of these stages has its own respective industry value chain. Thus, imagine the aforementioned set of hypothetical individual industry value chains, which all lead, in this case, to the focal industry in this example: Local Motors (and the 3D printing of automobiles). We can think of the whole set of interconnecting industry value chains as follows:

- Source code and design can be "open sourced" (i.e., anyone has access to it); this whole process of crowd-sourcing (and institutionalizing the process) has its own value chain.
- Source code can be "closed sourced" (i.e., proprietary); the development of the design (and putting it to code) has its own development and value chain.

- The generation of materials utilized in the process (i.e., from simple composites to advanced metal) is associated with its own set of industries, research, and value chains.
- The 3D printers constitute a market with its own value chain.
- The final assembly and tooling consist of multiple industries and multiple value chains (often borrowing and adapting processes and tools from traditional manufacturing).
- Distribution has its own value chain, which is potentially quite different from traditional distribution. In this context, we can produce locally, so the physical product may need to travel considerably shorter distances; however, the material input will need to be distributed locally, which involves a set of different issues.

And the list goes on. A 3D printing "platform" involves a whole set of interconnected value chains and interconnected industries. For our purposes, strategic control in one part of this platform can reverberate across other parts. For example, if you own a key patent on a more efficient and reliable nozzle (used in the printers), you can extract a disproportionate share of the margins in each of the aforementioned individual industry value chains.

If Local Motors has a strategic advantage in the community that designs and builds code, they can extend this (e.g., from vehicles to motorcycles to bicycles to drones and even to microwave ovens). Thus, in many markets today, the capabilities in one market or platform (e.g., designing, building, and selling automobiles) can be leveraged into almost countless manufacturing applications, industries, and industry value chains. The competitive ecosystem around additive manufacturing is limited only by the technological limitations of the material being used in the manufacturing. The "Visual Value Map" (figure 3.7) is a way of capturing the relationships in the industry:

The diagram in figure 3.7 expands the linear "level one" industry value chain to include the notion that each part of the level one value chain has multiple parts.

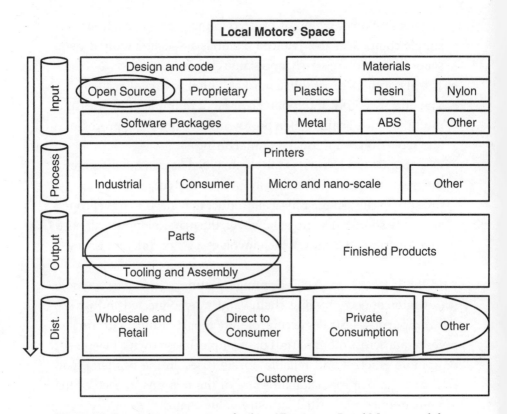

Figure 3.7 Expanding ecosystems further: 3D printers, Local Motors, and the "Visual Value Map"

Note that the "standard" level one industry value chain presented earlier is represented here (on the left side) via the value chain running from top to bottom. (It could also run from left to right [on top] – simply reversing the axis.) For each component, you can "sketch" out the relevant parts and present this visually. For any one component, you can explore further, now that you can visualize how the parts interconnect. For example, we can divide and explore the three circled parts, one by one:

1 *Open Source Code* – There is a community of code writers in this space; indeed, Local Motors has generated significant loyalty in

this area by providing not just financial success but also prestige to those who help them design (i.e., code) their new vehicles. To the extent that any one company, such as Local Motors, can have such a strategic advantage (e.g., attracting the best coders and designers), they will have a significant strategic advantage throughout this map.

2 *Parts* – This may be one of the more interesting and complex "sub-ecosystems" in the entire Visual Value Map; not only are parts (exactly forty-nine in the case of the Local Motors Strati vehicle) needed to manufacturer the vehicle, but the associated advantages, in this one area, also have the potential to reverberate through myriad sub-value chains, including (i) parts manufacturing (e.g., original equipment manufacturers [OEM], OEM suppliers, and replacement part manufacturers); (ii) parts distribution (traditional distribution will change, as the manufacturing of parts is now done locally and the number of parts to be distributed shrinks considerably); and (iii) auto parts retailing (e.g., stores will change from stocking inventory to printing parts – or shut down entirely).

3 *Distribution* – The process of distribution is now very different from that in earlier eras. Now, automobiles can be printed on-site – even in the back of an eighteen-wheeler. The sales process can be done via the internet, in a mobile "factory" – or just about anywhere.

Key Takeaway: Considering the "big picture" Visual Value Map (figure 3.7) makes it much easier to see how the parts interconnect and how an advantage in one section (e.g., parts manufacturing, 3D printing, or code sourcing) can reverberate through other, interconnected parts. Indeed, you can take any of the boxes above and dig down much deeper to acquire additional insights. So, try drawing one for your market. What do you learn from it?

Let's think back to a couple of examples already discussed. We initially explored how Google – which controls the information coming off its platforms – is profiting from the ability to extract margins from this activity by sharing some of this information with disparate industries, from insurance to advertising. Similarly, Amazon is able to extract a margin (approximately 20 percent) on every item sold in its Marketplace by virtue of the platform it has in place. Local Motors also has the potential to do this via the process technology it is building. If it can do this, the potential is limitless; however, if it can't, there may be little reason to be in the industry at all. Hence, the key to succeeding in today's interconnected world is understanding where the key *strategic control points* are inside an ecosystem – and how to leverage these across various parts of the ecosystem.

Companies can sometimes be part of multiple value chains across multiple markets; for example, as noted earlier, Apple controls its entire "ecosystem," from design and R&D to manufacturing to the requirements of apps to the retail sales in its Apple stores. When you purchase an iPad, you are actually purchasing a bundle of Apple offerings. As Walter Isaacson, the Steve Jobs biographer, stated in a *60 Minutes* interview, "Only a complete control freak like Steve Jobs could control all aspects of its business like this."[10] Amazon

---

10 Walter Isaacson noted that Steve Jobs had created a walled garden: if you wanted to use any of his products, it was easier to buy into the whole Apple ecosystem. It was something "only a complete control freak" could have pulled off. Source: CBS, *60 Minutes*, "Revelations from a Tech Giant," interview with Walter Isaacson, original air date 23 October 2011. To illustrate how this is true even today (and perhaps the reason why Tim Cook was tapped to be the successor to Steve Jobs), in 2015 the supply chain for Apple's products consisted of 198 global companies with 759 subsidiaries. Seamus Grimes of National University of Ireland and Yutao Sun of Dalian University of China studied each of the 759 subsidiaries and categorized the electronics components into core, non-core, and assembly-related, with the high-cost, intellectual property-dependent technologies being designated as core. They found that 336, or 44.2 percent, of these subsidiaries were manufacturing in China; 115 were in Taiwan; and 84 in Europe or the United States. When they looked into the ownership of subsidiaries that were manufacturing in China, they found that only 3.95 percent were Chinese and only 2.2 percent of the core component suppliers

is developing very similar capabilities, from one-click ordering to control of the retail interface online to the storage capabilities in the "cloud" to controlling the publisher's offering and terms – all to its strategic advantage. So, the notion that you need to own or control one key *strategic control point* is clearly too myopic.

Today, Google's has the ability to access and potentially control all aspects of internet and content delivery. Indeed, Google is trying to dominate the "hub" (i.e., ubiquitous high-speed internet access) – which will be a key *strategic control point* in the future – for the next generation of communication devices (beyond the smartphone). Google recognizes that every piece of information generally goes through one hub; if they were able to develop and run the ultra-high-speed broadband service in addition to the aforementioned "nodes" of content delivery, they could take margins from virtually any industry that needs information they have unique access to. The key is in owning the internet connection; indeed, they own that – and they own you.

Key Takeaway: Google has mastered the concept of the competitive ecosystem like no other company. Amazon and Apple come close; Jeff Bezos at Amazon and Steve Jobs (at Apple before him) both realized the importance of leveraging strength across multiple markets. This is the lesson for today's business environment – a lesson above all else.

---

were Chinese. The largest proportion – 32.7 percent – were Japanese; 28.5 percent were American; 19.0 percent were Taiwanese; and 6.5 percent were European. Thus, more than half of the components of Apple's products are imported into China, and Chinese companies make practically none of the important core technologies. Despite much of the production for Apple being conducted in China, Apple still controls virtually all of the core technology and intellectual property. Source: Vivek Wadhwa, "Trump's Demand That Apple Must Make iPhones in the U.S. Isn't Actually That Crazy": http://wadhwa.com/articles/. Accessed on 18 March 2019, and used by permission of Vivek Wadhwa.

The Three-Dimensional Chess Board of Today

Fans of *Star Trek* will recall that, in a number of episodes, Captain Kirk and Spock would be playing a three-dimensional variant of chess; on a par with this concept,[11] it is immediately apparent that the map in figure 3.7 is complicated. However, the complicated map (like three-dimensional chess) can be broken down into individual components in order to see the big picture.

Ultimately, strategically successful firms are not only able to do well at competing on these different levels; they are also able to compete successfully in multiple, interconnected areas – while also recognizing (and taking advantage of) how these parts interconnect.

This is important for your business, since building a Visual Value Map (e.g., as in the battle for internet provision) must anticipate the market impact. *Never* let the impact of interconnected markets catch you by surprise. The likely outcome of such a surprise is the business equivalent of "checkmate" on a three-dimensional chessboard.

In order to illustrate the interconnected nature of the world in which we live, let's now consider two articles published on the front page of the "Business and Technology" section of the *Wall Street Journal* on the same day back in April 2016.[12] At first glance, they are entirely unrelated: one is about earthquakes in Japan, and the other is about Airbus's satellite production.

The first article ("Japan Earthquakes Rattle Toyota's Vulnerable Supply Chain") discusses how the one-time envy of the world, Japan's "just in time" (JIT) production, has often led to disastrous production

---

11 Interestingly, while it had the appearance of being more complex, the board consisted of three 4 x 4 layers and four more 2 x 2 areas for a total of 64 squares – the same number as there are in chess.

12 Source for both articles: *Wall Street Journal*: 1) Yoko Kubota, "Japan Earthquakes Rattle Toyota's Vulnerable Supply Chain": https://www.wsj.com/articles/japan-earthquakes-rattle-toyotas-supply-chain-1460986805; and 2) Andy Pasztour, "Airbus Joint Venture Aims to Churn out Satellites": https://www.wsj.com/articles/airbus-joint-venture-aims-to-churn-out-satellites-1461011968, both published on 18 April 2016.

delays. In this case, Toyota temporarily shut down twenty-six car assembly lines in Japan. Lean assembly without disruption can be incredibly efficient; however, disruption in one part of the chain can reverberate throughout the entire chain and lead to costly delays.

The second article ("Airbus Joint Venture Aims to Churn out Satellites") discusses Airbus's joint venture to produce small, approximately 300-pound, advanced satellites at a rate never before achieved, even remotely (e.g., as many as fifteen satellites per week). Interestingly, the facility is slated to be located on-site at the Kennedy Space Center – next to Jeff Bezos's Blue Origin LLC.

So, what do supply-chain disruptions in Japan caused by a series of earthquakes have to do with satellites being produced in Florida? Well, the JIT production that made Japan great in the 1970s and 1980s is rapidly giving way to IoT, interconnected devices so that the supply chain – now interconnected through the cloud and guided by AI optimization algorithms – adjusts to any disruption automatically. These processes are connected globally through the internet, provided by satellite communications that Airbus, Boeing, Google, Facebook, Amazon, and others are frantically fighting over as you read this. Thus, information will reverberate to the cloud and then throughout the supply chain in a matter of seconds. As a result, supply-chain disruptions, like that mentioned in the article about Toyota's supply chain, will mostly be a thing of the past.

The winners in this battle will be the backbone of future production and remind us of how Japan's Lean Six Sigma and JIT production efficiency transformed factories worldwide back in the 1980s. The winner? Global growth. So, hold onto your hats; you may think the internet, as we now know it, has transformed our lives. However, we're about to witness unprecedented growth.

The old model of production efficiency is rapidly giving way to IoT (internet of things) cloud-based interconnectivity, led by automated robotics, artificial intelligence, additive manufacturing (3D printing), and interconnected devices, resulting in supply-chain efficiencies and factory automation in ways we have never seen before. Gartner group (in numbers that are likely inflated but not by as much as you might think) estimates that by 2025 the "Industrial Internet" will dwarf the "Consumer Internet," generating a staggering $32 trillion in revenue.[13]

For those of us running a business today, it is extraordinarily difficult to see – let alone correctly act on – all of the interconnected parts of the markets in examples like this. Often, the secondary effects reverberating across markets are not easily seen or anticipated – hence the importance of building the Visual Value Map, a tool to help us visualize the frequently disparate but connected parts.

The general concept of the Visual Value Map, as illustrated earlier (see figure 3.7), can be extended to other industries as well. Here, we can think about earlier discussions around internet provision and see that:

- Google's ability to provide the full range of services gives them a huge advantage over rivals; let's think of this in the context of a "Google ecosystem" consisting of a full range of disparate parts – on a par with Apple's "ecosystem," which allows it to sell small adapters for exorbitant prices.
- The key, however, is the provision of ultra-high-speed, ubiquitous, broadband internet connections. This *strategic control point*, if it were in place, would mean that Google could potentially be the only company in the market to be able to simultaneously provide all three key components: (i) the ubiquitous internet connection, (ii) all of the associated desired components, and (iii) a device that interconnects with the system (e.g., Google Glass or an Android-run smartphone).

---

13 As noted earlier, we are expected to have more than 50 billion connected devices by 2020 that will generate $11 trillion a year by 2025 and cumulatively $32 trillion by 2025. Source: McKinsey & Company, McKinsey Global Institute, "Digital America: Tale of the Haves and Have-Mores," December 2015.

- Once this "ecosystem" is put into place, the marginal related incentives of any potential rival (i.e., to introduce the ubiquitous internet connection, all of the nodes, and even the glasses themselves) are reduced substantially; indeed, what would be left for this new entrant is leftovers after Google's entry. In short, order matters.

Further, there are numerous ways to enhance profitability by strategically using the concept of a competitive ecosystem:

1 *Margin extraction due to advantageous competitive structure and competitive advantage.* This is the "classic" view of being able to extract profit by offering superior products in a market with a limited number of competitors and monopoly rents.
2 *Use of a key strategic control point.* Again, this is primarily about leveraging, owning, or controlling a *strategic control point* to extract greater margins in the competitive ecosystem.
3 *First-mover advantages related to strategic control points* (versus imitable attributes). The lesson from the literature (i.e., on advantages and disadvantages for early movers) suggests that when firms move early and gain control of *strategic control points*, they have sustainable competitive advantages over time.
4 *Owning back to front in a competitive ecosystem* (e.g., Apple and Amazon). If you don't own an important *strategic control point* in the competitive ecosystem that you can leverage, can you provide all aspects of the competitive ecosystem and combine them in a way that no one can match? Both Apple and Amazon have done a great job of utilizing this principle to attain strategic success.
5 *Leveraging the principle of asset specificity.* A recent area of research focuses on the utilization of "asset specificity" for aligning incentives across two parties. A small investment in assets specific to a relationship may align the incentives of the parties

in a market. We discussed this in great detail earlier and suggest that a horizontal and vertical incentive alignment is a crucial part of any strategy within any business-to-business (B2B) and/or business-to-consumer (B2C) market today.

What do you learn from this? The tools can be incredibly powerful, enabling you to spot opportunities that you might never have seen otherwise – or leading you to conclude that divestiture is the best option.

Either way, use this to your advantage.

Chapter 3: Key Foundations and Business Principles

- *Strategic control points* exist in contexts where access to (and control of) a certain part of the competitive ecosystem can result in substantial advantages throughout an industry's value chain – and in other markets more broadly.
- Developing Competitive and Capabilities Maps can help you understand gaps that may exist in your current capabilities.
- Visual Value Map analysis begins with the industry supply chain but then traces competition both horizontally and vertically.
- The business objective of Visual Value Map analysis is often to detect areas where advantageous margin opportunities exist and strategic leverage may be exerted.
- The process of expanding along the competitive ecosystem follows a classic sequence:
  - Determine the long-term strategic vision and work backwards to your current core – a step at a time.
  - Map out the competitive ecosystem in detail.
  - Identify key *strategic control points* and areas for potential value extraction.
  - Map out core competencies across all players in the market and across all areas of the competitive ecosystem.
  - For the areas where competencies are lacking (i.e., in key *strategic control points*), assess organic versus inorganic competency acquisition.
  - An exit or a "no entry" decision may be warranted in markets where (i) core competencies in areas of strategic control and/ or margin extraction are weak (relative to key competitors) and (ii) organic and inorganic competency acquisition is not feasible or financially realistic. Make the tough decision.
- Matching areas of competency in key areas of the competitive ecosystem can help guide strategic investment – particularly in areas where gaps may exist.

On the Outside Looking In: What Happens When Someone Else Owns a Strategic Control Point?

What can you do if someone else has a unique competency in a point of strategic control? Is it rivalrous or non-rivalrous?
If rivalrous, think like Rockefeller.

It was the early 1880s and John D. Rockefeller had a problem. While his company, Standard Oil, controlled some 90 percent of U.S. refinery capacity, Cornelius Vanderbilt and Tom Scott (owners of by far the two largest railroads) agreed to make their most significant client, Rockefeller's Standard Oil Company, pay "going rates" on shipping oil by rail.[1] Previously, Rockefeller had received significantly discounted rates, which provided him with a substantial cost advantage (over the few rivals that he did have) and better margins on the oil that he sold. Rockefeller viewed the rate increase as a declaration of war and vowed to find another way. Unfortunately for Rockefeller, rail was the only way to get oil from a number of oil fields to his refineries and was thus a classic *strategic control point*. When it came to getting his oil from point A to point B, he was "on the outside looking in."

Enter Tidewater and the pipeline.

Rockefeller's solution was to find his own alternative to the strategic control of the railroads – build a pipeline. Beginning with a

---

1   Source: The History Channel's *The Men Who Built America*, episode 2, www.history. com.

majority stake in the Tidewater Pipe Company, his companies laid one and a half miles of pipeline a day, eventually constructing a pipeline that was more than 4,000 miles long – connecting lucrative oil wells across Ohio and Pennsylvania directly to Standard Oil refineries. While it was a huge task that only a Rockefeller, Carnegie, or Vanderbilt could have undertaken at the time, it was also a huge success. The marginal cost of shipping oil to the refinery was now close to zero, and all margins were internalized to Standard Oil. Better yet, Rockefeller had won his war against the railroads by making what was once a critical *strategic control point* into something that was no longer even a part of the kerosene production value chain. Brilliant.

As a brief aside, it is ironic that once the pipeline was constructed, Rockefeller no longer needed the railroads; however, the railroads increasingly needed *his* oil as the volume of shipments by rail plummeted at the turn of the century. The railroads had forced him into a corner that pushed him to do something (i.e., construct a pipeline) that led to their own irrelevance.

We now focus on seven potential strategies for overcoming someone else's *strategic control point*. Specifically, what do you do when someone else owns that key point of strategic control? – something we refer to as being "on the outside looking in."

Seven Strategies for Overcoming Strategic Control

As with Rockefeller's solution of building a pipeline (the workaround for the stranglehold that the railroads had on oil shipments), there are various strategies for working around points of strategic control that are owned by someone else. We break these down into seven main strategies:

1 Find a release.
2 Seize the addiction.
3 Disintermediate, disintermediate, disintermediate.

4 Build a better mousetrap.
5 Proliferate and imitate.
6 Utilize the entire value chain and avoid the "commodity trap."
7 Surrender to the curve.

Let's now look at each of these in more detail:

1. *Find a release.* Lessen a rival's key point of strategic control.

Sometimes you can't easily access a point of control, and so you need to find a strategy to work effectively around it. Apple, with the success of its iTunes platform, had tied customers to its iTunes, iPod, iPad, and iPhone by pulling all of their music, apps, and information into a single, interconnected platform; given the early development of the App Store, users typically spent hundreds of dollars on apps. Thus, they would have to start all over again if they were to switch from Apple's iOS and still wanted the same, or similar, apps on their non-iOS-based smartphone. Indeed, for smartphones, the OS (operating system) is incredibly "sticky." How many of us have faced this same dilemma? You like that new Samsung; however, you have a number of Apple devices and are thus part of the Apple "ecosystem."

So, let's examine the strategic options available to Google when they developed a strategy for the Android operating system after purchasing Android, Inc., in 2005:

a. Become an iOS app developer. If you can't beat them, join them;
   after all, tough competitors (e.g., Nokia, RIM, Dell, Palm, and
   Microsoft) had tried to beat Apple at their own game and all had
   failed – often dramatically.
b. Go it alone and beat Apple at its own game. Move forward
   based on the belief that it is possible to do this better and
   more successfully – even with Apple's iTunes and App Store

dominance (and its point of strategic control growing stronger as the iPhone penetration and cumulative spend on existing iOS apps have increased over time).

c. Find a way to bring the collective of the industry together to fight Apple's iOS strategic control point – of course using the Android OS as the instrument.

Google wisely chose Option C, combined it with incentive alignment (Google gave carriers 30 percent of the Android app store cut), and attempted to develop a viable strategy to "find a release" from Apple's strategic control. Fred Vogelstein in *Dogfight: How Apple and Google Went to War and Started a Revolution*, tells the story well:[2]

But by 2010 it was also clear that Rubin and Android were playing a much more sophisticated game than Apple's previous competitors. To them the hub wasn't the laptop or the desktop computer, but the millions of faceless machines running 24-7 in Google's giant network of server farms – now often referred to as the cloud. Connecting and syncing with a personal computer – the way iTunes was set up – was necessary when devices didn't have wireless capability or when wireless bandwidth was too slow to be useful. But in 2010 neither was true, prompting Rubin and the Android team to ask, why tether users to one machine when the Wi-Fi and cellular chips inside smartphones are fast enough to let them have access to their content on any machine? Android now wirelessly synced with virtually all mail, contact, and calendar servers – whether stored at Google, Microsoft, or Yahoo!, or at a worker's company. Music and movies could be downloaded from Amazon in addition to the iTunes store. Spotify and Pandora offered music subscription services for small monthly fees. Developers were scrambling to make sure that all of the programs inside the Apple app store could be found inside the Android

---

2 Source for both the quotation and the 30 percent figure used in this section: Fred Vogelstein, *Dogfight: How Apple and Google Went to War and Started a Revolution* (New York: Farrar, Straus and Giroux, 2013), 141–2.

app store too. As for all that content trapped inside iTunes, Google and the rest of the software industry were writing programs that made it easier and easier to get it out and uploaded to Google – or anywhere. With many new ways to download and enjoy content on Android devices, the penalty for using a non-Apple device that wouldn't connect to iTunes was diminished. Freed from this control, users were choosing Android devices in droves. ...

Thus, Google incentivized carriers to adopt, sell, and push Android-based phones via an offer of 30 percent of the cut of associated Android app store sales; as a result, it was able to significantly lessen Apple's strategic control. As Android adoption grew and as the proliferation strategy of Samsung and others continued to succeed, the position of Google in this space only improved over time.

Google used the lessons discussed earlier by providing a "carrot," vis-à-vis incentive alignment (by giving 30 percent of Android app store revenue back to the carriers), and a "stick" (finding a way to effectively lesson Apple's point of strategic control) to fight back against Apple (methods more effective than those used earlier by Dell, Palm, Nokia, RIM, Microsoft, and other very strong players). How can you learn from this? What can you do in your industry?

Finding creative ways to lessen existing points of strategic control is not limited to high-tech solutions. Sometimes you can find low-tech solutions to high-technology problems.

"High-frequency trading" is a fancy name for an automated trading platform – used by large investment banks and institutional investors – that utilizes powerful computers at extremely high speeds. The speed of the trades is crucial, and those trades that are executed from locations closer to Wall Street in lower Manhattan can often have a micro-second(s) advantage on a trade, an advantage that can make a significant financial difference on high-speed, high-volume trading. In fact, locations closer to Wall Street command a real-estate premium, and the popular press has often commented that our financial system is not fair – that institutional investors have an advantage over the average investor like you and me. Michael Lewis addresses this in detail in his 2014 book *Flash Boys*.[3]

The star of that book is Brad Katsuyama. Brad started his career at the Royal Bank of Canada (RBC) and help developed a software solution to try to level the playing field. The solution was to put in a delay so that every order was executed on a level playing field: every order placed at the same time would arrive at the same time.

He decided to use this as the basis to start his own exchange, IEX, co-founded in 2012 with Ronan Ryan, to rival the giant NASDAQ and New York Stock Exchange (NYSE). He wanted an exchange where every order was executed fairly. His problem was that RBC owned the software – so his solution was ingenious and "old school." He built a box, a physical box, with thirty-five miles of fiber optic cable built in. Why thirty-five miles? It turns out that most high-frequency traders were located within a thirty-five-mile radius of Wall Street. Thus, he could put a physical delay into any order so that an order placed in the next building on Wall Street would be processed at the same time as one placed at the same instant somewhere in New Jersey thirty-five miles away. Leveling the playing field, in this case with an old-school, low-tech solution, was his strategy to break the *strategic control point* held by existing exchanges, NASDAQ and the NYSE (the Securities and Exchange Commission [SEC] approves all exchanges, and their regulatory approval was the key point of strategic control). With the significant pressure on the SEC to approve the "fairer" exchange, IEX was granted approval in June 2016 and began operating in September 2016.[4]

3 Michael Lewis, *Flash Boys: A Wall Street Revolt* (New York: W.W. Norton & Company, 2014).
4 The details here on IEX come from numerous personal conversations with IEX executives, including but not limited to Brad Katsuyama, Laurence Latimer, and Gerald Lam, and from their presentation at the Yale School of Management on 19 July 2017.

What is important to note here is that the existing point of strategic control held by NASDAQ and the NYSE (under the auspices of SEC regulatory approval) was overcome only by putting pressure on the SEC to approve a "fairer" exchange, thereby lessening the incumbents' point of strategic control. And it was achieved with an ingenious, low-tech solution!

Finally, recall the earlier example of placing sensors on windmills; this had a similar impact – namely, to lessen the point of strategic control owned by the two big windmill players, GE and Siemens. In this case, the company was finding a way to help weaken a point of strategic control that was also a barrier to others (e.g., in this case, smaller, Chinese windmill manufacturers), thus presenting firms with an entirely new business model.

2. *Seize the addiction.* Take advantage of a rival's lack of agility.

The classic strategy for overcoming another firm's point of strategic control is to take advantage of a rival's slow reaction to market change; this is something that often happens when a firm becomes addicted to the current revenue of existing products. This approach is classic and one that has been used in more industries than we can count. Indeed, companies often have a "cocaine problem" – not a literal cocaine problem, of course, but a metaphorical one. They are hooked on the drug of their existing business. The classic example is the now clichéd Kodak story. Indeed, Kodak should have owned digital photography; however, it was wedded to its film business, which made it slow to move to the digital world.

Modern-day examples of this include Nokia and BlackBerry. In 2005, BlackBerry (then called RIM [for Research in Motion]) controlled the enterprise smartphone market, and Nokia controlled the handset market. Apple recognized how both firms were slow to change in response to the emerging technologies (e.g., smartphones) that have since come into mass use. Ease of use and design – along with technological improvements – allowed everyday users to browse the internet, send email, and use apps. As with numerous other examples over time, Apple took advantage of Nokia's addiction to handsets and RIM's addiction to the corporate enterprise user and recognized that – precisely because of these addictions – these firms would not react quickly enough to a key emerging market (i.e., smartphones for the masses).

A more recent and perhaps more relevant example is that of Olli. Imagine needing a ride home from your favorite watering hole. You might call a taxi (or use Flywheel, Uber, or Lyft); however, there is little room in the existing "transportation" market for other competitors these days – particularly given the cost of vehicles and the regulatory environment. Until now.

Imagine pulling out your smartphone – or your wearable device – and simply saying "Olli, take me home." Olli comes and picks you up, talks to you on your way home, drops you off at your door, automatically bills your credit card, and sends an email receipt (much like Uber does). The only twist is that Olli is a small, personalized bus that is 3D printed by Local Motors, "powered" by IBM's Watson, and doesn't have a driver – it's fully autonomous. Further, Watson and Olli get to "know" you and your habits – if you want to know how the Giants did that day, just say "Olli, who won today?" Olli would know from your "favorites" list on your ESPN app that the Giants are your favorite baseball team and that they played the Yankees today. Olli would know the score and might even offer words of consolation to you if your team lost.

In fact, the autonomous vehicle market is becoming more and more competitive. If the major firms move into this space quickly, Olli's market may be small and may not be worth the investment; alternatively, if Local Motors can gain scale with Olli (i.e., before others can transition to a partially driverless world), Olli has a fighting chance. Thus, Olli has a chance to succeed – with the caveat that speed to scale is of the essence. It now has $150 million from Airbus and $1 billion in available funding for Olli customers, secured as of late 2017.[5]

3. *Disintermediate, disintermediate, disintermediate.*

We are living in the age of disintermediation – when a single player or technology can disrupt a market of 100 years or more.

> **DEFINITIONS: DISINTERMEDIATION AND CANARY**
>
> *Disintermediation*: a reduction in the use of intermediaries between producers and consumers. In English, this means that we no longer need traditional providers because we can get what we need more directly.
>
> *Canary*: an African finch with a melodious song, typically having yellowish-green plumage. The canary is popular as a pet bird and has been bred in a variety of colors, especially bright yellow; however, it is also known as the bird that warns of disasters. A canary can be sent down into a mine to warn of dangers. If it returns, it is safe to go in; however, if it doesn't return, that means the mine is unsafe for humans to enter.

A non-avian type of "canary" is disintermediating a whole host of businesses – from home security and monitoring services to branded smoke detectors. Some of you reading this have a home security system, most – if not all – of you have smoke and carbon

---

5 Source: Alan Boyle, "Airbus Ventures Dips into $150 Million Fund to Back 3-D Printing at Local Motors," *Geek Wire*, 16 January 2016: https://www.geekwire.com/2016/airbus-ventures-dips-into-150-million-fund-to-back-3-d-printing-at-local-motors/; and Local Motors website and the original announcement found on numerous sites, including *Mass Transit*, "Local Motors Secures over $1B in Financing for Olli Customers," 3 January 2018: http://www.masstransitmag.com/press_release/12389054/local-motors-secures-over-1-billion-in-financing-for-olli-customers.

monoxide detectors, and many of you have home security cameras and/or indoor air-quality monitors to check for temperature, humidity, and particulates.[6]

"Canary" is a device that sits in your home and has a camera that can be viewed and monitored remotely, can send pictures or videos of an intruder, and has a whole host of monitoring sensors (e.g., that measure air temperature, humidity levels, and carbon monoxide levels and can sense when a fire has started). Canary can potentially interact with your heating system to automatically turn down the heat – or turn on the dehumidifier. Such a device has the potential to disrupt a myriad of existing businesses, such as home security and monitoring companies like ADT, carbon monoxide and smoke detector brands like Kidde, and testing agencies such as Underwriters Laboratories (UL). This is much of the reason why there is such a fight going on for home-related connectivity (e.g., Alphabet with its Nest division; the Chinese manufacturer Huawei; "Home Hub" competitors like Wink, Z-wave, Zigbee, and Apple's Home Kit); many players are vying to control your home.

Canary is just one of many offerings that have the potential to disintermediate entire industries, much as Amazon did to traditional retailing many years ago, as Uber has done to taxi cabs, and as Airbnb has done to the traditional hotel business. Disintermediation can be one of the most effective methods of freeing the stranglehold that an owner of a strategic control point may have – witness the fact that large hotel chains controlled the hotel real estate in major cities only to be disintermediated through the internet, and taxi cabs controlled transportation via the medallion system only to be disintermediated by a sharing economy (via Uber). Technology-based disintermediation may now be the most effective and commonly used approach for disrupting markets; however, it's not the only one. Our economy is being disrupted daily in ways we couldn't have imagined just a few years ago.

---

6 I thank Christian Anschuetz, chief digital officer for UL, LLC, for this example.

Creative ways around a company's distribution dominance through disintermediation have become much more prevalent in recent years and extend beyond Canary. There is often a common theme across many of the examples of industries that have been disrupted in recent years: dissatisfaction with the current offerings in that industry (e.g., the high cost of eyeglasses and men's razors; the poor performance and lack of availability of taxi cabs).

Disintermediate through alternative "points of access." *Warby Parker.* Two Wharton students were on a camping trip when one lost a recently purchased – and very expensive – pair of eyeglasses. After much consternation, the pair (pun intended) set out to revolutionize the eyewear industry. On their website, they explain their rationale as follows:

> Every idea starts with a problem. Ours was simple: glasses are too expensive ... It turns out there was a simple explanation. The eyewear industry is dominated by a single company that has been able to keep prices artificially high while reaping huge profits from consumers who have no other options ... We started Warby Parker to create an alternative.[7]

They didn't attack incumbents directly through traditional retail outlets. Instead, they sold exclusively online, using "pop-up" stores (temporary stores located in prominent locations) and traveling buses to help promote the brand. Their business model is straightforward: a customer picks out five frames online, and Warby Parker FedExes a package with these frames for you to try on at home. You pick out the one you like, order online, and send the package back (prepaid) via FedEx – or send the package back and order a different set of five frames. You can try them on at the location of your choice, with your spouse,

---

7 Source: Warby Parker website, https://www.warbyparker.com/history.

partner, or friend to provide feedback ("Did you really choose THAT frame?!"), all at your convenience. The finished product is then delivered in a few days to your home. As a result, online sales of eyewear products in the United States have taken off, and in 2018 Warby Parker was valued at $1.75 billion in a pre-IPO investment of $75 million.[8]

Disintermediate by sidestepping regulatory authorities. *Uber, Lyft, Airbnb.* The stories of Uber, Lyft, and Airbnb have been told so many times, there is no need to repeat them here.[9] However, one could argue that each of these companies has been able to succeed because they have found ways to circumvent government regulations. Uber was able to "ride share" so that they would not (at least in theory) be subject to medallion restrictions, and Airbnb found a way around regulations that would have required room sharing to be regulated (and taxed) under municipal hotel codes.[10]

Disintermediate by going online and employing a subscription model. *Dollar Shave Club* and *Harry's.* Dollar Shave Club was founded by Mark Levine and Michael Dubin in 2011 after they met at a party and spoke of their frustrations with the cost of razor blades. There had to be a better way, they argued. Launched online in 2012, their company offered a subscription model with three tiers whereby razors are delivered to your door monthly rather than being purchased at a brick-and-mortar retailer. Five years and more than three million subscribers later,

---

8   Source: Jason Del Rey, "Warby Parker Is Valued at $1.75 Billion after a Pre-IPO Investment of $75 Million," *Recode*, 14 March 2018: https://www.recode.net/2018/3/14/17115230/warby-parker-75-million-funding-t-rowe-price-ipo.

9   See, for example, Uber's website, https://www.uber.com/newsroom/history/; *Logo My Way*, "The History of Lyft and their Logo Design," 31 October 2017: http://blog.logomyway.com/the-history-of-lyft-and-their-logo-design/; and Jessica Salter, "Airbnb: The Story behind the $1.3 Billion Room-Letting Website," *Telegraph*, 7 September 2012: https://www.telegraph.co.uk/technology/news/9525267/Airbnb-The-story-behind-the-1.3bn-room-letting-website.html.

10   Thanks to Keith Williams, president and CEO of Underwriters Laboratories, for this observation.

the company was acquired by Unilever for more than $1 billion (from Unilever's perspective, "If you can't beat them, join them"). Harry's, founded in 2013, uses both a direct-delivery and a retail approach to addressing the same concern (the high cost of men's razors) that prompted the founding of the Dollar Shave Club. Recently, Harry's has been valued at just under $1 billion.[11] Disintermediation through a "judo strategy" (not attacking larger rivals directly) pays – in men's razors, to the tune of $1 billion!

Disintermediate via a multi-faceted approach to distribution. *Globe Union.* To overcome traditional distribution brand concentration, Globe Union employs a multi-faceted approach. They use two private branded products, Danze and Gerber, to sell outside of big box retail (these two brands, by design, do not sell to big box stores). Instead, these two brands sell almost exclusively through two-step distribution (distribution to wholesalers to plumbers or builders). In big box, Globe Union's parent company, Industrial Corporation in Taiwan, manufactures and sells private label products for big box stores, giving them access to both big box (via the private labels) and plumbers/builders (via Gerber and Danze). It also uses Gerber ("the plumber's brand") to focus on the service plumber market.[12] Thus, via this multi-pronged approach, they are able to compete effectively across multiple traditional distribution channels, enabling them to grow in ways a single-branded/single-channel approach could not.

---

11   Source: Helena Ball, "How This $750 Million Shaving Startup Cuts Through the Competition," *Inc.com*, 23 November 2016: https://www.inc.com/helena-ball/harrys-2016-company-of-the-year-nominee.html.

12   Typically, when a service plumber responds to a call from a homeowner with a leaky faucet, he or she arrives with a truck that contains everything required for a repair job (e.g., equipment, tools, and replacement parts) – as well as a few "extras." One of the biggest sources of revenue for the modern-day plumber is the "upsell"; rather than just doing the repair job, they try to upsell you, for example, to purchase a shiny new faucet to replace the one that your grandfather installed back in 1927. Special thanks are owed to Brian Fiala at Globe Union for his help on clarifying details about the U.S. faucet market.

4. *Build a better mousetrap.* Find a better point of strategic control.

The classic example is, of course, Rockefeller's pipeline (as discussed earlier). Rockefeller decided to build an efficient, near-zero-marginal-cost network of pipelines to bypass the existing railroad stranglehold on crude shipments. However, there are analogous, albeit less dramatic, strategies that have worked quite well for other companies over the years. Examples are as varied as payment methods/systems, old-line manufacturing, use of unmanned vehicle technologies, and motorized bicycles in China.

Traditional credit cards as we know them, physical cards that are used at point-of-sale, are increasingly less relevant as the interface of retail payments is evolving – and converging – as in every other industry discussed in this book. In this instance, mobile payments firms such as Square allow a merchant or service provider to accept payments on their phones. Some companies are developing "payments by facial recognition." Indeed, over time, "virtual" credit cards using certain technologies (e.g., near-field communication, tokenization, and others) will likely make physical cards obsolete. I often joke that I go to Starbucks because I don't ever have to pay – "I just show them my phone." I do have to pay, of course, but using the Starbucks app or using Apple Pay, Visa Checkout, Samsung Pay, you-name-it pay – with your smartphone and a thumbprint or your face – is infinitely easier than using a card with a chip. I would even take this one step further and say that once some company has figured out a way to strike a deal with the government to digitize IDs, we will no longer have to carry a wallet. Anything can be done with some sort of scan of a smartphone or, with the launch of Apple's Watch 4, a watch on your wrist.

Amazon's Go stores and its Whole Foods acquisition aim to eliminate checkout stands entirely (Walmart has been experimenting with doing away with the checkout stand for years). The idea is that you could just walk out the door, an RFID chip (e.g., a chip on all of the products in your basket) would automatically charge your Amazon previously agreed payment method, and an itemized receipt would be sent to your smartphone. Amazon, with its efficient distribution network, is taking this to another level.

The concept of "building a better mousetrap" to loosen existing points of strategic control applies equally to "old line" industries. As noted earlier in this book, Owens Corning is one of a few national manufacturers of roofing shingles in the United States; however, like other roofing manufacturers, it has an important problem: highly regional, variable demand. As an owner of a house on the ocean in North Carolina, I have experience of this phenomenon. A storm or a hurricane hits, and the demand for roofing shingles surges. For the homeowner, the first qualified roofing contractor who can repair the roof often gets the contract.

Lead and fulfillment are crucial for contractors; the lead is the point of control – as is supply fulfillment, at times. Nationwide and Owens Corning have a unique solution: they use satellite images of roofs to calculate the number of squares of roofing material that might be needed in advance of a storm. Thus, when associated contractors show up at your door, they are ready with not only a secured/ready supply (and an estimate of how many roofing "squares" are needed) but also a preapproved insurance settlement (from Nationwide). Approximately 95 percent of estimates go to contract and result in completion of the job.[13]

The use of drones/unmanned aerial vehicles (UAVs) in home inspections and mortgage approvals is another example of "building a better mousetrap." Quality home inspectors are often in short supply in hot markets. Thus, some companies are using drones to do local appraisals, a strategy that can save both time and money and increase the number of appraisals that any one appraiser can complete. Similarly, Indiana Limestone uses drones to try to grow

---

13 Source: Numerous internal company conversations (original quote from Brian Chambers in 2016, president of Owens Corning, who was recently named as incoming CEO in 2019, replacing Mike Thaman).

the market in Asia: a customer in Korea, with a budget to spend, can log into an Indiana Limestone server and – literally – fly a drone over a limestone quarry in Indiana; from his or her desk in Korea, this individual can then pick out custom limestone from the quarry.

Still in the unmanned arena, a North Carolina company has an interesting solution to onerous but necessary OSHA requirements. For context, in quarries, vehicles are not allowed to dig in areas with vertical walls higher than six feet (i.e., the height of an average male), to guard against having a wall collapse on a driver. The solution: use an unmanned vehicle to cover the terrain – not only increasing the yield of the quarry but also saving on labor costs. They can now send an unmanned vehicle into the mine, at depths and heights that were not possible previously.

Finally, Chinese company Didi has an ingenious Uber-type app that is available in cities such as Shanghai and Beijing. China, like many other countries today, has a "zero tolerance" alcohol policy. If you drink any amount of alcohol and then drive, you go to jail – and you don't want to go to a Chinese prison! Thus, the Uber-style app enables you to quickly find a driver who can drive you home; via the app, you can see the drivers' faces and check their driving records. They actually show up driving a motorized bicycle that folds up and fits in your trunk. After driving your car home for you, the driver then takes his or her bike out of your trunk and drives to the next job. You, however, wake up the next morning, in your bed, and with your car right at home.

5. *Proliferate and imitate.* Make cool uncool (Samsung versus Apple – today).

Samsung chose an interesting strategy to fight Apple's stranglehold on not only the mobile phone market but also the entire value chain in mobile devices. Recall the earlier discussion about how Apple – back in the era of Steve Jobs – was able to control its entire value chain. How do you break into this market with the switching costs so high? How did Samsung succeed where others (e.g., Sony Ericsson,

Nokia, and BlackBerry) had failed? They imitated and improved the attributes of the Apple lineup.

Of course, Samsung could not have succeeded were it not for Google. Apple's *strategic control point* was significantly weakened by Google (e.g., by Google's Android OS and Google Play). Thus, Google's "building a better mousetrap" loosened Apple's *strategic control point*, thereby presenting an opening for Samsung.

Proliferation, the business strategy of offering numerous variants of the same base product, can have a profound impact on entry success and create significant entry barriers. For example, Richard Schmalensee studied the ready-to-eat (RTE) breakfast cereal market a number of years ago and came to some interesting conclusions.[14] Imagine a market opportunity for a repeat purchase product (e.g., a breakfast cereal) with 1,000 customers and no one supplying the market. If you enter first, you have the potential (sometimes referred to as available) market opportunity of 1,000 customers. Next, imagine that a competitor is thinking about entering this market after you already have. This firm would normally expect, on average, a 50 percent market share, since there would be two firms (you and this new entrant) in the market after they entered; in this context, their available market opportunity would be, at most, half (500) of yours when you entered (1,000).

Now, imagine that, after these two firms have entered the market, a third firm is also contemplating entering this market. They naturally might expect at most one-third of the market or about 333 customers (i.e., far less than your original 1,000). Thus, the incentive to enter decreases after more and more firms have entered.

Alternatively, now imagine that, before the second firm has entered, you introduce a total of nine products – each somewhat different from the others – so that your offerings cover every available option in this space. With nine products in the market, each product

---

14 See Richard Schmalensee, "Entry Deterrence in the Ready-to-Eat Breakfast Cereal Industry," *Bell Journal of Economics* 9 (2) (October 1978): 305–27.

might, on average, be expected to get one-ninth of the total market. *Now*, if the aforementioned second entrant decides to enter, this firm might be expected, on average, to get one-tenth of the market (i.e., just 100 customers), since there are now ten products in the market (assuming that all products split the market roughly equally). Taking this one step farther, imagine that you introduced nineteen slightly different products spanning the options in the market. Then, if this firm considers entering the market, it might reasonably expect just one-twentieth of the market (or just 50 customers).

So, we've gone from the original new entrant with a market opportunity of 1,000 customers down to just 5 percent (50 customers) as a result of the first firm's strategy of proliferating the number of offerings in the same market. As incumbent firms "proliferate" their offerings, the motivation to enter for any new firm is reduced. Thus, proliferation can provide significant entry barriers, something that has been confirmed in multiple industries.[15]

6. *Utilize the entire value chain and avoid the "commodity trap."*

What if there is no way to differentiate your product? What if you are increasingly commoditized and there is no way out? Do you exit the business or are there ways to win even here? Occasionally, when evaluating the value chain in their own – and related – markets, firms find that there are no avenues for strategic control and little in the way of margin opportunities within the market (i.e., a classic "commodity trap") – a market that should generally be avoided at all costs. However, a few recent developments suggest that some ideas might be worth pursuing before you decide to give up on a market. The first,

---

15 For further reading on the effects of product-line proliferation, see Barry L. Bayus and William P. Putsis, Jr, "An Empirical Analysis of Firm Product Line Decisions," *Journal of Marketing Research*, 38 (1) (February 2001): 110–18; and William P. Putsis, Jr, and Barry L. Bayus, "Product Proliferation: An Empirical Analysis of Product Line Determinants and Market Outcomes," *Marketing Science*, 18 (2) (1999): 137–53.

used by Intel and others to extract higher margins on largely commodity products, is illustrated by an example involving sushi and sushi rice. The second example is one that posits that a marginal advantage can be parlayed into a much bigger one via the right strategy. The key is utilizing the entire value chain – much as Amazon has done over the years. Sometimes owning the value chain back to ront can, in and of itself, give you a point of strategic control that no one can match.

Sushi restaurants and one-way fares – other leverage opportunities. Recent research has pointed out another potential way to extract margins within the value chain – even for commodity or low-value-added products. Imagine the following example: you own a sushi restaurant. You obtain two basic ingredients from key suppliers: 1) sushi rice, a commodity product that can be stockpiled and for which a continuous and regular supply is available; and 2) fish, which is perishable and volatile in terms of its demand (due to often highly unpredictable restaurant traffic flows) and which also requires a fair amount of customization from the supplier. One would think that the margins on the rice (a commodity product) would be small and the margins on the fish would be extremely high. In fact, research[16] has uncovered that the margins on the sushi rice were relatively high. Why? Simply because the rice is consistently in demand and can be stored; for this reason, "overpaying" on the rice makes sense for both parties and facilitates contractual supply on the fish (including delivery, customization, and support) that is required on a daily basis.

Can you connect a commodity product to a value-added product so that the steady supply of the value-added product is guaranteed by the supply of the (now higher-margin) commodity product?

This is an interesting twist on the age-old practice of connecting supply issues with customization, perishability, and commoditization.

---

16 Cristina Nistor and Matthew Selove, "Pricing and Quality Provision in a Channel: A Model of Efficient Relational Contracts," Working Paper, 14 February 2018: https://papers.ssrn.com/sol3/papers.cfm?abstract_id=3123844. Available at SSRN: https://ssrn.com/abstract=3123844 or http://dx.doi.org/10.2139/ssrn.3123844.

Whenever possible, leverage strengths in one part of the competition to extract better terms in another part of the chain.

Another example illustrates a firm's advantages associated with owning the value chain back-to-front. Imagine two airlines competing on a given route between City 1 and City 2. Airline A has ten trips a day from City 1 to City 2 and ten trips back. Airline B has only one a day in each direction. So, on average, Airline A has a ten-to-one advantage over Airline B in each direction (since they have ten times as many choices in each direction).[17]

We can diagram this as shown in figure 4.1.

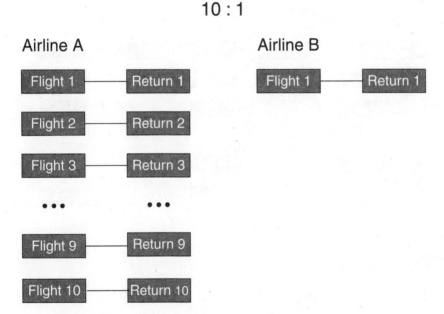

Figure 4.1 Airline purchases

---

17 This is, of course, assuming all other things are held constant. That is, it may be that the optimal thing for Airline B is to schedule its one flight at the peak travel time; however, if there is excess capacity at other times of the day, the advantage is less than ten to one. There are other nuances that may make the advantage different (versus precisely ten to one), but the essence of the argument made here remains the same.

Question: Under this structure, how can Airline A dramatically increase its advantage in the market?

Answer: Do not allow one-way ticket purchases. If Airline A does not allow one-way ticket purchases and requires customers to purchase round-trip tickets (essentially "bundling" the two one-way tickets), its ten-to-one advantage grows to a hundred-to-one, since there are 100 combinations that you can purchase from Airline A but only one combination that you can purchase from Airline B (as figure 4.2 suggests).[18]

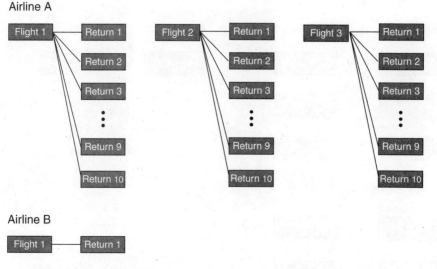

Figure 4.2 Airline flights

By changing the rules of engagement, the company has turned a commodity into a strategic advantage. Although it's often not possible to change a commodity into anything but a commodity,

---

18 Thanks to Barry Nalebuff for the framing of this example.

when there is a chance to do so, creative strategies can be effective. The sushi and rice example was derived from Intel's strategy across customized versus non-customized chips, for example. The airline example is a real one involving a common practice on certain routes.

By way of analogy, Amazon controls its entire value chain back to front. We can't order from Amazon, arrange delivery from someone else, and pay the seller directly; everything goes through Amazon. Moreover, today they are using what is known as an advanced programming interface (API) as a point of strategic control across platforms. Amazon gives companies an API tunnel to develop an offering to integrate into their systems, and you can run with it; furthermore, the more that is available throughout Amazon's system, the more they control the value chain. The result is on a par with the airline example – magnifying an advantage that is already there (the whole is greater than the sum of the parts), which is something exceedingly difficult to imitate.

7. *Surrender to the curve.* Recognize that the only way to compete is to leverage someone else's point of control.

In extreme cases, the market throws you a curve. For example, Blockbuster had a great business model years ago, renting video-cassettes and then DVDs until other companies (e.g., Redbox and Netflix) came along and made the rental business fiercely price competitive. Also, Netflix had a great business model years ago, distributing DVDs via mail until streaming became mainstream. How then, if you are Netflix, do you address today's fiercely competitive, mostly commoditized content-streaming market? You surrender to this curve, recognize that it is inevitable, and give in. Focus on other ways to achieve strategic advantage. For Netflix, this means two things: (i) original content that is unique to Netflix and generates a loyal set of viewers/customers, and (ii) analytics so that they appear to know your tastes better than you do and always seem to have the right movies for you.

There's an old saying: "Find a way." Good leaders find a way. When it comes to strategic control and you're on the outside looking in, find a way. Use this to your advantage – sketch out your industry and, if you find yourself "on the outside looking in," deploy one of these approaches. It's better to be on the inside looking out!

Chapter 4: Key Foundations and Business Principles

- Recall the story of Rockefeller's pipeline – and the stranglehold that the railroads once had on oil shipments. There are often strategies for working around points of strategic control that are owned by someone else (and they are usually less dramatic and costly than the Rockefeller solution).
- We break these into seven main strategies:
  - ○ *Find a release.*
  - ○ *Seize the addiction.*
  - ○ *Disintermediate, disintermediate, disintermediate.*
  - ○ *Build a better mousetrap.*
  - ○ *Proliferate and imitate.*
  - ○ *Utilize the entire value chain and avoid the "commodity trap."*
  - ○ *Surrender to the curve.*
- As we noted in in the previous chapter, first-mover advantages associated with strategic control can be sustainable and lasting; however, first-mover advantages associated with product attributes are typically ephemeral.
- In the event that you are in a commodity business, the best option may be to exit; however, in the event that you are committed to the market, certain strategies (referred to as tying and bundling) may be effective – albeit subject to antitrust scrutiny.

What Can Go Wrong When You Own a Point of Strategic Control? The Concept of Blowback to the Core

In this story, the perfect storm happened during a time of prosperity. It was late 2012, and Apple could do no wrong. It had been able to control the value chain from front to back with complete autonomy – and extract superior margins as a result. Apple, like many companies before it, felt that it could do anything and everything better than its competitors.

Enter lightning plugs and Apple Maps.

Apple was convinced, correctly, that the future was not in wired devices. The "cloud" was connecting devices to the internet, and devices were becoming interconnected in houses wirelessly – this was the future. However, Apple was saddled with ten-year-old plugs on all of their devices that interconnected audio and video, and they still needed to encourage customers to move over to a wireless world.

If you think about it, Apple had every incentive in the world to facilitate this changeover back in 2012 because of their interconnectivity (e.g., of iTunes libraries with iPhones, iPads, and computers). This is what had made Apple "sticky": once you bought into the Apple "ecosystem," another type of product wouldn't be able to interconnect with other devices (by design), and hence the barrier to switching to another system of devices was formidable.

So, what were Apple's options at the time as they switched to a new system that consisted of a charger and sync device (i.e., the "lightning" plug), which were combined with wireless playback of video and audio via your Wi-Fi network at home and a cloud-based system outside your home? Apple had two main strategic options:

1 Leverage its strong brand name and the "lock" it already had on its customer base by leveraging every penny out of the new cords and accessories (via huge margins and high prices). After all, much of this book has been about leveraging strength in one market for gain in another. Apple had the potential to extract huge margins on cables and related accessories and – as this line of thinking goes – they should have extracted every penny that they could.

2 Recognize that the key is creating – and keeping – a "lock in" ecosystem for users; thus, Apple needed to avoid creating product-related purchasing barriers – and thus facilitating a switch to rival products. Think of this as the razor/razor blades problem in reverse: (i) give away (or nearly so) the cables, cords, and devices that let customers interconnect all of their wireless devices and (ii) make your margins on the actual products (e.g., iPhones and iPads). If you want to encourage customers to move to the system of the future (wherein devices are interconnected wirelessly), you should do everything you can to make it easier for them to do so.

What did Apple do? They overplayed their hand and overestimated the willingness of their customers to pay *anything* at all for Apple products. They introduced new cables and accessories at exorbitant prices (e.g., $29 for a simple charging cord). Further, all of the old accessories became obsolete even though there was a simple solution to keep them functional: Bluetooth adapters (which came into the market in force about a year later). Moreover, a rival (Samsung) was about to introduce a successful rival product (i.e., the Galaxy S4) that *gave away* a *wireless* HDMI audio/video adapter.

Add to this the perfect storm – the Apple Maps fiasco. Apple forced users to use their new proprietary map app – one that quite often got the directions wrong! At the time, Google Maps worked quite well; however, it wasn't approved for the new phones and operating system. Not coincidentally, Apple began to appear fallible, and its stock price reflected this – falling from a record high of more than $700 a share to, at one point, less than $400 a share.[1]

We call this "blowback to the core" – when you overplay your hand and it negatively affects your core business. Apple made a fundamental mistake: while they may have been able to extract huge margins on accessories, it made little sense for them to do so. Customers *had* to spend money to replace old cables and accessories precisely at a time when rivals were catching up.

> **Key Takeaway**: Know and protect your core. Any attempt to leverage strengths in other parts of the market or value chain should always be done when it makes it more likely that customers will choose your core.

Apple's lightning cable fiasco pushed customers away from their core. By contrast, as discussed earlier, when Jeppesen Marine needed to leverage its core in digital navigation charts, it was able to get onto the bridge of ships and give customers an integrated suite of tools to navigate and save fuel. Pushing hard to gain such access enabled them to charge better rates for their core navigation products. Never jeopardize your core. Never.

---

1 Source: Wharton Wharton's WRDS data base (University of North Carolina at Chapel Hill license).

The Story of Ubuntu, Sapphire Glass – and "Best-Laid Plans"

Canonical Limited, a U.K.-based software company privately held by South African entrepreneur Mark Shuttleworth, has more than 500 employees and $30 million in revenues in more than thirty countries. Canonical focuses on open-source software across a variety of applications.[2] Ubuntu is a leading Linux-based operating system produced by Canonical and is named after the southern African philosophy of *Ubuntu* (which is often translated as "humanity towards others").

One of Canonical's recent areas of focus has been on mobile operating systems (OS); it first announced plans for an Ubuntu mobile OS at the beginning of 2013 – and has been attempting since to become the third leading mobile platform in the industry (behind Apple iOS and Google's Android). Even more ambitious, Chinese phone makers BQ and Meizu, anxious to differentiate themselves in the market, announced their plans to manufacture smartphones based in the Ubuntu Linux-based operating system – potentially a huge coup for Canonical because of the size of the Chinese market and the power of BQ and Meizu.

The "human-ness" of Ubuntu as "open-source" and free has taken on a somewhat ironic twist in the market as it faces the "stick" strategy of strategic control exerted by one of its most powerful competitors; this illustrates the potential power and pitfalls of strategic control to keep new entrants and rivals at bay.

In an absolutely classic application of the concept of a *strategic control point*, Apple bought up enough sapphire glass to supply other

---

2 This section relies on the following: Jasper Hamill, "Help: Apple Has Snaffled the WHOLE WORLD'S Supply of Sapphire Glass," *The Register*, 20 February 2014: http://www.theregister.co.uk/2014/02/20/apple_eats_whole_worlds_supply_of_sapphire_screens/; http://en.wikipedia.org/wiki/Canonical_Ltd.; and "Ubuntu," Wikipedia: http://en.wikipedia.org/wiki/Ubuntu_%28operating_system%29.

companies for years – effectively buying up the world's supply of sapphire glass for three years. This is key, because sapphire glass was thought at the time to be a critical component in today's smartphone manufacturing because of its super-tough, scratch-resistant properties. How many of us have dropped our iPhones and marveled at how – somehow – they didn't break or scratch?

It's all about strategic control.

Imagine Canonical's frustration. They've seemingly done everything right. They developed a well-supported, open-source, free operating system that is highly rated and sourced key manufacturers in a critical region of the world to manufacture new smartphones based on its mobile operating system; however, they found that a commodity needed for the production of its phones was now owned, for three years, by a key rival – Apple. In a seemingly brilliant move, akin to Minnetonka's buying up of the world's supply of pumps when it introduced Softsoap®, Apple could now focus on what matters most to their success in mobile phones: competing with Google's Android platform – with all other competitors kept safely at bay. Brilliant. Or so it seemed.

"Best-Laid Plans"

What is most interesting about this story is how it backfired for Apple.

Apple's control of sapphire glass was a classic example of a strategy that went awry – not for strategic but for operational reasons. Apple delayed introducing sapphire glass during the launch of its steel and gold Apple Watches; there were quality issues associated with the new furnaces at its supplier's Mesa Arizona plant. Apple's chief supplier of sapphire crystal – GT Advanced Technologies (GTAT) – committed to building larger furnaces to meet Apple's scale requirements only to find out that the quality of the sapphire produced by the furnaces didn't meet Apple's quality requirements. GTAT also found the terms of its contract with Apple "oppressive and burdensome," according to court papers, and eventually filed for bankruptcy. The end result was that Apple wrote off more than $1 billion on the furnaces at GTAT's Mesa facilities.[3]

Even with *strategic control points*, "the best laid plans of mice and men often go awry" – and this is no less true for Apple and sapphire glass.

The Importance of Customer Service and Employee Empowerment

In business, convoluted logic abounds. One recent example involves AT&T U-Verse, which gave up a no-cost annuity by refusing to correct an employee error. The following is a true story. We had just moved into our beautiful new home within walking distance of shops, tree-lined streets, and other quaint houses. Since I often work at home, internet provision was important. So, we focused on ensuring that we had internet ready to go from the start.

We decided to equip our new home with AT&T's U-Verse service – which included internet, television, and phone service for about $200 a month. AT&T came on-site and installed all services, and we were up and running. However, just three days after closing on our new home, we received an "overdue" bill from AT&T stating that we owed them $260 – now overdue for more than a month. Obviously, this was an error of some sort since we had just moved in within the past week. We called AT&T and were told that this was due for the previous six weeks of service. When we told the customer service

---

3 Source: Philip Elmer-Dewitt, "Apple Got a Mess on Its Hands in Mesa, Arizona," *Fortune*, 11 October 2014: http://fortune.com/2014/10/11/apples-got-a-mess-on-its-hands-in-mesa-arizona/.

representative (and her supervisor) that this must be an error since we had only been in the house three days, we were told that we were being billed from the time the previous owners had called to stop service – a full six weeks before we had even owned the house or moved in! I then told the supervisor that we obviously weren't going to pay for the previous owners' service. AT&T then had two choices: (i) take the previous owners' charges off our bill and correct this error or (ii) connect me to whomever could immediately disconnect and cancel our service.

From a business perspective, let's examine AT&T's choices:

1 They could correct this error and remove any charges from before we moved in – essentially refunding the incorrectly billed $260 (and presumably contacting the previous owners to collect what they owed). Even if we legitimately owed this $260 (which we did not), refunding $260 would have enabled AT&T to keep us as a customer. This would have given them an annuity of $200 per month for the next 10 years (the time we expect to be in this home) with essentially no marginal cost of service provision – all for a one-time "cost" of $260. Under this choice:

   Gain to AT&T: 10 years × 12 months × $200
   per month = $24,000
   Loss to AT&T: $260 (which may be collected from the previous owners)

2 Refuse to budge on their error and lose us as customers. At best, they might collect $260, but they would lose 10 years × 12 months × $200 per month in revenue. Under this choice:

   Gain to AT&T: $260 (if we actually pay and $0 if we refuse)
   Loss to AT&T: 10 years × 12 months × $200
   per month = $24,000

What did they do? They connected us to the disconnection department. Within about three minutes, they had lost us as a customer forever – losing approximately \$24,000 in revenue over 10 years![4] We are now happy Comcast customers.

Interestingly, research on "service recovery" has indicated that customers are considerably more likely to buy from companies associated *with* service errors that were handled in ways that exceeded expectations than from companies with no errors.

It's Easy to See the Writing on the Wall, for the Sign Is the Signs

The old saying that "the writing is on the wall" is relevant when spotting trends in business. Holden Beach is a small town in Brunswick County on the North Carolina shore; it was home to two small hardware stores (including a local True Value store) that competed with the larger Home Depot and Lowe's that are twenty minutes away in the "booming" big town of Shallotte. About two years ago, the True Value store reorganized the floor space – shrinking the hardware floor space by 50 percent and opening a consignment store in the other half. This was a surefire sign that the store's bankruptcy was not far behind. Sure enough, shortly thereafter they liquidated inventory with a "Going out of Business" sign on the storefront, and the store has since closed. Similarly, the True Value in Durham, North Carolina, rented space to a pharmacy and closed its doors about six months later. These "signs" are the first indication that the end is in sight.

Conversely, the sooner you know that you have won the war the better; it tells you when you can afford to take your foot off the pedal. In *Compete Smarter, Not Harder*, I told the story of Blockbuster's early dominance of the video rental business, based on a strategy of "stocking deep" (i.e., having enough of the current titles on hand so

---

4 For simplicity purposes, we ignore present value and other considerations here.

that you can always get the most recent title at Blockbuster). Local "Mom and Pop" video retailers generally couldn't afford to match such a strategy since they didn't have the "deep pockets" of a Blockbuster. Wayne Huizenga, the CEO of Blockbuster at the time, said that Blockbuster knew it had won the war (beating out the local video rental stores) the minute the Mom and Pop stores would put up the "2-for-1" signs on their doors.

These signs are incredibly easy to spot when you know where to look. For example, retailer Barnes & Noble generated $3.66 billion in 2018, down from over $5 billion back in 2013.[5] Worse yet, they experienced a series of *declines* in *online* sales over much of this time period as well (e.g., 15 percent and 14.4 percent year-on-year declines in 2015 and 2016, respectively).[6] To add to these woes, the *Wall Street Journal* noted Barnes & Noble's "Mystery of Vanishing Sales"[7] – the fact that a smaller and smaller proportion of Barnes & Noble's sales at its brick-and-mortar stores are associated with books. Toys, games, e-readers, and novelties make up a larger and larger portion of their sales. Sales continued to fall through at least the second quarter of 2019 (when they reported a net loss of $18.7 million, or 26 cents a share).[8] These are all telltale sign of things to come. Just

---

5 Source: Barnes & Noble, "Barnes & Noble Net Sales in Fiscal Years 2012 to 2018, by Commerce Segment (in Million U.S. Dollars)," *Statista - The Statistics Portal*, Statista, www.statista.com/statistics/199008/barnes-und-noble-net-sales-by-commerce-segment/. Accessed 23 March 2019.

6 Source: Stefany Zaroban, "Barnes and Noble Grows Its Internet Sales for the First Time in Four Years," *Internet Retailer*, 22 June 2017: https://www.digitalcommerce360.com/2017/06/22/barnes-noble-grows-annual-web-sales-for-the-first-time-in-four-years/.

7 Jeffrey A. Trachtenberg, "B&N's Mystery of Vanishing Sales," *Wall Street Journal*, 27 June 2013: https://www.wsj.com/articles/SB10001424127887323689204578569903094947598.

8 Source: Andria Cheng, "Barnes and Noble's Problem Is No Longer Just Amazon," *Forbes*, 6 September 2018: https://www.forbes.com/sites/andriacheng/2018/09/06/barnes-nobles-problem-is-no-longer-about-amazon/#664ca69344d0; and Allison Prang, "Barnes & Noble Narrows Loss, but Sales Decline," *Wall Street Journal*, 19 June 2019: https://www.wsj.com/articles/barnes-noble-narrows-loss-but-sales-decline-11560949387.

like the Mom and Pop retailers being forced into 2-for-1 sales and the True Value store allocating space to a consignment shop and a pharmacy, Barnes & Noble (with shrinking online sales and having to fill brick-and-mortar space with things like toys and games) showed signs that it wouldn't exist in its current state for long.[9]

The lesson here isn't the need to move away from the core as industries and sectors evolve; rather, it is that good companies use core strength to invest in new businesses. A telltale sign of a company in trouble is a shrinking core concurrent with a failure to invest in new market opportunities; indeed, this has predicted the failure of countless firms (e.g., Borders, Kodak, Dell, BlackBerry), whereas the number of successes is considerably less (e.g., IBM, Xerox). If you're caught in a business with a shrinking core (and fail to transform the business away from the core), you're fighting an uphill battle; a "fire sale," at the core, is one surefire sign that the battle is being lost!

Overplaying Your Hand – Green Mountain Coffee Roasters, Keurig, and Digital Rights Management[10]

Playing from strength is often crucial when utilizing points of strategic control; however, sometimes companies overestimate their

---

9 Indeed, in June of 2019, it was announced that Barnes & Noble agreed to be bought out in a private equity deal by Elliott Management Corp. for $475 million in cash, a figure that was criticized by many. Allison Prang, "Barnes & Noble Narrows Loss, but Sales Decline," *Wall Street Journal*, 19 June 2019: https://www.wsj.com/articles/barnes-noble-narrows-loss-but-sales-decline-11560949387.

10 This section relies heavily upon the following court filing: Treehouse Foods, Inc., Bay Valley Foods, LLC, and Strum Foods, Inc. v. Green Mountain Coffee Roasters, Inc. and Keurig, Incorporated, United States District Court for the Southern District of New York, Civil Action No. 14CV0905, court filing 2/11/14, as well as the following sites:

Jarrett Bellini, "Apparently This Matters: Keurig 2.0," *CNN Business*, 7 March 2014: http://www.cnn.com/2014/03/07/tech/social-media/apparently-this-matters-keurig-drm/; and Tricia Duryee, "Keurig Brewing up Controversy over DRM-enabled Coffee Maker," *Geek Wire*, 4 March 2014: http://www.geekwire.com/2014/keurig-brewing-controversy-drm-enabled-coffee-maker/.

market strengths and overplay their hands for a variety of reasons (e.g., arrogance, a lack of strategic discipline, overzealous senior management). One recent example is that of Green Mountain Coffee Roasters (GMCR) and its Keurig brand of coffeemakers.

Question: Do you own a Keurig "K-Cup" coffee maker? Have you ever used one?

If you have, you know how convenient – and expensive – they can be.

GMCR is a company with a rich, colorful history. In 1981, GMCR began as a small café in Waitsfield, Vermont, roasting and selling brewed coffee. If you visit its visitors' center in a restored Waterbury, Vermont, train station, you will read about and hear quaint stories of small-town values; an organic, fair trade product; and wholesome roots.

Keurig, founded in 1990 by entrepreneurs Peter Dragone and John Sylvan, pioneered single-serve coffeemakers via a patented K-Cup brewing system. The K-Cup system consists of single-serving "K-Cup" plastic packets (i.e., the grounds and paper filter are inside a plastic cup, with a foil seal on top). GMCR purchased a 35 percent interest in Keurig in 1996 and acquired it outright ten years later (in 2006) for $160 million.

A Brief History of the Coffee Market in the Post-World War II United States

In order to fully understand GMCR's overzealous approach – and how they overplayed their hand – some background on the market for coffee and single-serve makers and packets is key. By the end of World War II, a handful of large companies dominated the U.S. coffee industry – Chase & Sanborn, A&P, and Maxwell House controlled a combined 40 percent of the U.S. coffee market (Folgers, Nestlé, and Hills Brothers controlled much of the rest). Starting in the early 1960s, however, coffee consumption in the United States declined from 3.1 cups per person per day (in 1963) to less than two cups per day in the early 1980s. Due in large part to a market that was shrinking, the major players were forced to compete vigorously for market share, and the U.S. coffee market became increasingly dominated by mass-produced coffee throughout the 1970s and 1980s. Inferior-quality beans were distributed through grocery retailers, and brewed coffee was sold through delis and 7-Elevens; this resulted in an opening for "specialty," higher-quality coffee.[11]

Enter Howard Schultz.

At the age of twenty-six, Howard Schultz began working for Hammerplast, a U.S. subsidiary of Perstorp, the Swedish housewares company. While working for Hammerplast in Chicago, he became curious as to why a small company in Seattle – Starbucks Coffee, Tea and Spice – was ordering so many plastic coffee filters. In fact, despite having just a few outlets, it was ordering more filters than large retailers such as Macy's. After traveling to see this small company in Seattle, he was so impressed that shortly thereafter, in 1982, he joined the company as the director of operations and marketing. At around the same time, he visited Milan on a buying trip and became convinced that there was a market for high-quality coffee inside a coffee culture (i.e., a "third place" to drink coffee besides the home and office) – all of this aided by, as he described it, the "swill" that came from mass-produced, cheaper coffee that was the norm in the United States at the time.

In 1986, Schultz opened his first retail store in Seattle and named it *il Giornale* after the Italian word for newspaper. He eventually bought Starbucks in August 1987, and the rest, as they say, is history. As the specialty coffee market grew in the United States over the ensuing twenty years, new opportunities appeared in the home-brewed market – somewhere between the "upmarket"

---

11 The source for much of this section about the U.S. coffee industry at this time and about Howard Schultz specifically is Nancy F. Koehn, "Howard Schultz and Starbucks Coffee Company," Harvard Business School case 9-801-361, February 2001. (Revised September 2005.)

(and expensive) Starbucks and the lower-end, "automatic drip" coffeemakers of the past.

While Starbucks and others pushed high-quality (and more expensive) beans into distribution for home use, others – most notably Keurig – pioneered the "single-serving" pods for home use. The main advantage of "single-serve" pods was *ease of use* – you could just drop a pre-manufactured "pod" into the coffeemaker, press a button, and a single serving of coffee would be produced in seconds; the quality of the coffee was determined by the coffee inside the pods. Starbucks even developed, licensed, and continues to sell pods with Starbucks coffee inside the original "K-Cup" version (patented by Keurig).

When February 2014 rolled around, GMCR (which now owned Keurig) controlled about 89 percent of the market for single-serve machines and approximately 73 percent of U.S. sales of single-serving packets, with margins of approximately 50 percent. Much of this dominant market share – and margin – was controlled via the original patents on the K-Cup system that GMCR had acquired (along with Keurig) in 2006.

However, most of the key patents expired in 2012, and therein lay the issue.

GMCR's revenue share and earnings growth started to decline after the key patents expired,[12] since competitive, "unlicensed" pods (sold and distributed by third-party providers) began to penetrate the market with prices, not surprisingly, up to 25 percent lower than that of the "official" licensed pods. Without ongoing patent protection, GMCR seemingly had few available options to stem the tide of competitive, "unlicensed" K-Cup pods that were flooding the market and forcing the company to lower its 50 percent margins. Or did it? Since its acquisition of Keurig in 2006, GMCR actually possessed two points of strategic control and was playing them well.

---

12 Source: Green Mountain Coffee Roaster annual reports, accessed online.

GMCR's Strategic Control Points

Strategic control point 1 (2006–12) – patents. When GMCR acquired all of Keurig in 2006, it also acquired its K-Cup patents and enforced them vigorously – quite rightly: the U.S. patent system (one of the most vigorous and viable in the world) is set up to reward innovation and provide a return on investment for companies that innovate. In 2012, however, GMCR and Keurig faced the expiration of key patents.

Strategic control point 2 (2006–present) – distribution. GMCR's "textbook" purchase of Keurig in 2006 was indeed a "strategic nirvana": the dominant player in a fast-growing segment of the U.S. coffee market (single-serving brewers) combined with a company – GMCR – that was able to acquire a ready distribution vehicle for its coffee and had a nearly captive audience as a result of its patents. If you wanted a single-brew, easy-to-use coffee system, Keurig machines were sold at every major retailer, as well as online, and Keurig was the dominant system. The accompanying patented K-Cups were distributed in every major grocery chain, large retailers (e.g., Walmart, Target, and Costco), and were available online and via virtually every distribution channel imaginable.

Through 2012, GMCR masterfully played distribution penetration – and Keurig's dominance in the brewers. Distribution combined with the K-Cup patents almost guaranteed dominant market share (which it had developed by 2012, with almost 100 percent of K-Cup pods and 89 percent of the single-serve brewer market). If another competitor were to enter, it would not only have to develop a new brewing system that didn't infringe on GMCR's patents but would also have to find a way to match GMCR distribution (on both the brewer and K-Cup side) – an enormous undertaking and a significant barrier to entry for any potential entrant/competitor.

GMCR's dominance may have led to arrogance, however. In 2014, GMCR overplayed its hand by attempting to introduce a third point of strategic control, a move that invited competition into this space via the creation of a huge gap in the market – resulting in what we call "blowback to the core."

What Were GMCR's Options for Strategic Control after Patent Expiry?

Patents as a source of strategic control were no longer an option for GMCR, since they had expired; thus, GMCR turned to leveraging two other potential points of strategic control – distribution and technology – which were both implemented via coercion.

Potential strategic control point 1 – distribution. Once the patents expired, distribution became a key point of strategic advantage, as it was hard to replicate. The inevitability that competitors would enter with lower-priced, competitive K-Cups was clear; with 50 percent margins, there was just too much to be gained by third-party manufacturers and retailers alike. Wise, proactive steps would have been to recognize and move into adjacent markets ahead of the competition (e.g., as Starbucks has done so well over the years by expanding from stores to grocery retailers to new geographies and new product lines) and to lower margins on GMCR K-Cups (to decrease the incentive for competitors to enter).

What GMCR chose to do, however, invited antitrust intervention; it cut off the suppliers and partners (by agreement) that also chose to distribute "non-licensed" K-Cups. With its dominant market share in these markets, this was almost guaranteed to produce competitive lawsuits under the Sherman and Clayton acts and/or via Department of Justice/Federal Trade Commission action. (See the section in this chapter describing these key U.S. antitrust acts.) Such aggressive actions by a near monopoly – in order to cut off suppliers in an attempt to prevent competitive entry – would almost certainly raise the attention of regulators. Here, GMCR overplayed its hand, essentially inviting litigation and/or government intervention.

Potential strategic control point 2 – technology. Once the patents expired and revenue and profit growth slowed (see figure 5.1), GMCR decided to force its dominance on customers in another "creative" way. GMCR announced in early 2014 that it was instituting a "Digital Rights Management" (DRM) system on all of its new coffeemakers – in essence, a chip that would be placed on all licensed K-Cups; if the K-Cup wasn't a Green Mountain K-Cup (i.e., if it was manufactured and sold by a competitor), the Keurig system wouldn't work; thus it *forced* customers to buy GMCR K-Cups. In the absence of competitive entry (i.e., when there are other barriers to entry), such a strategy could indeed work; however, in this instance – since GMCR could no longer enforce key K-Cup patents – its 50 percent margins on K-Cups opened the door for competitors on *both* the machine *and* the K-Cup side.

Thus, in this instance, the implementation of DRM on all new Keurig machines *strongly* encouraged other manufacturers to enter; it created a *huge gaping hole* in the market for lower-priced, machine alternatives that didn't have DRM chips built in. Thus, GMCR overplayed

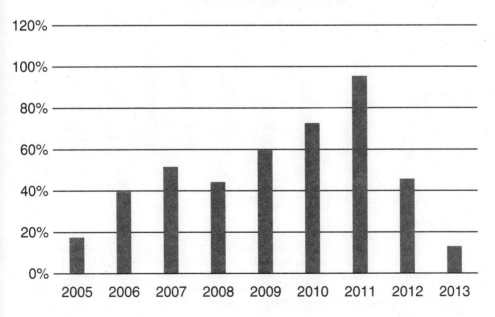

Revenue Growth

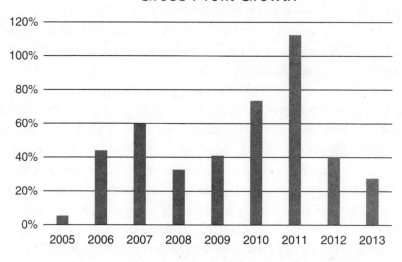

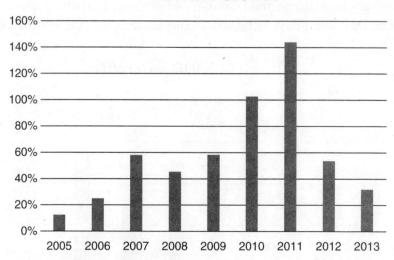

Figure 5.1 Green Mountain profit growth[13]

---

13 Figure 5.1 is author-created from Green Mountain Income Statements, all accessed
through Capital IQ. The original data came from the following link using sliders to
adjust for the years of data to include (at the time of the making of the three charts,
the time period used was 2002 to 2013). See the following link for details: https://
www.capitaliq.com/CIQDotNet/Financial/IncomeStatement.aspx?CompanyId=
334622&statekey=2feea69739a345e59d3aa540866a2b18.

its hand and encouraged competition in the context of both machines and K-Cup alternatives. The implementation of a DRM chip was *not* a viable option for strategic control but a potential source of alienating its core customers. No customer needs or wants a DRM chip after all!

So, what would you have done under these circumstances? What should GMCR have done?

One solution would have been to use its strengths and revenue in the single-serve market to develop other, related markets ahead of its competitors. GMCR still had a huge advantage in distribution and revenue in existing markets that could facilitate entry into adjacent markets (e.g., alternative beverages, commercial markets, and even markets in new geographies). Indeed, to the extent that the DRM system was used as a "sand fence" strategy (see the earlier discussion), such a "stall" strategy could have made sense; the problem with it, however, was that it had the potential to hasten the demise of the company's core revenue-generating product line – a scary proposition in any case!

Epilogue – The Worst-Laid Plans of Mice and Men ...

Sometimes it just works out.

In December 2015, it was announced that Keurig Green Mountain, Inc., would be acquired by a JAB Holding investor group for $13.9 billion in cash – a deal completed on 3 March 2016. Since GMCR stock had been battered on Wall Street for a year after the Keurig 2 DRM strategy was initiated – its share price was down over 62 percent – JAB Holdings was able to buy the stock at $92 a share (which was 89 percent higher than the company's twenty-day moving average prior to the announcement). This was the largest premium for any acquisition in the beverage industry ever compiled by Bloomberg.[14]

---

14 See Jennifer Kaplan, "Keurig to Go Private in $13.9 Billion Buyout Led by JAB," *Bloomberg.com*, 7 December 2015: http://www.bloomberg.com/news/articles/2015-12-07/keurig-to-be-bought-by-jab-led-investor-group-for-13-9-billion.

How, then, given the discussion above, does this make sense? Sometimes there is a fit, and sometimes it just works out. In this instance, JAB is a closely held, Luxembourg-based investment firm that (i) manages the $19 billion fortune of Austria's Reimann family,[15] (ii) is run by a trio of seasoned consumer-industry executives (who were planning to mount a challenge to global leader Nestlé SA in the coffee industry), and (iii) owns a controlling stake of Jacobs Douwe Egberts, Peet's Coffee & Tea, Caribou Coffee, Einstein Noah Restaurant Group, Espresso House, Pret-a-Manger, and Baresso Coffee. Thus, the JAB GMCR acquisition is part of a much larger strategy, making GMCR uniquely valuable to JAB (versus to the market at large on their own) – which has ready-made, tailored distribution outlets (all of these retail businesses) at the ready for its K-cups![16]

JAB plans to consolidate coffee – on a par with how Anheuser-Busch InBev consolidated the malt beverage industry. As such, Keurig and GMCR – and likely Dunkin' Donuts – fitted within a much larger strategy. Peet's, Caribou, Einstein's Bagels, Pret-a-Manger, and other locations provided a natural outlet for Keurig K-Cups (and a distinct positioning advantage for its Espresso House and Baresso coffees). Thus, for JAB Holdings, GMCR was uniquely positioned to provide value to JAB in ways that others were not (more recently, in July of 2018, Keurig Green Mountain, in turn, acquired the Dr. Pepper Snapple Group for $18.7 billion).[17]

---

15 Max Jedeur-Palmgren, "The Secretive Billionaire Family behind the $13.9 Billion Keurig-Green Mountain Deal," Forbes, 7 December 2015: https://www.forbes.com/sites/maxjedeurpalmgren/2015/12/07/the-secretive-billionaire-family-behind-the-13-9-billion-keurig-green-mountain-deal/#64ab2b5d3b51.

16 See https://www.cbinsights.com/research/jab-holding-us-coffee-consolidation/ for a list of recent acquisitions by JAB.

17 The combined company was renamed Keurig Dr. Pepper and began trading publicly again on the New York Stock Exchange under the ticker KDP. Shareholders of Dr. Pepper Snapple Group own 13 percent of the combined company, with Keurig shareholder Mondelez International owning 13 percent to 14 percent of that fraction. JAB Holdings owns the remaining majority stake: https://en.wikipedia.org/wiki/Keurig_Dr_Pepper#cite_note-13.

In short, GMCR and Keurig got lucky; it is exceedingly unlikely that they built the company and positioned it for this one acquisition. Don't build your strategy around expectation of a fortunately positioned acquisition, for it is rare when such a suitor saves the day!

Some important items to think about when planning for impending patent expiry include the following:

- Plan for patent expiry ahead of time. Leverage strengths in your core market well before your advantage dissipates. For GMCR, this would have been between 2010 and 2012 – long before they responded to declining revenue and profits by instituting the Digital Rights Management (DRM) chip. Always play from strength.
- Don't overplay your hand; recognize the inevitable. GMCR's DRM system had the potential to alienate existing customers and hasten competitive entry.
- Proliferate as a way to deter entry but be careful. Proliferating your product line as GMCR did by introducing a wide variety of coffeemakers and beverage pods significantly reduces the incentive for rival entry. Combine this with reduced margins (i.e., below the current 50 percent) and entry is considerably less likely than if you introduce a DRM system to preclude entry. Always seek legal advice here, as potential antitrust violations abound.
- Expand to adjacent markets before patent expiry; know that competition and margin erosion are inevitable. Starbucks has been a master at this over the years (e.g., by moving into other product lines, retail channels, and geographies).
- Find features and attributes that your customers value (rather than making them angry by *forcing* them to buy your metaphorical razor blades if they buy your razors).

- And, finally, don't expect your industry's equivalent of JAB
  Holdings to come to your rescue – such a fitting and happy
  outcome is rare indeed!

A Very Important Caveat: Antitrust Considerations

We would be seriously remiss if we didn't discuss antitrust issues;
indeed, leveraging *strategic control points* should always be done
with the involvement of legal counsel. U.S. antitrust law is a bit of
an oxymoron in that it is actually a combination of federal and state
laws, federal agencies (U.S. Department of Justice [DOJ] and the
Federal Trade Commission [FTC]), U.S. "antitrust" laws and policy,
and legal decisions required to interpret and enforce existing laws.

There have been countless papers, books, and courses devoted
to the subject; however, the origins of current "antitrust" law go
back to the Industrial Revolution. The fact that we call it "antitrust"
speaks to its origins. The backbone of federal antitrust law in the
United States is the Sherman Act, which was passed in 1890 – at the
height of the "trust" era wherein such titans as Rockefeller, Carnegie,
and Morgan ruthlessly dominated the competitive landscape and
drove countless smaller players out of business.[18] The Sherman Act
makes it illegal to attempt to form a monopoly or to restrain trade.
In 1914, Congress passed the Clayton Act, which prohibited certain
practices (e.g., certain forms of price discrimination and tying), and
the Federal Trade Commission Act (which formed the FTC). Later,
the Robinson-Patman Act of 1936 restricted a firm's ability to give
advantageous deals to large sellers in cases where the impact would
substantially lessen competition.

---

18 For an entertaining view of the time, see the History Channel's *The Men Who Built
    America*.

All of these acts – and a series of related ones – are enforced at the federal level by a combination of the DOJ and the FTC. How industries and cases are allocated/divided across the two agencies is largely based on history, agreement, and a de facto division that has evolved over the years. In addition to this federal oversight, various state laws are enforced by state attorneys general and, in some cases, state agencies. Furthermore, individual companies also have the right to bring an action, under both federal and state law.

At the federal level, the use of "monopoly power" to substantially lessen competition is often a trigger for initiating antitrust enforcement action when it results in consumer harm. Think of this as containing three parts: (i) the existence of monopoly power; (ii) the lessening of competition; and (iii) consumer harm. There are various definitions and measures of monopoly power and its impact on competition; however, the "Lerner Index" and the "Hirschman-Herfindahl Index" (HHI) are perhaps the two most important indices that have historically been used. The HHI is defined as the sum of the market shares of the firms in a given industry squared. Since a monopolist has a market share of 100 percent by definition, the maximum value of HHI is 10,000 (100 × 100). Conversely, in an industry with many small players, the index can approach zero. (Imagine an industry with a very large number of firms, each with infinitesimal market shares; the sum of those market shares would be close to zero.) Highly concentrated industries with HHI greater than 2,500 will likely generate interest and potential action by the FTC or the DOJ.[19]

The Lerner Index measures how much a firm can raise price over marginal cost – expressed as a percentage of marginal cost.

<hr />

19 See the DOJ page http://www.justice.gov/atr/public/guidelines/hhi.html for merger guidelines; and http://www.justice.gov/atr/index.html for a comprehensive coverage of U.S. antitrust policy developments.

The rationale here is that monopolists have the ability to raise price over marginal cost, but firms operating in a perfectly competitive (e.g., a commodity) business would have little or no ability to raise price; thus, the higher the Lerner Index, the greater the monopoly power in the industry – and the more consumers are harmed as a result.

This topic could fill many books; however, for our purposes, it is important to note that much of this book discusses the use of *strategic control points* and leveraging strength to gain competitive advantage – even using examples from Carnegie and Rockefeller that today would be subject to immediate and swift antitrust intervention. In the technology space, various antitrust actions have been taken by (and against) IBM, Microsoft, Apple, Samsung, Google – and many other firms that are held up as examples of good strategy. For example, Apple and Google were both afraid of Microsoft when the original iPhone and Android operating systems were being developed:

> Google executives were convinced that if Windows on mobile devices caught on, Microsoft would interfere with users' access to Google search on those devices in favor of its own search engine. The government's successful antitrust trial against Microsoft in the 1990s made it difficult for the company to use its monopoly on desktops and laptops to bully competitors. It could not, for example, make Microsoft's the default search engine in Windows without giving users a choice between its search engine and those from Google, Yahoo, and others. However, on smartphones, few rules governed how fiercely Microsoft could compete. It didn't have a monopoly there. Google worried that if Microsoft made it hard enough to use Google mobile devices and easy enough to use Microsoft search, many users would just switch search engines. This was the way Microsoft killed Netscape with Internet Explorer in the 1990s. If users stopped using Google's search engine and began using a competitor's such as Microsoft's, Google's business

would quickly run aground ... "It's hard to relate to that [fear of Microsoft] now, but at the time we were very concerned that Microsoft's mobile strategy would be successful," Schmidt said in 2012 during testimony in the Oracle v. Google copyright trial.[20]

Thus, we would be remiss if antirust considerations were not raised in this book. If you were to exert monopoly power (i.e., via utilizing sufficient market share in a way that has a detrimental impact on consumers and is based on the strategies discussed here), you might very well face unwelcome regulatory antitrust interventions. While more detailed coverage of the nuances of antitrust policies and regulatory interventions is well outside the scope of this book, always remain aware of the issues and get legal counsel at every stage – forewarned is forearmed.

Uber and Airbnb are facing similar issues – many drivers and property owners are becoming unhappy with their increasingly "consumer-friendly" terms. Thus, many drivers and property owners are opting to drive for Lyft or rent with Vacation Rental by Owner (VRBO). As companies like Uber or Airbnb become bigger and more powerful, they need to heed local regulatory hurdles; as a result, they may impose more stringent regulations on their suppliers (i.e., the drivers and owners). Further, discussions about "breaking up big tech" (referred to earlier in this book) have been in the forefront of the popular press for some time now, focused on the FANG companies – Facebook, Amazon, Netflix (to a lesser degree), and Google.

---

20 Fred Vogelstein, *Dogfight: How Apple and Google Went to War and Started a Revolution* (New York: Farrar, Straus and Giroux, Kindle Edition, 2013), 51.

Chapter 5: Key Foundations and Business Principles

- Be aware of the hazards of "blowback to the core"; be sure not to overplay your hand, particularly if loosening of a key *strategic control point* is possible as a result.
- Know and protect your core always. Any attempt to leverage strengths in other parts of the market or value chain should always be done when it *increases* the likelihood that customers will choose your core.
- When you can't build on the core (as was the case when Keurig's patents were expiring), use your core strengths to move into adjacent markets. Grow outward from the core (e.g., Starbucks has been a master at this).
- One bad business decision and poorly trained employees (e.g., who are not taught to "do the right thing") can cost you dearly. Empower your customer service staff to minimize the likelihood of blowback to the core.
- The sign is often in the signs – be aware of the telltale signs of demise (e.g., a need to shrink core businesses versus utilizing strong core sales to invest in your company's future). The writing is often on the wall. So always be on the lookout for it.
- Always be aware of antitrust considerations, and utilize legal counsel throughout.

PART III

THE CARROT AND THE STICK: STRATEGIES FOR TODAY'S INTERCONNECTED ENVIRONMENT

The Concept of Aligning Incentives ("The Carrot")

Vertical Incentive Alignment, "Asset Specificity," and "Virtual Vertical Integration"

Procter & Gamble, Windmills, Sensors, and Asset Specificity

Today, one of the keys to business success rests with the concept of "vertical incentive alignment," which is the design of vertical relationships in the value chain so that the incentives of all players are aligned with your best interests – so your buyers and suppliers have your best interests at heart by virtue of the structural relationship that you have set up.

One classic example goes back to the early 1990s, when Procter & Gamble (P&G) proposed jointly investing in an inventory control management system that would be jointly owned, managed, and run by P&G and Walmart.[1] The system would track every P&G product sold by Walmart in the United States, recording sales as the product was run through the checkout scanner. Pre-specified stock levels would be set up so that if one of P&G's products went below a certain level, P&G would replenish each store's stock just in time. The result was that Walmart would never (or at least almost never)

---

1 Much of the detail of this section comes from personal conversations with John Pepper at P&G during this period, all occurring at the Yale School of Management.

run out of P&G stock. Furthermore, P&G estimated that Walmart's inventory holding costs on P&G products would be reduced by about 60 percent, since Walmart would receive P&G products to the store just in time, rather than have to warehouse and internally distribute them (today, Walmart doesn't hold inventory, but back then it did).

So, what was in it for Walmart back in 1990? Clearly, it must have been appealing to have one of its major suppliers (P&G) reduce Walmart's inventory holding costs by as much as 60 percent; indeed, to have a supplier contribute financially to this system (which Walmart was planning on investing in anyway) was clearly desirable. Furthermore, this arrangement had the potential to enable Walmart to make similar requests of other manufacturers. From Walmart's perspective, there was little downside.

From P&G's perspective, they were able to solidify a key relationship with their most important customer, Walmart. P&G also benefitted from having timely access to information: P&G could see sales in real time and get feedback on what sold well and where. Consequently, P&G could efficiently adjust their product mix for regions of the country – even down to the individual store level. While the list of benefits goes on, this still doesn't get at the *real, most important* benefit and the reason why it was such a brilliant business move. Indeed, the strategy's brilliance is inherent in the dynamics of any channel relationship.

The Brilliance of P&G's Strategy

A retailer is motivated by a number of things; margins and inventory turnover are clearly two important items. This system significantly reduced Walmart's inventory holding costs on P&G products and P&G products alone; as a result, *the effective margins that Walmart saw on ONLY P&G products went through the roof*. Furthermore, since Walmart streamlined inventory, the turnover rate on P&G products increased substantially as well. What did Walmart want to do as a result? Sell more P&G product, sell more P&G product. *P&G took a behemoth like Walmart, its number one customer, and perfectly aligned its incentives – all with a (relatively) small investment in the inventory control system.* Better yet, P&G didn't have to assess Walmart's adherence to any contractual agreement; instead, it could just sit and watch. Why? Because P&G knew that Walmart would do what was in P&G's best interest since *it was in Walmart's best interest to do what was in P&G's best interest.* Brilliant.

Interestingly, just a few months back, I had a conversation with someone who was the head of Walmart's supply chain in the early 1990s. When I told him this story, his reaction was "That's why they were telling me that!" Back in the early 1990s, he was being told, "P&G products get out the door first – they get priority." However, until a few months ago, he hadn't known why!

Today, Walmart runs on consignment, holds no inventory, and the entire supply chain is run to Walmart's advantage; however, in 1990, this wasn't the case. While P&G's competitors eventually did break into the system at Walmart, P&G enjoyed almost a decade's worth of competitive advantage in a hotly competitive business as they rolled the system out to other retailers, staying consistently one step ahead of the competition. P&G used the concept of *asset specificity* to its advantage.

DEFINITION: ASSET SPECIFICITY
Asset specificity refers to a joint investment – often well short of a full-blown merger or acquisition, and unique to the parties at hand – that aligns the incentives of the parties to the investment.

In order to see how the principles of *vertical incentive alignment* and *asset specificity* are even more important in today's environment, recall the earlier example of the sensors on the windmills that can sense vibration and temperature changes so that they can anticipate an impending part or motor failure before it happens; data that are

Table 6.1 Incentives and costs for key players in the windmill industry

Entity	Incentive	Direct Costs
Windmill Owner/Operator	Reduced maintenance costs	Zero
Windmill Manufacturer	Ability to compete directly with larger players (e.g., GE and Siemens) in ways they could not on their own	Zero
Sensor/maintenance provider	Lock in on high-margin maintenance contracts, install stickiness	Sensor, Analytics, Maintenance

"out of tolerance" are sent up to the cloud, analyzed remotely, and trigger maintenance crews to be dispatched on-site. The advantage to the windmill owners and smaller manufacturers includes better "uptime," lower maintenance costs, and the ability to compete with services provided by the big players, GE and Siemens. We can think of the windmill owner/operator as having a joint investment with the sensor provider/installer – they jointly share in windmill access. Let's examine the incentives of the key players, as shown in table 6.1.

The installation of the sensors provides perfect alignment across all players in this system and is both a method to align incentives and a point of strategic control: as seen above, (i) the windmill owner/operator gets lower maintenance costs; (ii) the smaller windmill manufacturers get to compete with the "big boys"; and (iii) the sensor manufacturer gets an effective lock on the maintenance business, since it can provide better, more cost-effective maintenance at margins that are the same as or better than those of its competition. This is indeed a brilliant approach and a "win-win-win" for the windmill owner/operator, the windmill manufacturer, and the sensor provider in this space.

So, what are the lessons to be learned from all of this?

1 Think about the things that have the potential to disrupt the existing way of doing business. What are the inevitable trends in your industry that, if you take advantage of them now, would give you a competitive advantage – even if it were in the short term only?

2 Use *asset specificity* to your advantage. Once you have identified the part of the value chain where you are competing and have identified gaps in competencies required to compete effectively – or to access a key *strategic control point* – use the concept of asset specificity whenever possible to align the incentives. Don't immediately think merger and acquisition (M&A). You may be able to achieve the same result with a substantially smaller investment (and smaller managerial headache).

3 Managing customers and suppliers (i.e., vertical relationships) is all about incentive structure. It's not simply about cooperating with suppliers; it's also about how to align the incentive structure – using points of strategic control whenever possible. Often, a joint investment can help align parties to the same incentive, as it did for P&G.

Virtual Vertical Integration

The P&G and windmill sensor examples highlight the use of a (relatively) small investment that aligns the incentives of both parties. So, what is an investment (i.e., an asset specific to the relationship) that would align conflicts in the value chain in *your* industry?

DEFINITION: VIRTUAL VERTICAL INTEGRATION

Virtual vertical integration entails the integration across two (or more) firms whereby the form of the integration aligns the incentives of the firms involved. Virtual vertical integration can take the form of material movement (e.g., inbound and outbound logistics), financial instruments (e.g., automated payment systems), time, people, and any operational aspect of the organization that can be configured to the interests of both (or of multiple) parties but does not generally involve asset transfer or joint ownership.

Virtual vertical integration almost always involves some sort of asset specific (hence the term "asset specificity") to the relationship between the parties involved, although this isn't always necessary: for instance, financial integration (e.g., automated processing and payment of invoices) may involve little or no joint ownership of an asset unique to the venture. However, if it can be made unique to the relationship of the two parties, it can align the incentives of the two parties, with few or no specific assets involved. Today, examples of virtual vertical integration are numerous; the terms that firms use to integrate variations of the principle fit under "integrated materials management" and "performance-based logistics." The key to all of these is not simply providing convenience to customers – rather, they need to be undertaken in such a way as to align incentives across both buyers and suppliers.

Key Takeaway: Use the concept of asset specificity to align incentives to your advantage across the value chain by first sketching out the existing value chain and then finding areas where incentives might be misaligned. From here, joint investments (e.g., sensors on windmills or P&G's inventory control system) can facilitate alignment.

Google's Incentive Alignment and the Android Operating System

In the late 2000s, cellphone carriers were concerned that the proliferation of Android-based phones combined with iPhone and iOS-dominated devices would commoditize the carriers and that Google's Android proliferation strategy would hasten this development. However, Google used the "carrot" (i.e., incentive alignment) to its advantage. Google allowed each carrier to add its own software and applications on top of the Android operating system in order to enable differentiation – and gave 30 percent of the Android app revenue back to the carriers.[2]

Google's objective was to create as much competition between the carriers and manufacturers as possible, thereby pushing adoption and distribution. The carriers and manufacturers recognized that none of them could beat Apple individually; however, together, they could collectively gain by taking back strategic control from Apple. The lesson in all of this is that Google used the concept of incentive alignment flawlessly to get everyone on board with the then fledgling Android OS – the only way anyone had a chance to fight back against the Apple machine. Later, we will discuss how this notion of strategic control (the "Stick") and vertical incentive alignment (the "Carrot") can be effectively combined to generate better overall firm financial performance and success in the markets of today and the decades to come.

This same set of incentives brings up a myriad of issues. Imagine the complex web of incentive minefields that this presents. For example, when you are looking at a collection of online sites or stores, what deal is going to pop up first? Is it the one mostly closely aligned with your interests or with the retailer's interests? Can a store "buy your eyes" and influence what pops up on your screen – much as sponsored search advertising does on the internet version of Google? Who gets the revenue? Stay tuned; all of this is being played out even as you read this.

Channel Conflict, Moral Hazard, and Principal Agent Problems

Groupon, Living Social, Square, BMW, Apple, Google, and Amazon – they all face similar issues with the most crucial part of their business: information. The use of information – and the way information can

---

2 Source: Fred Vogelstein, *Dogfight: How Apple and Google Went to War and Started a Revolution* (New York: Farrar, Straus and Giroux, 2013), 120.

alter modern-day incentives – is perhaps the driving force behind successful companies today, whatever the industry. For example, BMW created a video version of a hypothetical future entitled "Breakdown." A businessman is in a rental car on his way to the airport listening to a voiceover in the car – much like a navigation system or Apple's Siri. The voiceover is reading his email back to him when an interruption overrides the reading with an urgent message: "WARNING, BREAKDOWN IMMINENT"; the voice then proceeds to direct him, turn-by-turn, to the nearest service station where a service attendant is waiting for him in clean white overalls – iPad in hand. The attendant informs the businessman that he was expecting his arrival and that his plane reservation and afternoon meetings were moved to accommodate his detour. The man responds by saying, "All I need is a taxi." A yellow taxi then instantly arrives. The spot ends with the businessman saying, "All I need now is a million dollars ..." and, of course, nothing happens – much to his disappointment.

This isn't just a Madison Avenue advertising fantasy; in many ways, the video mirrors what is already present in diverse industries. Performance-based logistics (PBL) in many manufacturing industries, "power by the hour" leasing agreements, and the embedded use of information in aviation markets are examples of how this fantasy is now a reality. To illustrate how information can play a pivotal role in the inter-firm incentive structure, let's examine the use of advanced technology sensors aboard modern aircraft (e.g., Boeing's 787, 747–8, or 737-NG, or Airbus's A380). In the newer aircraft, onboard sensors determine when a part has failed and, in many cases, when it is about to fail. Embedded onboard communications notify ground crews before a plane touches down. Maintenance and repair facilities can be notified in advance so that the crews are waiting at the gate to replace the malfunctioning part. The result is more efficient maintenance operations and higher aircraft utilization rates (a key to operator profitability) as aircraft downtime is reduced – potentially significantly. Thus, there is a material and often significant competitive advantage in the market for maintenance, repair, and overhaul (MRO) organizations and airplane manufacturers that are better able to introduce, coordinate, and manage information flows in this regard.

The lesson here, however, is less about the particulars of the aviation industry than about what this does to the incentive structure across players in the industry. For instance, think about what this does to airline operators (e.g., American Airlines, Southwest, and Lufthansa) after such technology is embedded on board an aircraft or a family of aircraft (e.g., Airbus A320s or Boeing 737s). First, at low levels of "technology embeddedness," one would expect a fair amount of resistance on the part of incumbent players in the industry. The operators would have few savings, since the technology is not incorporated into the maintenance and repair organizations on the ground; in fact, their costs might actually be higher because of the maintenance costs of the technology. Furthermore, for the MRO organizations, this is clearly a threat to their very livelihood; any cost savings to MRO operations would only come if the information on the plane was incorporated into the on-the-ground maintenance – and there is no incentive to do this if the level of embeddedness is still low.

As the information technology makes its way into a higher percentage of aircraft in the air, however, the incentive structure exactly reverses. For instance, with more sensor technology onboard the aircraft, the potential impact of sensor utilization increases dramatically (e.g., on operational utilization and efficiency). Once there is a broader diffusion of the information sensor (and related on-the-ground infrastructure support), it becomes economically viable to support the ground operations that will be waiting for inbound aircraft should an issue arise in flight. Furthermore, technology adoption turns from a threat into a potential source of growth and revenue generation for MRO facilities to the extent that they can extract higher margins by capturing some of the value of the

Table 6.2 Incentives for key players across the aerospace value chain

Part of Value Chain	Incentive
Manufacturer (e.g., Boeing, Airbus, Embraer, COMAC)	Increased sales and value capture possible *only* if there exists enough of an installed base to make unique MRO capabilities of aircraft scalable – thus, penetrate as quickly as possible to gain scale; if not, technology has no clear advantage and only adds cost. Furthermore, the solution needs to be proprietary (i.e., to manufacturer planes) or there is no differential competitive advantage.
Operator (e.g., American, United, Lufthansa)	Since the technology has the potential to produce huge gains in efficiency and aircraft utilization rates – but entails a significant upfront investment – adoption will only occur once enough aircraft possess the technology. Furthermore, gains only occur if there is an advantage over rivals. For "single-fleet" operators, incentive is closely aligned with manufacturers; for "mixed- fleet" operators, incentives depart significantly from manufacturers.
Maintenance, repair, and overhaul (MRO) (e.g., Lufthansa Technik)	This is where it gets complicated. When standalone MROs work on mixed fleets, there is little incentive to scale – unless technology solutions, across manufacturers, are compatible. For standalone MROs focusing on single fleets (e.g., Boeing), scale gives them a competitive advantage, provided that the technology is proprietary. For operator-owned MROs (such as Technik) or operators that do their MRO work in-house, there is a significant threat of being incentivized out of the business.

increased efficiency of the operators. Of course, the tipping point between seeing the new technology as a threat and seeing it as an opportunity depends upon a complex set of cost, scale, and adoption considerations, the level of previous penetration, and when the transition is undertaken. An analysis of the value chain (as discussed earlier) may be essential for identifying this tipping point.

Table 6.2 outlines the incentives for key players in the market across the value chain. For example, it reveals that the technology (which aircraft manufacturers spent billions of dollars developing) only adds manufacturer costs and little in the way of benefit to the other players in the value chain – *unless* sufficient scale can be achieved so that the potential cost savings and efficiencies can be fully realized in the market.

Scale (size) lowers the cost of the network of maintenance and repair benefits associated with the information transmitted from the plane; without that scale (i.e., if only a small fraction of planes in service have these capabilities), such an offering will not likely take off in the market. Hence, the focus of early strategy should be on gaining scale at all costs. The first to market with a service that gains scale – and, accordingly, takes advantage of that scale – will most likely win in the market. Once the market has been won, the ongoing advantage would be significant, since the original need for scale makes additional entry at this point unattractive (given that one firm is in the market with significant scale). For start-up after start-up, similar issues are emerging today. For example, Pandora's ability to compete against other competitors (e.g., iHeartRadio, iPods, iPhones, smartphones, and internet radio) depends upon their ability to rapidly grow installed base in an attempt to build entry barriers.

The importance of scale is certainly recognized by private equity firms; after "investing in the person" (i.e., betting on the main visionary behind the proposed business), the ability to scale an idea is often cited as the main reason to invest – or not invest – in a proposal. Yet, the discussion around table 6.2 (on the aviation industry) suggests that major players in this market may not understand this important point (an observation not unique to this market). To illustrate, think about the following:

1 Services are being launched by major players (e.g., Boeing, Airbus, and Lufthansa Technik) with the goal of having them earn money out of the gate. However, short-term profitability should not be the priority: a focus on gaining early penetration should preempt every urge to focus on profitability. If there is a long-run play in this market, then whatever determines long-run success should drive short-run strategic decisions. The winner will be the one that can gain scale as quickly as possible,

not the one that is profitable out of the gate. Spend to build scale initially, and reap the benefits later.

2   On the "platform" side, scale is huge; however, one of the main benefits to scale, on selling an airplane, is the potential for the annuity of services (e.g., flight and maintenance training, service, and support) that come from selling an airplane. As the market for services grows, new entrants (e.g., Honda Jet, Embraer, Bombardier, and Russian and Chinese firms such as COMAC) compete for the smaller, passenger (i.e., "commuter") end of the market; as more and more routes use smaller jets (e.g., a doubling of regional jets in service through 2035 is expected),[3] the ability to grow scale on the maintenance side for the two major players in the industry (i.e., Boeing and Airbus) diminishes over time. Thus, the move to services *now* becomes increasingly urgent.

More generally, speed to critical mass can hinder future entrants. Think of YouTube, Google, Skype, Facebook, and others; not only would a potential competitor have to produce a platform as good as (or better than) each of these in order to compete effectively, they would have to battle the installed base issue. Indeed, if "everyone" is on Facebook, where else would you go to connect to friends? Thus, growth to scale can be a barrier to entry by competitors – if you get in first and grow scale, this reduces the incentive for secondary entrants to come into the market. Combine this with a point of strategic control in the market and you have significantly increased your chances of success.[4]

---

3   Source: Boeing Commercial Market Outlook (CMO): http://www.boeing.com/resources/boeingdotcom/commercial/about-our-market/assets/downloads/cmo_print_2016_final_updated.pdf.

4   More generally, the academic literature has studied this phenomenon from a variety of perspectives. Perhaps most relevant to the discussion here is the "diffusion" literature, which studies the rate and size of the adopting pool for any new innovation. See Antonio Ladrón-de-Guevara and William Putsis, "Multi-Market, Multi-Product New Product Diffusion: Decomposing Local, Foreign, and Indirect (Cross-Product) Effects," *Customer Needs and Solutions*, Springer, Institute for Sustainable Innovation and Growth (iSIG), 2 (1) (March 2015): 57–70, for a recent example.

This concept extends in a number of other directions, including corporate governance. Recently, I gave a talk on the topic of corporate governance at the Yale Law School to a group of corporate board members from a variety of large multinational corporations. At the beginning of the talk, I played a video featuring various wearable projects (ranging from contact-lens versions of Google's Glass to virtual reality [VR] glasses by Oculus to holographic projected iPhones to cameras embedded in contact lenses). The result of many of these technologies is that, in the future, a meeting could be broadcast live without the participants even knowing. The point for corporate governance is that companies can't govern by rules anymore; governance needs to happen by incentives – firms will need to ensure that participants do not *want* to broadcast meetings surreptitiously.

Information Economics and Incentive Alignment

Today, many markets are characterized by what economists have called "asymmetric information," which is just a fancy term for instances when a buyer and seller have different information. For example, sellers of an automobile may know about a defect in the car that they are selling, but unless they reveal this, the buyer doesn't.

There are numerous, classic examples of this, including the "lemons" market (suggested by George Akerlof many years ago).[5] The principle is simple, yet chilling. When there is asymmetric information between buyers and sellers in a market, the bad quality products will drive out the good ones so that we are only able to buy "lemons" (i.e., poorer quality products) or, worse yet, nothing at all.

In order to illustrate this principle, imagine that two companies – Company A and Company B – both have products in the widget

---

5   George Akerlof was awarded a Nobel Prize in Economic Science in 2001 for his work in this area. See George.A. Akerlof, "The Market for 'Lemons': Quality Uncertainty and the Market Mechanism," *Quarterly Journal of Economics*, 84 (3) (1970): 488–500.

market; however, Company A's product is of superior quality to that of Company B, and it costs more to produce higher-quality products. Assume further that each company knows more about the quality of the product than any potential buyer. We call this "asymmetric information," since the information is "asymmetric" between the buyer and seller. In this example, a buyer can only ascertain quality after purchasing and using the product; and when the product has been used, it cannot be returned. Since buyers cannot ascertain the actual quality level before buying, they would only be willing to pay for average quality in the market. Indeed, why would you pay for higher quality when you could not tell that a product is indeed of higher quality?

Under these circumstances, it makes little sense for the high-quality producer, Company A, to continue to produce – at a higher cost – a higher-quality product, since the market is not rewarding the higher quality with a higher price. Thus, all above-average quality products will be driven out of the market. Once this happens, we can tell the story again with the remaining products in the market, and once again the above-average quality products will be driven from the market. This will continue, of course, until either only poor quality or, in the extreme case, no products remain. Thus, a market can fail due to uncertainty and asymmetric information; if "bad" (low-quality) products drive out "good" (higher-quality) products from a market, only a market for "lemons" (i.e., poorer quality products) can exist!

In practice, of course, there are various reasons why this may not play out as Akerlof had described; these include repeat buying behavior; the existence of intermediaries, which are sometimes referred to as "Akerlof intermediaries" (e.g., internet ratings services like Yelp, Epinions, and CNET); and good old-fashioned word of mouth.

Philip Nelson once claimed that advertising contained relevant information[6] (i.e., when products were associated with more frequent

---

6 Philip Nelson, "Advertising as Information," *Journal of Political Economy*, 82 (2) (1978): 729–54. (Professor Philip Nelson was an advisor of mine as an undergraduate and a gifted, albeit animated and eccentric, teacher.)

advertising, they were actually of higher quality). The logic, which is provocative, is also intriguing. Take our example above wherein Company A's product is of superior quality. In this instance, if this quality could be discerned at point of sale (POS) – such as a pair of trousers whose fabric and stitching can be evaluated – companies that advertise more will attract more customers to their stores (assuming the advertising works). Since quality can be evaluated at POS, this will generate a higher level of sales, thereby providing a return on the advertising investment. We thus may not expect to see advertisements for products of inferior quality (e.g., those made by Company B). Company B may not have an incentive to advertise, since they could only really hope to get customers into the store; once the customers got there, they would likely observe that the product was of inferior quality and most likely wouldn't purchase it, and thus the advertising cost would be wasted.

For products associated with "search" qualities (i.e., the quality could be ascertained prior to purchase), the advertising actually contains information about quality. Note that this would also be true for products with qualities that may not be investigated prior to sale and that are largely successful as a result of repeat purchases. Thus, advertising contains credible information (and can actually serve to reduce the asymmetric information between buyers and sellers) for products with qualities that can be investigated (i.e., searched) prior to purchase or qualities that can only be ascertained after purchase but generate a substantial number of repeat purchases.

Research in this area generally defines "search" qualities (aspects of an offering that can be evaluated prior to purchase), "experience" qualities (qualities that can only be evaluated after purchase, such as in a can of soup or a can of paint), and "credence" qualities. Credence qualities are qualities that we can't evaluate even after the purchase and consumption process; for example, when your car is repaired, do you really know if the mechanic replaced the part with an original, manufacturer-certified part or a cheaper refurbished part? When competing in a market – and competing in the information game with rivals – knowing and understanding the nature of information is crucial. Think of Amazon and eBay. It is in their best interest to turn the information "game" into one of search qualities (i.e., provide credible, user-based ratings, return guarantees, and support). Informational asymmetries are reduced between buyers and sellers (e.g., the buyer knows more about the probability of seller service or quality gaps as a result of the ratings), and Amazon and eBay turn the products in their offering lineups (think Amazon Marketplace) into more of a search offering, thereby providing an informational strategic advantage over less "omnipresent" competitors.

For many companies today, the strategic use of information and informational asymmetries presents radically different problems; however, some companies (e.g., Amazon, eBay, Facebook, and Alphabet) face almost the reverse issue – that of too much information. Such companies process extraordinary amounts of data every minute; firms that use the data most efficiently reduce buyer-related informational asymmetries and thus gain strategic advantages in the market. The game – like the games discussed earlier – is real, alive, and well. Only this time, the game is one of information and signaling. Thus, knowing the nature of the informational game is the first step toward using it for your strategic advantage.

Chapter 6: Key Foundations and Business Principles

- Align incentives, align incentives, align incentives. A key part of strategic planning is the alignment of incentives throughout the value chain.
- Today's successful companies align incentives upstream and downstream in the channel – with suppliers and customers alike.
- The best type of business to business (B2B) relationship benefits both the seller and the customer.
- Identify the inevitable trends in your industry that could give you a competitive advantage – even in the short run only. How might you turn them into a sustainable competitive advantage?
- Use the notion of *asset specificity* as follows:
  - Once you have identified your key part of the value chain (i.e., where you are competing) and gaps in the competencies required to compete effectively in that part of the value chain (or to access a key *strategic control point*), use the concept of asset specificity, whenever possible, to align incentives across the board.
  - Don't immediately think mergers and acquisitions (M&A). You may be able to achieve the same result with a substantially smaller investment (and smaller managerial headache).
  - Managing customers and suppliers (i.e., vertical relationships) is all about incentive structure. First and foremost, spend time understanding (i) where the power is in the channel and (ii) what incentivizes each player in the value chain.
  - Connect these incentives to your ultimate objective of maximizing profits in the high-priority segments of your market.

o Use both the "carrot" (via incentive alignment, the subject of this chapter) and the "stick" (via the utilization of *strategic control points*). Research, which is discussed in the next chapter, has shown that using this type of carrot and stick, in concert, can be particularly effective for generating long-term success in today's market.

CHAPTER 7

Why Utilizing the "Carrot" and the "Stick" Matters and What to Do about It

Strategies Necessary for Success in Today's Environment

In an attempt to be provocative, I often tell audiences that if I was working for an organization needing to be more innovative, I would want to give my team two weeks' vacation, all expenses paid, with just one stipulation: that they spend their time in the San Francisco Bay area doing nothing but going to parties. Indeed, it is truly a different world in the Bay area. Everyone is interested in starting a new business; in fact, it is not uncommon to go to a party and find that the majority of people you meet – each with a PhD from Caltech or Stanford – are working for startups at a small salary without benefits. They know that if they work for three-to-five start-ups, on average, one of the start-ups will get sold or do an IPO (initial public offering, i.e., go public), and they'll be able to retire wealthy. I've even had a clerk at a local Safeway approach me to try out her new app!

After I delivered a presentation in Santa Clara, California, in the heart of Silicon Valley, about a year ago, someone came up to me and asked, "What is it that has differentiated the winners from the losers for all of the new start-ups in the San Francisco Bay area over the years?" Of course, there are innumerable answers to this question; however, after she left, I thought about the answer over and over.

What I came up with was certainly true of the technology winners – within and outside the San Francisco Bay area:

1 They had built some form of strategic control (e.g., an operating system or scale that was difficult to replicate).
2 They found a way to align incentives across both buyers and sellers (e.g., Google's decision to give a 30 percent cut of app store revenue back to the carriers).
3 They recognized that they needed to exert control and influence across a series of interconnected industry value chains (i.e., they recognized a broader "ecosystem").

Based on these observations, I developed some working hypotheses. We then began compiling data from multiple sources to test whether strategic control and vertical incentive alignment were indeed key factors for succeeding in today's environment. The first data set included data on the financial performance of publicly traded U.S. companies from the Wharton Research Data Services (WRDS) database on financial performance.[1] Specifically, data on measures of financial performance – stock price; net income; return on net assets (RONA); earnings before interest, taxes, and depreciation (EBIT); and earnings before interest, taxes, depreciation, and amortization (EBITA) – was collected for every U.S. firm in the S&P 500 (the largest 500 publicly traded firms) from 2009 to 2016.[2] For the second database, managers and industry analysts were interviewed in order to (subjectively) assess each firm's ability to align incentives and exert strategic control. Specifically, we asked them to rate each firm within their domain of expertise in terms of (i) the level of incentive alignment throughout

1 Thanks to Chanil Boo, then a PhD candidate at University of North Carolina, Chapel Hill, and now an assistant professor at City University of New York, for much of this work.
2 We excluded data during the "Great Recession," since this is an anomalous period in U.S. economic history, noting that this limits some of the interpretation of the results (as will be discussed later in the chapter).

the value chain (both upstream and downstream) and (ii) the firm's ability to capture point(s) of strategic control in the value chain – both measures on a scale of 1 to 10.[3] The two data sources were combined into a large database that was analyzed in two ways:

1 through the use of statistics, specifically using multiple regression techniques; and
2 through examination of the data for patterns and groupings.

DEFINITION: MULTIPLE REGRESSION
Multiple regression is a statistical technique for examining the impact of one variable on another – in this case on stock price, income, or earnings – holding all other variables in the study constant; it gives us the ability to isolate the impact of one variable, such as strategic control or vertical alignment.

Our hypotheses were strongly confirmed by this analysis. Companies that are succeeding today utilize both a "stick" (strategic control) and a "carrot" (vertical incentive alignment); they find points of strategic control, leverage them in the market, and align external incentives effectively. The utilization of both strategic control and vertical incentive alignment has a profound impact on a firm's success – particularly with respect to financial performance. Table 7.1 lists just a few of the companies that our research has identified as either a success or failure in the game of strategic control (SC) and vertical incentive alignment (VIA).

---

3 To the extent that the "experts" were not able to do a good job of assessing the degree of strategic control and vertical incentive alignment (for example, if their assessments were random or subject to a significant degree of error), this would work against us – that is, make it substantially *more* difficult to find any result at all. Thus, the existence of any expert error actually makes these results stronger, since we would be finding these strong results in spite of error that would make it less likely to find any result at all.

Table 7.1 Winners and losers based on strategic control (SC) and vertical incentive alignment (VIA)

Winners (High SC and/or VIA)	Losers (Low SC and VIA)
Amazon	Borders, Geeks.com
Walmart	JC Penney, Sears, Toys-R-Us
Alphabet (Google)	Yahoo
Apple, Samsung	Canonical
Netflix	Blockbuster
LinkedIn	Groupon
Eastman Chemical	USPS
FedEx, Facebook	Zynga

Amazon, for example, has recognized that owning points of strategic control throughout the value chain (and owning the value chain from back to front) can provide a dominant strategic advantage that others cannot match. However, Walmart learned from P&G's initiative in the 1990s and now aligns incentives throughout *its* supply chain (e.g., via inventory management processes and "scanbacks").

To illustrate how important this can be, we conducted a detailed econometric analysis, employing advanced multiple regression techniques to ascertain the post-downturn (from 2009 forward) financial performance of the companies in our data set via Compustat and Wharton's WRDS data. This detailed analysis revealed that:

- 23 percent of earnings growth (from 2009 to 2016) can be explained by strategic control alone;
- 34 percent of net income growth is explained by strategic control and vertical alignment;
- a full 41 percent of share price growth (from 2009 to 2016) is explained by just three factors: strategic control, vertical alignment, and net income.

That's startling – to explain 41 percent of the (cross-sectional) variation in share price growth with just three factors is phenomenal. In order to put this in perspective, an increase in strategic control from a 3 to an 8 on a 10-point scale (from low to high, where a 3 might be a company like Hulu, whereas an 8 might be a company like Amazon) would increase share price growth by a startling 35 percent. This drives home how important strategic control is to financial performance.

In short, strategic control and vertical incentive alignment are material to a firm's financial performance.

We then divided the companies into four quadrants and gave each quadrant a name: *"Update the Résumé"* (because you'll be looking for a job soon); *"Don't Quit Your Day Job"* (because the company will do well and you should stick with it); *"It's Fixable"* (because it is); and *"It's a Matter of Time"* (because it's not fixable and it's a matter of time before the company faces hard times).

Update the Résumé. Thirty-two percent of the S&P 500 rated low on both incentive alignment and the ability to form points of strategic control. These firms were the least successful in terms of share price return, market share, and long-term prospects for growth.

Don't Quit Your Day Job. Nineteen percent were high on both strategic control and incentive alignment, and these firms outperformed the rest of the sample in every metric, from share price and market share appreciation to long-term success and growth rates. This is not surprising, since aligned incentives and control of key points of strategic control (e.g., Amazon's obsessive control of the value chain and Apple's control of the "Apple ecosystem") make it nearly impossible for a rival to displace the company that executes on this well.

It's Fixable. Nineteen percent of the firms in the S&P 500 had reasonably high points of strategic control (e.g., Microsoft's Office and Facebook's social network); however, they were relatively weak on incentive alignment outside the organization. For example, Surface sales or Microsoft mobile OS have performed nearly as well as the previous group in terms of

short-term market performance; however, they will be under
pressure unless they can solve the incentive alignment issue.
Thus, their success is tenuous moving forward but fixable.

It's a Matter of Time. Thirty percent of firms in the S&P 500 had low
points of strategic control but reasonably well-aligned vertical
incentives (e.g., Time Warner Cable's control of geographies
and apartment complexes). These firms have done well in the
sales channels and/or with customer acquisition and retention
strategies but will continue to be under the threat of competitive
entry unless points of strategic control can be formed.

Figure 7.1 depicts the continuum that exists across points of strategic
control (from low to high) and across degrees of vertical incentive
alignment (from weak to strong), in addition to some of the companies that fit into each quadrant (note that the companies listed

Point of Strategic Control

		Low	High
Vertical Incentive Alignment	**Weak**	**Update the Resume** (Others will dominate) Barnes & Noble JC Penney Nokia 32%	**It's Flexible** (Dominance Under Pressure) Microsoft Facebook Twitter 19%
	Strong	**It's a Matter of Time** (Unsustainable Dominance) Comcast Time Warner Cable 30%	**Don't Quit Your Day Job** (Sustainable Dominance) Amazon Walmart Google, Netflix, Apple 19%

Figure 7.1 Quadrants and points of strategic control

Table 7.2 Financial performance across the "2x2" categories based on share price; return on net assets (RONA); earnings before interest and taxes (EBIT); and earnings before interest, taxes, and amortization (EBITA)

	Share Price	RONA	EBIT	EBITA
"Update Résumé" (LL)	0.256	−2.19	−0.560	−0.261
"Matter of Time" (LH)	0.498	1.44	−0.035	0.0389
"It's Fixable" (HL)	0.347	1.55	0.332	1.057
"Don't Quit Day Job" (HH)	0.698	1.45	0.495	2.238

in Figure 7.1 are for illustration purposes only – not all of these companies are in the S&P 500). Some companies have moved significantly over time, and their position may differ from country to country. For example, Nokia earns more than 500 million Euros (i.e., approximately $700 million U.S.) in patent revenue annually but has essentially fallen out of the handset race in the United States despite a significant presence in other parts of the world. Hence, in the market for handsets in the United States, Nokia would fall into the "Update the Résumé" quadrant, but would fit in other quadrants for other lines of business and in other parts of the world.[4]

We provide further perspective on why this matters financially by examining financial performance across the four groups and reporting this in table 7.2 (all numbers represent percentage change from 2009 to 2016; the LL [Low/Low], LH [Low/High], HL [High/Low], and HH [High/High] designations refer to strategic control [Low or High] and vertical alignment [Low or High], respectively, and correspond to the four quadrants identified above).

These numbers suggest the following:

- Those in the "LL" category (low in both strategic control and vertical incentive alignment) had a 25.6 percent increase in share price from 2009 to 2016 (2009 as base); in contrast, companies that were

---

4 See Renee Schultes, "Nokia Could Take Time to Mine Patents," *Wall Street Journal*, 13 December 2013, B14.

high on both appreciated almost 70 percent over the same period.

- Return on net assets (RONA), earnings before interest and taxes (EBIT), and earnings before interest, taxes, and amortization (EBITA) were all *negative* for firms that were low on both strategic control and vertical incentive alignment; all these measures were positive and grew significantly for those companies in the "Don't Quit Your Day Job" (HH) category.
- Whereas EBITA more than doubled for those in the HH ("Don't Quit Your Day Job") category, it was actually negative for those low on both (i.e., in the "Update the Résumé" category).

Conclusion: The "Carrot and Stick" approach of developing businesses around points of strategic control and vertical incentive alignment matters financially; firms that succeed in today's markets have effectively developed points of strategic control and have aligned external incentives. You can utilize this analysis to help identify key strategic issues and invest in moving forward. Use it to your advantage by sketching it out for your business.

An Important Caveat

In this study, we address only U.S. data during a period of economic growth (i.e., coming out of the "Great Recession"). Furthermore, we focus only on larger firms (i.e., those inside the S&P 500). As such, we can at this time offer only anecdotal evidence as to how these results translate to economies outside the United States, and how they would play out in a downturn or recession and for smaller firms. We think it likely that this analysis would be relevant to other situations, countries, economies, and economic climates; however, this would be pure speculation without further, detailed study. That said, much of the logic of this book is about how points of strategic control and vertical alignment are utilized by small and large firms alike, in the United States and abroad (e.g., Alibaba and Tencent in China and Tata in India). So, although this chapter focuses only on how these concepts relate to the financial performance of U.S. firms during a period of economic growth, we still believe that the concepts do apply universally in today's global markets.

Lessons for First Movers – Sources of Advantages and Disadvantages via Strategic Control

While much has been written about "first-mover advantages," there is an important distinction to be made here. When first movers are in product areas where attributes and features can be easily imitated, this may actually lead to a strategic disadvantage, since rivals may subsequently enter the market with improved and/or lower-cost alternatives or imitated attributes. Conversely, when firms can move first and secure critical *strategic control points* (e.g., the pumps for Softsoap®), they can potentially attain long-term strategic gains, since these gains can be protected. Thus, first-mover advantages are generally considerably stronger with respect to *strategic control points* versus attributes.

> *Business Lesson: First-mover advantages involving product attributes are generally fleeting, since the attributes can often be replicated and imitated. On the other hand, a first-mover advantage that involves securing a point of strategic control is sustainable and often long-lasting by definition. Thus, always try to move first on points of strategic control, and be wary of any advantages gained on offering attributes alone.*

There are exceptions, of course. Certain attributes can be protected and thus can potentially be a source of long-term and sustainable competitive advantage. For example, in order to achieve superior fuel efficiency, Boeing developed longer wings on its new plane (the "777-X"), which can't fit between planes at gates at airports. Its solution? Folding wingtips, which make the planes 28 percent more fuel efficient than competitors' planes (vis-à-vis the longer wings) while allowing the planes to fit in airport gates. It will take competitors from five to ten years to incorporate such a design into their products. In agrichemicals, one ingenious company had the idea to put green dye in the chemical used to treat lawns and golf courses – as a visible "sign" that the product was "working." Customers loved it and *perceived* it to be better at controlling the weeds that made lawns unsightly (even though it made absolutely no difference to the efficacy of the product). It would take competitors from three to five years to develop competitive products (i.e., with a comparable green dye), since even inert ingredients require regulatory approval for "labeling." Thus, the first mover had a sustainable advantage in the interim.

These are exceptions, however; most attribute-based advantages can be imitated, replicated, or even made better. Thus, you must determine what you can defend versus what are more typical attributes that competitors can copy. For example, the mapping industries (e.g., paper, digital, aviation, marine, land, online, and mobile) illustrate the fast-moving pace of today's markets and how first-mover advantages that are created by owning points of strategic control work better than advantages based on product features or attributes. Although the battle for maps has been dramatic and far-reaching, and has involved a myriad of players (e.g., Rand McNally, Garmin, TomTom, NavTech, MapQuest, Google, and Apple), probably the most visible mapping battle has been between Apple Maps and Google Maps on the mobile platforms (Apple's iOS in particular), so that is the focus of the present discussion.

The Battle for Maps Isn't about Maps

Imagine the following: you are about to embark on a journey from your home address to a place you haven't been before. How do you figure out how to get there? In the "old days" (i.e., before about

2005), you would consult your handy Rand McNally atlas, write down the preferred route on a piece of paper, and you were on your way.[5] By July 2006, MapQuest (then a division of AOL, now a division of Verizon Media) had launched its beta version of an online tool that would allow you to "build your route," so you could go online and plan each portion of your route, print it out, and then follow the printed page throughout your journey – hoping that traffic was clear during that time of day.

At around the same time that this service was being launched, Google was acquiring Where 2 Technologies, a small mapping-related start-up co-founded by two Danish brothers, Lars and Jens Rasmussen. Building on this acquisition, Google launched Google Maps in June 2005 with U.S. road maps and then followed with integrated Google Earth and Satellite imagery in January 2006. Google Traffic was integrated into the maps in February 2007, and "Street View" was added in May 2007. Much of this was happening behind the scenes with few of us really noticing.

The launch of the iPhone, the iPad, the Android operating system, and digital maps with turn-by-turn navigation integrated into other third-party apps began a heated rivalry for an entirely free mapping service. From the time of the launch of the first-generation iPhone (on 29 June 2007) until 18 September 2012, mobile applications, through both Apple's iOS and Google's Android operating systems, used Google Maps for turn-by-turn navigation by employing GPS location-based services. However, Apple replaced Google Maps with Apple Maps as the default mapping system integrated in Apple (iOS) devices on 19 September 2012. On 13 December 2012, Google Maps was re-launched inside the Apple platform as a standalone app, although Apple Maps remained the default application for all other key apps.

---

5 These histories of MapQuest, Google Maps, and others were taken from the companies' websites and supplemented by the author's recollection (i.e., most of us remember driving with one hand and holding a MapQuest route path printed on a piece of paper in the other hand).

Concurrently, a small Israeli start-up, Waze Mobile, had introduced a free mobile map app that contained innovative, "community-driven" features. Originally launched as "FreeMap Israel" in 2006, it expanded to the United States and contained innovative features that allowed users to report accidents, traffic jams, and speed and police traps and identify the cheapest nearby fuel stations. In June 2013, Google purchased Waze for $1.1 billion, adding the crowdsourced, community-driven features of Waze to their existing maps.[6] Thus, the "old" days (i.e., six to seven years ago) of paper maps are an ancient memory; now the "market" is focused on *free* maps with integrated navigation, directions, and local "crowdsourced" information, and the battle is now not just about travel routing but also about indoor mapping and promotional planning.

But, you may wonder, why would Apple spend so much development time competing with behemoth incumbents (e.g., Google and MapQuest)? Why are companies like Apple and Google so obsessed with winning the exceedingly expensive battle to give away *free* digital map applications?

Before 2010, Apple faced a difficult dilemma that had nothing to do with maps but had everything to do with maps. Specifically, the online environment was being driven more and more by location-based *mobile* advertising revenue (versus traditional desktop and search-based advertising). For example, Google has been increasingly pushing advertisements within all mobile apps in order to diversify its ad revenue stream, as traditional search and desktop advertising prices and revenue growth fall.[7] Both Google and Apple knew that the future of revenue for mobile applications was correlated with location-based services that Yelp, OpenTable, and others need in order to bring their offerings to market. Furthermore, if you

---

6   Source of the background information on Waze: https://en.wikipedia.org/wiki/Waze.
7   See Tony Danova, "Google Maps Is Losing iOS Users in the US," *Business Insider*, 12 November 2013: http://www.businessinsider.com/apple-maps-is-catching-up-to-google-maps-in-the-us-2013-11#ixzz2mFI8JWeO.

allow your map to access your locational "geo tag" (i.e., where you are), as the vast majority of us do, your map provider knows where you are and how fast you're going. This type of information is often quite valuable, as noted by the aforementioned insurance executive from Latin America (see the introduction).

Apple, like Google, has recognized that the future is about (i) information (e.g., where you are, what you are doing, how fast you are going, and what you are buying) as *the* point of strategic control that can be used to acquire mobile-based advertising revenue, and (ii) aligning incentives with players in this space. So, the search for a local hardware store on an Apple iOS device (e.g., via an app like Yelp) will ultimately lead to an integrated iOS maps program (i.e., Apple or Google Maps). This map contains a myriad of advertising opportunities and locational information (e.g., subscriber movements and actions), which are huge revenue sources. Thus, if one firm can harness the power of any app using locational data by offering a popular mapping service, they have a huge strategic advantage in the battle for the information coming off your smartphone.

Utilization of principles in this chapter leads us to address the following two questions:

1 *What is the strategic control point for mobile-based data?* The valuable item is the data. When a firm owns access to such data, the revenue opportunities are almost limitless. Here, we suggest that there are two important points of data access control that we should focus on: the connection and the map. Currently, connection is fragmented. On your smartphone, you can connect in numerous ways (e.g., through various Wi-Fi hotspots and cellular carriers); however, only the map is common to every application on the planet. Own the map and you own access to virtually all of the data coming off the phone. This is why the battle for maps has been so fierce; this is reminiscent of when

Rand McNally locked up the distribution of paper maps in gas stations, 7-Elevens, and Kmarts back in the day. Today, however, the control of "distribution" is very, very different. Good companies get this.

2 *What is the point of aligned incentives?* Note that if Apple Maps was the only integrated map in the apps on iOS devices, the incentives are aligned, since the objective is for the customer to use the app in a user-friendly, seamless fashion. This would be true regardless of the map (i.e., Apple or Google) that is integrated; however, the winner of the battle for default integration also wins the war. Hence, the *strategic control point* is key, and aligned incentives enable the point of strategic control to work effectively. By integrating Apple Maps, Apple tried to move its model into the "Don't Quit Your Day Job" category (the bottom right in figure 7.1), which is an area rich in revenue opportunities that are growing exponentially. The problem, of course, is that Apple Maps doesn't work well enough to be effective in this market. In any market, if your offering doesn't work – or isn't competitive – nothing else matters.

So, let's now look back with "20/20 hindsight" and think of the choices that Apple had available to them during the latter portion of the last decade. We can represent these under the following two broad headings:

Choice A was for Apple to cede the "maps market" to Google and focus on revenue from hardware, software, and its apps store. Google, via various location-based services, would dominate the market for location-based advertising revenue. However, because of Google's penchant for competing on hardware, software (Android OS and Google Play), and in the internet-provision space (through projects like Fiber, and more recently Loon), this could prove disastrous for Apple as Google developed the revenue to dominate across multiple markets (including Apple's core).

Choice B was to compete directly with Google on maps in an attempt to gain a significant share in the mobile-based advertising space. Not only would this add to Apple's ability to compete across multiple markets; it would cut into Google's revenue base as well. This would also give Apple ownership of a key *strategic control point* (i.e., ownership of the maps that are integrated into the operating system and apps on Apple iOS devices), in the same way that Google owns the same point on Google's Android-based platforms.

So, who is winning the revenue-rich, "free" maps, digital mapping market today? Well, let's do the math. In the United States, Google has 185.2 million map users (154.4 for Google Maps, 25.6 million for Waze, and 5.2 million for Google Earth), whereas Apple has a total of 23.3 million map users. Allowing for rounding error, that gives Google approximately an 80 percent market share with Apple at 10 percent, MapQuest at 10 percent, and Yahoo! Maps at 1 percent.[8] The evidence is clear that Google is winning this war across the board. This battle will continue, however, as its importance to information access is pivotal in multiple market opportunities.

The business lesson associated with key strategic control points in these examples is that the future of advertising-based revenue is in location-based mobile applications, which are rich in sponsored advertising and tracking data.[9] The key strategic control point for this revenue source (which depends on location- and customer-based information) is the mapping application that is integrated into the operating system (as the default application), giving the map provider access to critical information coming off the phone. This also

---

8 Source: Verto Analytics, "Most Popular Mapping Apps in the United States as of April 2018, by Monthly Users (in Millions)," *Statista – The Statistics Portal*, Statista: www.statista.com/statistics/865413/most-popular-us-mapping-apps-ranked-by-audience/. Accessed 23 March 2019.

9 This has progressed indoors; retailers are tracking movements and offering location-based promotions as well. See *CBS 17 (WNCN)*, "Some Retailers Tracking Shoppers' Movement Habits": http://www.wncn.com/story/24077303/some-retailers-tracking-shoppers-movements-habits.

aligns the incentive structure of both end users and app developers. Missteps on attributes (e.g., Apple's horrible reviews and the fiasco after its initial Maps launch) can be overcome as long as the strategic control points are in place and the incentives are aligned; conversely, you can have the best attributes in the world (e.g., Google Maps on iOS devices) and if someone else owns the point of strategic control, the attributes won't matter.

> **Bottom Line**: The battle for the maps is really about the battle for mo-
> bile, location-based advertising revenue (illustrating the key points
> raised earlier in this chapter).

This example translates to related industries as well. For example, Rand McNally faced a difficult choice when Patriarch Partners LLC acquired it in a distress sale in 2007. By 2007, the paper maps company had essentially missed the digital revolution in the consumer market (where Google and Apple have been fighting so vigorously). "You have to get one step ahead of everybody else, not redo Google Maps. You tear the company thread by thread and try to find the thread that allows you to leapfrog and innovate," according to Lynn Tilton, head of Patriarch Partners, back in 2009.[10]

Let's step back in time a bit and examine the choices faced by Rand McNally in 2009, shortly after the acquisition:

1 One option the company considered and dismissed was attacking Google Maps (and eventually Apple Maps), MapQuest,
   and others in the consumer mapping and mobile applications
   market head-on by building their own maps app. Why was this
   dismissed? Clearly, Rand McNally had a brand presence and,

---

10 Source: Greg Burns, "Rand McNally Maps a Digital Future," *Chicago Tribune*, 5 October 2009: https://www.chicagotribune.com/news/ct-xpm-2009-10-05-0910040209-story.html.

had they invested heavily in this option in the early 2000s, they might very well have been the winner in this market – one that we've already established was a key *strategic control point* in the market for mobile, location-based advertising spend – a key growth driver in 2014 and beyond. However, in 2009, they were in absolutely no position to compete (and spend) head-to-head against Google and Apple, both of which were flush with cash to defend their market position in maps; this was not a fight Rand McNally could win, no matter how hard they tried.

2 So, if they couldn't realistically win this *strategic control point*, was there another attractive market wherein they already had a brand presence, expertise, a reasonable chance at succeeding, competencies, and a *strategic control point*?

Fortunately, for Rand McNally, there was. They have become the "go to" app for truckers. In the last decade, they have dramatically transformed their business model to focus on location-based information in trucking, fleet management, mileage, routing, and recreational vehicles (RVs). Because of their decision to refocus on fleet management and trucking (e.g., fleet location, mileage, and optimization services), they – in principle – have found a key point of control in these markets, albeit in a smaller niche. If you own the data, you are able to lead in routing and management in trucking and RVs; you can also lead in areas where Google and Apple have no real investment and no significant expertise.

Why is this so important to Apple, Google, Rand McNally, and others – and why isn't it about the maps per se but about the data? For the truck driver, location, revenue-generating deals, ads, restaurants, truck stops, and other local information and opportunities pop up on the screen. By owning (or at least leading) in fleet, trucking, and RV opportunities, Rand McNally has put itself in a similar position to that of Google and Apple in iOS and Android platforms – albeit in a much smaller opportunity space.

One could argue that given the situation Rand McNally faced from 2007 to 2009, this was likely the only viable competitive play they could have made. The research discussed earlier in this chapter would suggest that a key to their success in this area will be how well they can align incentives (e.g., truckers, fleet managers, and local merchants catering to these segments). To the extent that they can align incentives, the strategy might actually pay off – and may have been the only smart move available to them. Time will tell if this will be successful; however, recognizing the points of strategic control and aligning incentives are key points to recognize above all else. After all, the battle for the maps isn't about the maps.

In figure 7.2, the lower arrow represents what happened over time to Rand McNally as the market shifted to digital (moving from point 1 to point 2). The upper arrow (from point 2 to point 1) represents the direction that Rand McNally has been attempting to

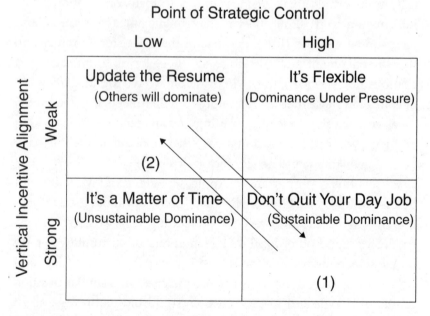

Figure 7.2 The quadrants revisited

achieve today, albeit in a smaller part of the market (i.e., inside the transportation and travel sector). To date, they have been successful in being the "go to" app for truckers in the United States. Moving to dominate in a smaller, niche market is a strategic direction that makes sense for them today.

Based on this example, you can extend the framework to your firm and industry, building on earlier examples:

1 Using the scale presented earlier on strategic control (where 10 means you own the patent or standard [i.e., complete control] and 1 represents a commodity product), rate your current level of strategic control.
2 How aligned are your external partners? Use a 10-point scale where 10 means perfectly aligned (as in the P&G/Walmart example), 1 means "everyone is in it for himself or herself" (i.e., no alignment), and 5 is the midpoint (i.e., between the two extremes).
3 Plot your business on the four-quadrant diagram shown in figure 7.2, and then plot your major competitors on the same diagram. In an ideal world, your business is on the bottom right and your competitors are on the top left (or at least somewhere on the left). If so, you're fine. If not, this can indicate what you need to focus on (as a business).

The example extends to multiple industries.

The pace of transformation cuts across multiple industries. For example, in aerospace, Jeppesen, the leading company in commercial aviation mapping, is replacing reams upon reams of paper (distributed within plane cockpits via pilots) with iPads.[11] For decades, they printed key information (e.g., routes, warnings, and changes in the approach structure) out of their massive facility in Englewood,

---

11 See Susan Carey, "IPads Help Airlines Cast off Costly Load of Paper," *Wall Street Journal*, 27 June 2013: https://www.wsj.com/articles/SB1000142412788732399860455 78567720762762606.

Colorado (just outside of Denver), and, via FedEx, sent the paper plans, routes, and information to pilots for their next route assignments. The sheer scale of this operation created a barrier to entry that made small-scale entry (i.e., competition) nearly impossible. In fact, at one point, they were the largest FedEx printing facility in the world.[12] Jeppesen's move to digital formats – both in aviation and in their marine division – presents both opportunities and dangers. On the one hand, their strategic control is weaker (because of the lack of physical printing scale and distribution); however, Jeppesen may be able to align incentives (e.g., with pilots and local merchants) in much the same way that Rand McNally is doing in the trucking industry (via links to other local businesses, information, and opportunities). In short, the digital revolution has moved them to a more vulnerable position, and unless they can maintain a point of strategic control, others will be lured into the market for revenue (from ancillary services and advertising) – eventually eroding Jeppesen's enviable market share in the aviation market.

There are multiple examples across multiple industries where this process is replicated. Detailed examples include: (i) Amazon's use of its clout (i.e., *strategic control point*) to launch Amazon Local (a local services version of Amazon.com), Amazon Go (if you've ever visited one of its pilot stores, you know how amazing it is), and Whole Foods; (ii) Google's Project Loon (an attempt to secure a point of strategic control for internet provision via low-altitude balloons); (iii) the battle for home automation (e.g., Microsoft's HomeOS versus Google), and the list goes on. Indeed, the convergence revolution has transformed entire industries by lowering the points of strategic control. For example, traditional hotels have lost a key point of strategic control because of the introduction of Airbnb (and similar sites), and taxi companies have lost their point of strategic control (the medallions) through apps such as Uber, among others.

Always know where the points of strategic control are.

---

12 Source: Author visit to company headquarters in Englewood, Colorado.

Chapter 7: Key Foundations and Business Principles

- Successful companies today use both a "carrot" and a "stick" approach to compete effectively in a converging world of interconnected information.
- The "stick" is leveraging points of strategic control and the "carrot" is aligning incentives – both upstream and downstream.
- Understand and map out your "2 × 2" table of position ("Don't Quit Your Day Job," "It's Fixable," "It's a Matter of Time" and "Update the Résumé"). Know where you are and where you need to be. These are key areas to consider, since they will affect the success of your business.
- It is possible to place firms along a continuum (i.e., between the carrot and stick); in fact, evidence from firms in the United States inside the S&P 500 indicates that:
   o 19 percent are high on both strategic control and vertical alignment (categorized as "Don't Quit Your Day Job"), and these firms have the greatest chance of success;
   o 19 percent have high strategic control but relatively weakly aligned external incentives ("It's Fixable"), and their focus should be on aligning vertical incentives to ensure success;
   o 30 percent have low levels of strategic control despite strongly aligned incentive structures ("It's a Matter of Time"), and unless they can find points of strategic control, it's a matter of time before their market position erodes;
   o 32 percent have low levels of strategic control and aligned incentives ("Update the Résumé"); these firms will fail unless both are remedied – and remedied quickly.
- Market advantages associated with strategic control can be sustainable and lasting; however, market advantages associated with product attributes are typically short-lived and fleeting.
- Both points of strategic control *and* vertically aligned incentives are required for sustainable success in today's business environment.

Game Theory, Signaling, and the Strategic Use of Information

How to Use These Concepts Strategically and Anticipate Competitive Response

So far, we have discussed the importance of strategic control points and how points of strategic control and vertical incentive alignment are crucial to success in markets today; however, implementing strategies by utilizing these principles is often easier said than done. Further, and perhaps more importantly, any plan to leverage strategic control points is likely to meet with a response from rivals in the marketplace. Fortunately, we have research, utilizing both mathematical and empirical models in the field of game theory, to guide us.

In emphasizing why you should be concerned not only about the "static" strategy of the carrot and the stick but also the "dynamic" strategy that incorporates competitive and market response over time, one of the more compelling stories is that of a consulting client of mine. In 2015, I was working with a company that was looking to obtain board approval for a brilliant strategy designed to steal share from rivals in what is essentially a zero-sum slow-growth market. The company's board, which included the renowned business gurus Jack Welch and A.G. Lafley, pushed back. At a board meeting seeking board approval for this new strategy, the company's CEO was asked, "Surely, any strategy designed to steal share from rivals will

知己知彼，百战不殆；不知彼而知己，一胜一负；不知彼，不知己，每战必殆

From the wisdom of Sun Tzu: if you know
yourself as well as your enemy, you will
fight a hundred battles and win them all;
if you only know yourself but not your enemy,
you will have one victory and one defeat;
if you know neither your enemy nor yourself,
you will lose all of your battles.

Figure 8.1 "The Stone Boat": The wisdom of Sun Tzu[1]

generate competitive response. Have you 'gamed out' this competitive response?" The leadership team had not – and based on this astute pushback by the board, we worked through a detailed game theory exercise in just over four months. At that stage, armed with a game plan based on competitive response, the team went back to the board and secured approval for their strategic plan. This strategy generated a 27 percent growth in revenue one year after implementation – inside of what was a relatively static and slow-growth market segment. It's important to realize that the best-laid plans may not succeed if the competitive environment is such that you will be fought tooth and nail. Be ready and prepared. That is the idea behind the wisdom of Sun Tzu (quoted in figure 8.1) and what this chapter is about.

This is particularly true in today's markets. Rita McGrath, in *The End of Competitive Advantage*,[2] argues that, given how fast markets move today, competitive advantage is "transient." In contrast, this book has argued that finding and securing points of strategic control is a key way to prolong competitive advantage and keep

---

1   Translation by Linda Jin. Photo by William Putsis.
2   Rita Gunther McGrath, *The End of Competitive Advantage: How to Keep Your Strategy Moving as Fast as Your Business* (Boston: Harvard Business Review Press, 2013).

competitors at bay: when you use strategic control points to stay ahead of competitors in markets that are indeed transient, you can generate unique competitive advantages.

In the 1990s, Adam Brandenburger and Barry Nalebuff argued that "cooperating" with competitors and suppliers can analogously provide unique competitive advantages in many markets.[3] As we saw earlier in the banking and "Fintech" example, this is a double-edged sword. On the one hand, cooperating has unique and distinct advantages. On the other hand, those initiating the cooperation (e.g., banks and "peer-to-peer" lending) do so only when it is to their own advantage. Although a strategy of cooperation fits neatly into the framework of this book, it should be used with caution. Game theory can help guide us in this respect.

The Halley's Comet Effect

All comets, including Halley's Comet, contain a center – a nucleus – that is usually only a few kilometers in diameter and is composed primarily of rocks and ice. What is less well known is that most comets actually have two tails, one of which is usually much brighter than the other. The tails form as a result of the sun's solar wind – the stream of charged particles that emanate from the sun. The solar wind dislodges gas and dust from the comet and forces the material into very narrow (relative to their length) tails.

In business, we often compete (or end up) in the part of the market that is the metaphorical equivalent of a comet's tail. We prepare our strategies for current market conditions and relative to the positions of our competitors; however, by the time we put these strategies and tactics into place, the market and our competitors have moved on,

---

3 Adam M. Brandenburger and Barry J. Nalebuff, *Co-opetition: A Revolution Mindset That Combines Competition and Cooperation: The Game Theory Strategy That's Changing the Game of Business* (New York: Doubleday, 1996).

and we end up one step behind – in the market's metaphorical tail. We then try to adjust, reacting to the new market equilibrium. By the time we respond anew, the market has moved again, and we are once again in the market's "tail." And so it goes. Over and over. The proverbial "Halley's Comet effect."

How do we stay at least one step *ahead* of the competition? How do we avoid remaining in the market's tail, chasing a continually moving target? This chapter focuses on the use of a structured and disciplined approach for (i) establishing priorities, (ii) becoming more competitive, (iii) meeting customer needs profitably, and (iv) managing competition rather than just reacting to it. Tools and approaches are available to us that can be used in concert to avoid the Halley's Comet effect – enabling us to always be ahead of our competition, customers, and market trends.[4]

The Story of the Girl on the Wing[5]

In a classic episode ("Nightmare at 20,000 Feet") of Rod Serling's *Twilight Zone*, Bob Wilson (played by a very young William Shatner) is on his first flight since his nervous breakdown six months earlier. At 20,000 feet, he repeatedly sees a creature on the wing, but whenever he points the creature out to someone else (his wife, the flight crew, fellow passengers), the creature has jumped out of sight. When the creature starts to tamper with the plane's wing and wiring, he grows increasingly concerned for the plane's safety. What should he do? If he ignores the creature, the plane might crash. If he

---

4 Interestingly, it turns out that the comet's tail always points away from the sun, which can produce a counter-intuitive event – when the comet is traveling away from the sun, the tail also faces away, so the comet is, in effect, following its own tail. Game theory, a concept underlying much of this book, enables us to know how to be in front of the comet (read: market) and when to lead in order to influence our competitor's actions.

5 Many of you have seen and can recall this classic episode; the summary here comes from seeing the episode countless times: somehow, the ending is so chilling that it never loses its impact no matter how many times you've seen it.

continues to go on about a creature no one else has seen, he might likely end up back in the sanitarium. What would you do?

If you've seen the episode, you may recall that he steals a sleeping policeman's handgun (it truly was a different time back then, before 9/11 and Transport Security Administration pre-flight checks) and proceeds to open the exit door and successfully shoot the creature. Since no one else has seen the creature, the end result is that Bob is taken off the plane in a straitjacket, back to the sanitarium, since for sure he was having yet another breakdown.

Spoiler alert: in case you haven't seen the classic episode and plan to as a result of this narrative, the twist at the end is about to be revealed.

At the end of the episode, as Bob is being carted off to the sanitarium in a straitjacket, the camera zooms in on the wing to reveal the damage done to the wing and wiring by the creature. Bob wasn't having a breakdown after all: in fact, he might have just saved everyone on the plane.

That was a Rod Serling fiction; the following account actually happened.

Recently, a very bright – and rambunctious – eight-year-old girl was traveling with her parents on a Boeing 747 from London to New York. They were sitting two rows ahead of me, and the girl was running up and down the aisle, reaching over seats to play with other people's computers and generally creating havoc throughout the cabin. Her mother tried everything to control her – but to no avail. The father sat detached and oblivious to everything that was going on around him, head buried in an academic journal. After about twenty-five minutes of this, however, he had had enough. Kneeling in the aisle, he grabbed the girl by the arm and sternly said, "If you don't behave, I am going to put you out on the wing!"

So, let's examine the decision at hand for this astute young girl. Clearly the mother had little influence; but when the father became involved, the girl had two options: (1) ignore the father and keep on misbehaving; or (2) sit down and be quiet. Her choices are represented in figure 8.2.

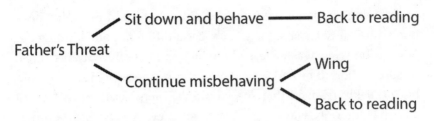

Figure 8.2 Child's decision tree

The girl had to assess the probable outcome of her choice of options. What would the father do if she sat down and behaved? Clearly he would do nothing except go back to his reading; but she wouldn't get to do what she wanted, namely wreak havoc on the rest of the passengers! On the other hand, if she continued, she would have to consider whether her father would follow through on his threat of putting her on the wing. She was a smart girl – it was clear he wasn't going to follow through and put her out on the wing. Any eight-year-old child would realize that this is simply not a *credible threat*. Consequently, she continued to misbehave (much to the dismay of the other passengers), and the father went back to his reading. Smart girl.

Backward Induction and Tactical Moves

What the story illustrates is the power of backward induction – logic forward and reason backward. When we are faced with a strategic choice, we can use logic to play out all of the alternatives and work through the logical outcomes and responses related to each. This enables us to identify the most desirable outcomes. We can then choose the actions that lead to the most favorable outcomes and monitor the process so that we stay on the correct path. The first part requires the use of decision trees; the second part can be played out via a tool called "Bayesian updating."

In the case of the little girl, she knew the outcome she wanted (continuing to misbehave). She quickly realized that she wouldn't end up on the wing no matter what she did. But what could the father have done differently to have the girl choose a different path? Putting her out on the wing wasn't feasible, which is precisely why his threat wasn't credible; if he had played out the girl's decision tree, he would have quickly realized that she wouldn't listen based on this threat and that the only way to get her to sit down would have been to incentivize her – either positively or negatively. For example, he could have threatened to withhold her allowance for a week (and then follow through); he could have purchased an interesting movie for her to watch on the plane's inflight entertainment system; or he could have suggested anything else that was (a) credible and (b) provided the proper incentive to move to the "right" path on the decision tree. Clearly, however, he wasn't playing the game from *her* perspective.

Chess or Checkers Anyone? Sequential Games Involving Asymmetric Imperfect Information

We can use this same set of principles to analyze the logic of competitive moves in business – as we do when playing chess or checkers. Think about a contemplated price cut, impending capacity decisions (e.g., whether to build a plant, renovate an existing one, or take one offline), a potential acquisition, or a whole host of strategic decisions you might be considering for your business. Now, think back to the little girl on the plane. Imagine drawing a decision tree for your business and following these guidelines:

- List the set of potential options available to your business for the strategic issue at hand. Be complete.
- Draw one branch of a tree for each potential strategic move; each branch will represent one available option.
- One at a time, list the set of options available for each of your competitors for *each* branch of the tree you just drew. Imagine

you actually did what was listed on each branch in turn – what is the complete set of feasible responses by rivals? Note that the tree is getting increasingly complex.

- For each and every branch, assess the outcomes for your firm – how good or bad would this be if the sequence of moves (first yours and then theirs) were actually to happen?

- Pick the best branches for your firm. What are the common elements of a "good" outcome? Is there a common first step? Are some of the outcomes particularly bad for your firm? If so, can you limit the likelihood of these bad outcomes by NOT doing the first step that leads to that bad outcome (by moving first, picking the strategic option for your firm first)? You can essentially take the bad outcomes "off the table" by choosing first, but this requires some work and forethought.

Decision trees can become very complex. For example, (i) probabilities and weights can be added to each branch; (ii) an outcome assessment (beyond simple "good" or "bad") can be done for each final branch; (iii) simulations (e.g., Monte Carlo analysis) and probability distributions can be placed on each note and branch; and (iv) software programs (ranging from simple to complex) can aid in the analysis. Regardless of the sophistication and complexity of the analysis, decision trees share a common principle: logic forward and reason backward. We use logic to draw a comprehensive set of branches for a decision tree; thus, whether you use complex computer programs, a large whiteboard, or simple paper and pencil, the process is the same – "logic" all the sets of possible alternatives. Be comprehensive and complete. Once this is done, pick the outcomes that are desirable and then reason backward to initial actions that can maximize the likelihood of the best outcomes for your firm. Let this guide your initial actions. No matter how complicated or simple, the principles are the same.

For any of you who have played a game of chess or checkers, you already apply this process to the game. You can choose a current move to maximize the likelihood of a favorable end result when you think several moves ahead (i.e., for a current set of strategic alternatives) and reason backward. If you understand chess and/or checkers, applying decision trees to sequential games is something that should be quite intuitive. In addition:

- We can update the moves over time – as events unfold, we can remove (or sometimes add) branches, depending upon what is happening. We can even adjust the outcomes and probabilities as a result. This is a process that, when conducted more formally using certain principles, is known as Bayesian updating.
- We can use different metrics to guide what the outcomes will look like (e.g., in terms of our sales, market share, and profits). We can integrate this information into a comprehensive model of choice for each branch.
- We can bring in competitive responses and, at each node, assess the best and optimal rival response to get a more precise sense of likely rival actions. For example, for those familiar with simulations and Monte Carlo analysis, we can use such techniques to better gauge the likely probabilities across the branches.

From this, a complex and rich analysis of the competitive space can be detailed in such a way that no market outcome comes as a surprise and you can choose your initial actions to influence both your competitors and market outcomes. The order of actions matters; you need a structured approach to ensure that the order unfolds to your advantage.

Let's think about the complex decision-making processes for a modern-day manufacturer selling through a channel. A firm needs to think about optimal tactical decisions based upon the market's total or *net* response. Furthermore, typically tactical (e.g., pricing, promotion, and communication) decisions are made within the channel; however, actual buying behavior is determined at

point-of-sale (POS) based, in part, on the "pass-through" from manufacturer to end users through the "waterfall" of decisions along
the channel. The complex, interconnected set of moves, reactions,
and equilibrium can be understood and influenced through such
things as game theory, choice analysis, pass-through metrics, decision optimization, and Bayesian updating. Using knowledge from
a these fields, we can now formalize strategic and tactical decisions.

The key is the importance of order. Order matters.

Order Matters. Setting the Game to Incentivize Your Rival to Do What's in Your Best Interest (conditional optimality is not the same as unconditional optimality)

Game theory is, if used strategically, setting the game to be played to
your advantage – getting your rivals to do what is in *your* best interest by *incentivizing* them to do what's in your best interest. Thus,
order matters – taking advantage of conditional (versus unconditional) decision heuristics is crucial to understanding how game
theory can make a difference in strategic decisions.

To illustrate, imagine a hypothetical competition between two
companies. Let's call them Company Avocado and Company
Paraná.[6] They are both focused on producing the next generation of
tablet devices, and they are deciding between producing a 10-inch or
a 7½-inch screen (assume that they each can only produce one size
of screen). We can represent the relative profits achieved by the two
firms as a result of their choice of which screen to produce through
something called a "payout matrix" (figure 8.3), where X\Y in each
of the four quadrants in figure 8.3 denote the "payouts" (here in

---

6 This example is a classic one, originally presented in somewhat different form by
Avinash Dixit and Barry J. Nalebuff, in *Thinking Strategically: The Competitive Edge in
Business, Politics and Everyday Life* (New York: W.W. Norton & Company, 1993).

An Example
Understanding the Competitive Game

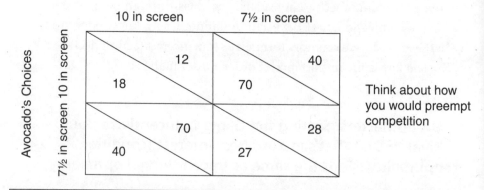

Paraná's Choices

Nash Equilibrium Strategy: A strategy pair (X, Y) is an equilibrium if each player has no incentive to change.

Figure 8.3 An example: Understanding the competitive game

profits) for Company Avocado and Company Paraná, respectively. As an example, if both companies choose to produce a 10-inch screen, the figure shows that Company Avocado would earn $18 million in profits and Company Paraná would earn $12 million in profits; or, if Company Avocado decides to produce a 7½-inch screen and Company Paraná decides to produce a 10-inch screen, then Company Avocado will earn $40 million in profits and Company Paraná will earn $70 million in profits. The same logic applies to the remaining two boxes in the payout matrix.

Simultaneous outcome. If both companies decide which screen size to produce at the same time, the best outcome for each firm would be a profit of $70 million. For Company Avocado, this means producing a device with a 10-inch screen, hoping that the other company chooses to make a device with a 7½-inch screen. Conversely, for Company

Paraná, this also means producing a device with a 10-inch screen and hoping the other company makes a device with a smaller screen.

Hence, if the game were played simultaneously, each firm would produce a device with a 10-inch screen. If this were to happen, Company Avocado would earn $18 million and Company Paraná would earn $12 million. That is, if each company acts according to its own best interest, both firms do not end up with optimal profits. In fact, both companies end up in the least attractive quadrant.

If you're Avocado, how can you do better? The best outcome for Company Avocado is to produce a 10-inch screen with Company Paraná producing a 7½ inch screen. Here, Company Avocado would earn $70 million and Company Paraná $40 million. So, if you're Company Avocado, how do you get Company Paraná to produce a 7½ inch screen? Do you call up their CEO and say, "It's better for us if you make a 7½-inch screen, and so can you please do so?" Aside from antitrust reasons why you couldn't/shouldn't do that, the CEO certainly wouldn't oblige simply because it's in your best interest and because you asked!

The answer is that order matters. Going first turns a simultaneous game into a sequential one – you can choose your initial move in a way that alters the incentive of your rival to your advantage. Imagine that Company Avocado chooses first and recognizes that its choice will affect how Company Paraná reacts. If Company Avocado goes first, what should they do?

In order to answer this, we "unravel" the game as shown in figure 8.4 (where each pair X, Y represents the profits of Avocado and Paraná, respectively).

If Company Avocado were to commit to producing a 10-inch screen first (the circle in figure 8.4), we end up in a new equilibrium whereby Company Avocado ends up with its desired outcome (with $70 billion in profits, denoted by the arrow in figure 8.4). Think about it this way: by going first, Company Avocado has eliminated the entire right-hand side of the tree diagram, as shown in figure 8.5.

Solving the Game
An Unraveled Game

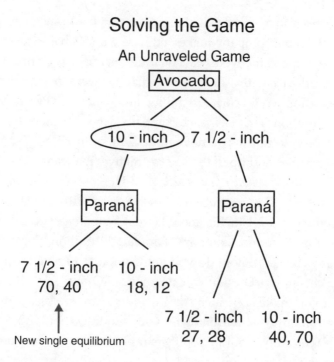

Figure 8.4 Solving the game: An unraveled game, part 1

After Company Avocado announces it will be producing a 10-inch screen, the only two choices left for Company Paraná (see the branches in figure 8.5) would result in either $40 billion in profits (if they produce the 7½-inch screen) or $12 billion (if they produce the 10-inch screen). What would you rather have if you are Company Paraná, profits of $40 billion (by producing the 7½-inch screen) or $12 billion (by producing the 10-inch screen)? The choice is clear. By "unraveling" the game and going first, Avocado has ended up with the outcome that it wants – producing a 10-inch screen – with its rival, Company Paraná, voluntarily choosing to produce a 7½-inch screen.

Solving the Game

An Unraveled Game

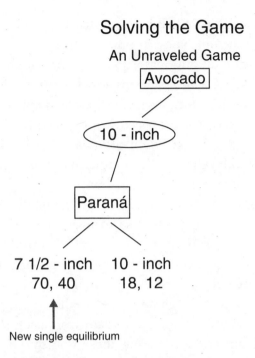

Figure 8.5 Solving the game: An unraveled game, part 2

The key here is that Company Paraná's "unconditional" (in the original, *simultaneous* game) choice is very different from its choice of which screen to produce *conditional* on Company Avocado's preemptive decision to produce a 10-inch screen. Essentially, by choosing first, Company Avocado has eliminated the entire right-hand side of the tree diagram (the only side with a potential bad outcome for Avocado). In short, Avocado moved first to eliminate their potential bad outcome.

If Company Avocado had simply waited for Company Paraná to choose first, it would not have controlled the market outcome to its advantage; in fact, by committing first, Company Avocado has forced Company Paraná's hand to its own advantage.

In reality. Finally, note that in this stylized example, we assumed that we knew the outcomes; in practice, however, we can't know these outcomes with any reasonable certainty in advance. However, we may know which is the preferred versus the less desirable outcome. Hence, in reality, instead of specific numbers in a payout matrix like the one just described, we might use a sliding "heat scale" that can vary from bright red (really bad) to bright green (really good), with yellow in the middle, allowing for a continuum of (subjective) outcomes in each quadrant.

In practice, I have worked numerous "game theory" sessions with various clients (e.g., Owens Corning, World Kitchen, Globe Union, and others), with each session mirroring the stylized example above. In these sessions, companies begin by simply listing (in some detail) all of the potential strategic options available to them. They then "game out" all of the potential sequences of competitive moves that could result from each of the potential strategic options, evaluating these one by one (with subjective probabilities for those moves). From this, they evaluate the outcome of each sequence (good or bad, typically using the sliding heat scale to evaluate the attractiveness of the outcome). They then identify their initial strategic move that eliminates all of the bad outcomes and try to select the options that result in the best outcome, as in the stylized example described for Company Avocado.

Order Matters. Use It to Your Advantage.

A real-life example of this played out in practice in the aviation industry as the major players struggled in the 1990s with the decision to build big versus small. The result of this strategic game was Boeing's decision to produce what is now known at the 787 "Dreamliner" and Airbus's decision to produce the A380. The 787, a smaller, more fuel-efficient plane, was designed to be efficient in "point-to-point" routes, carrying 200-plus passengers and generating fuel savings of approximately 20 percent because of its lighter-weight, all-composite design. By contrast, the A380, carrying from 500 to 900-plus passengers, was designed for long-haul, "hub-to-hub" routes.[7] The history, as it played out, wasn't unlike the stylized story told above:

- In January 1993, Boeing announced a consortium to build a "Very Large Commercial Transport" or "VLCT."
- In June 1994, Airbus responded by announcing a commitment to build an "A3XX" as an answer to Boeing's new large aircraft successor to the 747. The A3XX eventually became the Airbus A380.
- Shortly after Airbus staked its reputation on building the A380, Boeing announced plans to "drop the VLCT" in January 1995. Note that this happened only after Airbus's commitment to build the A3XX.

Meanwhile, Boeing's commitments signaled a very different strategy than Airbus's super large "bus in the sky":

- Boeing's interest in producing a "sonic cruiser" – with speeds near the speed of sound (Mach 0.98) – was proposed in 2001, at about the same time that Airbus broke ground on the A380.
- The 787, originally the "7E7," was announced in January 2003; the focus was on its smaller size (210 to 290 passengers), reduction in fuel consumption (by 20 percent), composite

---

7 Specifically, the 787–8 was designed for approximately 210 passengers in a three-class configuration, and the 787–9 was designed for 250 to 290 passengers. The A380–800 was designed to carry 555 passengers in a three-class configuration and up to 850 passengers in a configuration that had only one class of service: economy. The A380–900 "stretch" was designed for between 650 and 950 passengers. Source: internal Boeing.

construction, lower humidity levels in the cabin, larger windows, and overall advanced technologies.

- The 7E7 was renamed the 787 "Dreamliner" in July 2005 as a result of a global contest started online (in July 2003). The first firm order was in 2003, and there were more than 500 orders in mid-2006. The A380 was certified in February 2006.
- The 787 Dreamliner was rolled out in a public unveiling on 8 July 2007 with 677 firm orders (and the first delivery to ANA in September 2011).

By most accounts, the Boeing 787 has been the most successful product in aviation history. Its success began with Boeing's announcement of a decision to build and fund a "VLCT," which pushed Airbus to beat Boeing to market. Push your competitor to where you want them, so that you can do what you really wanted to do all along. Brilliant. By contrast, in 2019, Airbus announced that they would stop manufacturing A380s, admitting stunning defeat. The origins of this outcome were set by the game being played in the 1990s.

In short, order matters.

In a similar vein, big box retailers like Home Depot can be quite effective with pitting suppliers against each other. The retailer creates "line reviews" whereby competing suppliers are invited, in real time, to compete on price. Home Depot, Lowe's, and other firms know that the minute they get multiple suppliers competing against each other in the same location – or in real time online – they have already won. The trick for a supplier is to compete ahead of time (so that the decisions have already been made beforehand); the "trick" for the buyer is to force real-time competition (i.e., a "simultaneous game" across rival suppliers). If you are a buyer, you would generally prefer a simultaneous game; if you are a seller, you generally prefer a sequential game, where you go first. Indeed, Mike Thaman, recently retired CEO of Owens Corning, often told his people, "If we get to a line review, we've already lost."

The key for firms, of course, is putting all this together – and forming a coherent strategy. In order to do this, we need the right priorities, set up in a way that incentivizes the competition to do what is in our best interest.

Commitment Matters – Use It to Your Advantage: The Story of Nike, Marathon, a Heart Attack, and the Persians[8]

Do you think U.S. politics is dangerous these days? Well, back in 500 BC, the Persian Empire was the greatest and most powerful of the time. However, in some cases, brains beat brawn. Just ask the Athenians.

In 504 BC, the growth and dominance of the Persian Empire had led the Athenians to reluctantly agree to a protection doctrine with the Persians. However, after the Athenians achieved a clever victory over another local foe, they became emboldened and decided to change their minds and tell the Persians, "We don't need you anymore; we're pulling out from the agreement." This left a bitter taste in the mouth of the Persian ruler, Darius (known as "Darius the Great") – so much so that he had an aide whisper in his ear every night at dinner, "Revenge to the Athenians!" When the Persians went to collect the taxes due under the agreement (that they still recognized), the Athenians killed the collectors and threw their bodies in a well. This further agitated Darius, who then sent an army of 20,000 men to Athens to burn the city to the ground. "Not so fast," said the Athenians.

In the city of Marathon, 10,000 Athenian soldiers met the Persian army, and the Athenian general wisely and strategically surrounded them in a valley. In the first known executed "pincer" movement, the army from Athens killed more than half of the Persian army's

---

8 Source: History Channel *Barbarians* series.

20,000 men, while only suffering 198 deaths. (The names of these 198 are inscribed in the Parthenon in Athens to this very day.)

This huge victory led the Athenian general to send a messenger to Athens, 26 miles away to declare victory. Many runners today know that this is how the distance of the modern marathon came about: 26 miles and 385 yards (the distance from Marathon to the town square in Athens). What many don't know, however, is that when the runner reached the town square and proclaimed "Nike, Nike" (for the Greek goddess of victory), he dropped dead of an apparent heart attack!

The Persians escaped to their remaining fleet of almost 100 ships and decided to make a beeline for Athens, 62 nautical miles away. The Athenian general then marched his troops to Athens, and when the Persian ships arrived in Athens and saw the troops waiting for them on shore, they decided to retreat back to Persia rather than fight.

This story illustrates two other key tenets of game theory – commitment (in this case, to fight on the part of the Athenian army) and a credible threat – in this case, the Athenian army's readiness to do battle to back up its aggressive posturing. Sometimes having both can force your rival to retreat without so much as a fight. The lessons from all of this include the following:

- Make credible threats – given the defeat at Marathon, the threat that the Athenians would fight to the death was certainly very credible.
- Show commitment – they were there after all!
- Live to fight another day.
- Sometimes the best battle won is the one *not* fought – the power of game theory and credible commitment.

Order matters, commitment needs to be made, and a credible threat needs to be out there in order for you to be taken seriously. As an example, when my son was very young, he quickly learned not to negotiate with me on snacks or cookies. He once asked, "Dad, can

I have four cookies?" I responded, "You can have two." He next tried to compromise by saying, "How about three cookies?" My response was not the one he wanted to hear: "You get one cookie, then." And he got one cookie. The next time I said that he could have two cookies, he said, "Thank you." Credible threats.

Of course, now he's twenty-two years old and does whatever he wants; I have no sway – cookies or otherwise!

Competitive Assessment – Measuring Competitive Response and Residual Demand Elasticities: Marshallian versus Residual Demand Elasticities

A theoretical construct illustrates the importance of "Marshallian" versus "residual" demand elasticities in a practical and business sense. Virtually all the measures of price responsiveness utilized in business today fit under the heading of "Marshallian" elasticities (named after the famous micro-economist Alfred Marshall, who came up with the concept in the 1920s). The concept of a Marshallian demand elasticity is something that you may remember from economics classes – namely, a measure of how responsive quantity demanded is to price (more specifically, the percentage change in quantity demanded divided by the percentage change in price).[9] In the more technical, academic "industrial organization" literature, this is referred to as a "unilateral" price elasticity because it measures "*ceteris paribus*" (holding all other things constant) price responsiveness; thus, it captures the impact of a firm's price change when its competitors leave their prices constant (hence the term "unilateral"). This measure does not consider rival actions; however, it is the form of demand elasticity that is used almost exclusively in business.

---

9 This is technically a "point" elasticity measure, not to be confused with an arc or other related measures.

Enter the concept of "residual" demand elasticity.[10] Residual (sometimes referred to as "partial" or "net") demand elasticities consider competitive responses. You can think of this measure as reflecting the *net* result from a chain of events occurring after a price change and as a measure of what happens after (i.e., net of) a competitive response. To illustrate, imagine, for simplicity, that we have duopoly (i.e., two firms competing in a market), noting that the same process would indeed unfold with multiple competitors. In this duopoly, imagine that Competitor A reduces its price by 10 percent on a key product it is selling. As a result of the price cut, its customers respond, and the demand for its product increases by 15 percent (and revenue increases accordingly).[11] This would suggest a standard "Marshallian demand elasticity" equal to –1.5 (i.e., a 15 percent increase in volume divided by the –10 percent price change). Competitor B sees the price decrease (which may very well have cut into its share); as a result, it decreases its price as well. The percentage change in Competitor B's price, as a result of a given percentage change in Competitor A's price, is known as the "reaction elasticity." In turn, some of Competitor A's customers may see that Competitor B has lowered its price and buy from Competitor B instead (which is called "cross-price demand elasticity").

We can think of the chain of events as follows:

Competitor A decreases its price. Customers react to this price decrease by buying more.
Competitor B reacts by lowering price in response.
Customers react to Competitor B's lowered price.

---

10 These studies generally fit under the heading of "Industrial Organization" in the academic literature, with the topic originally introduced by Baker and Bresnahan: Jonathan B. Baker and Timothy F. Bresnahan, "The Gains from Merger or Collusion in Product-Differentiated Industries," *Journal of Industrial Economics*, 33 (1985): 427–44.
11 A price decrease for a product with elastic demand increases revenue. Think of it this way – revenue is simply price times quantity; if quantity increases by 15 percent with a 10 percent decline in price, then the product of price times quantity (i.e., revenue) must increase.

Table 8.1 Estimated "Marshallian" versus "residual" demand elasticities for national brands versus private label brands across three categories

	Instant Coffee	Canned Soup	Milk
Leading National Brand "Marshallian" Elasticity	−3.03	−1.39	−2.07
Leading National Brand "Residual" Elasticity	−0.12	−0.917	−2.05
Private Label Brand "Marshallian" Elasticity	−0.374	−6.38	−0.942
Private Label Brand "Residual" Elasticity	−0.314	−0.438	−0.878

Ultimately, if we initiate a price decrease as Competitor A, we are concerned with the final or *net* response after this chain of events has concluded (not just the initial reaction of our customers).

Thus, in order to calculate residual demand elasticities, we need to know three things:

1 the regular or "Marshallian" demand elasticity,
2 the competitive "reaction" elasticity, and
3 the "cross-price" demand response.

Think of points 2 and 3 above as "feedback effects" – what happens to Competitor A's demand when Competitor B responds.

In published papers in leading academic journals, we have estimated regular "Marshallian" as well as "residual demand" elasticities using advanced game theory models and advanced econometric estimation techniques for more than 200 fast-moving consumer goods (FMCGs) categories across the United States over a two-year period.[12] The results for three representative categories (i.e., instant coffee, canned soup, and fluid milk) are shown in table 8.1; in the table, we

---

12 William P. Putsis, Jr, and Ravi Dhar, "An Empirical Analysis of the Determinants of Category Expenditure," *Journal of Business Research*, 52 (3) (June 2001): 277–91. See also the elasticities reported in Ronald W. Cotterill, William P. Putsis, Jr, and Ravi Dhar, "Assessing the Competitive Interaction between Private Labels and National Brands," *Journal of Business*, 73 (1) (January 2000): 109–37.

show only the leading national brand and the leading store brand (i.e., a private label) in each category – although results were obtained across multiple brands in each category.

These three categories are chosen, in part, to illustrate the differences we often see across categories. Here, in the canned soup category, there is a substantial difference in the Marshallian (holding all else constant) demand versus residual (net) demand response measure for the leading private label product. In fact, examining the competitive response using a traditional "Marshallian" demand elasticity would lead to an incorrect pricing decision: at first glance, a price cut would generate a large consumer response (vis-à-vis a "Marshallian" demand elasticity of –6.38), but once competitive reaction is accounted for, we realize that it would generate very little net response (a "residual" demand elasticity of –0.438). For a second category (milk), competitive response doesn't matter at all ("residual" and "Marshallian" demand elasticities are almost identical for both national brand products as well as for both private label products). Accordingly, using the Marshallian demand elasticity would be just fine in this case. Unfortunately, differences between the two elasticity measures, holding all else constant (versus net of competitive response), are idiosyncratic to the category; thus, until the estimation is complete, one never knows whether or not there will be differences – or how important the differences will be.

Let's quickly examine the three categories in a bit more detail since each has very different results:

1   *Examining traditional* ceteris paribus *"Marshallian" demand elasticities would lead to erroneous conclusions and pricing decisions for one brand (i.e., the leading national brand) but not for the other (i.e., the leading private label) in one category.* In the instant coffee category, there is a huge difference between the Marshallian and residual demand elasticity for the leading national brand (–3.03 versus –0.12) but not for the leading private label (–0.374 versus –0.314). This

is not atypical (i.e., it is not unusual to see significant differences for one brand in the category but not the other). Sometimes this is because of lack of rivalry and competitive response by competitive brands in the category, and sometimes it can be the result of a lack of cross-brand customer response to rival price changes.

2 *Examining traditional* ceteris paribus *"Marshallian" demand elasticities would lead to erroneous conclusions and pricing decisions across the board.* Take a look at the private label elasticity measures estimated in the canned soup category from the table above (−6.38 Marshallian versus −0.438 residual demand elasticity); had you simply estimated a Marshallian demand elasticity (holding all else constant), you would have concluded that a 10 percent price cut, for example, would produce a whopping 63.8 percent jump in volume – a no-brainer price cut. However, net of competitive response, a 10 percent price cut would only actually have produced a paltry 4.38 percent increase in volume. Clearly, looking at the *ceteris paribus* Marshallian versus net residual demand elasticities can make a huge difference to what you want to do tactically!

3 *Examining traditional* ceteris paribus *"Marshallian" demand elasticities would lead to the same results as the residual demand elasticities in another category.* For example, the −2.07 estimate in the milk category indicates that, for the leading national brand (i.e., in the milk category), the "Marshallian demand elasticity" was −2.07, which suggests that for a given percentage price cut (increase), the demand for milk sold by the leading national brand would increase (decrease) by just over twice that percentage. For example, for a 10 percent price cut, the demand would increase by 20.7 percent, *assuming that nothing else changes ("ceteris paribus")*. In this category, it just so happens that after we examine the chain of events that follows this initial price cut, the net response is almost exactly the same (−2.07 versus −2.05). This may be for one of two reasons – either

competitors didn't respond to price cuts by rivals (which is indeed the case in the category and data studied here) or customers were extremely brand loyal and didn't respond to competitor price moves (i.e., the "cross-price elasticity" was low, which, as it turns out, is not the case here).

Residual elasticities are constructs that are inherently estimable – do not accept simple survey "willingness to pay" (WTP) instruments or even traditional "Marshallian" demand elasticity measures using econometric estimation techniques – we can do better.[13] Accepting even accurate customer willingness to pay or demand sensitivity measures will quite possibly put you in the position of having unreliable, or even wrong, information – getting accurate information about the demand response but missing the key chain of reactions that take place as a result. Again, we can do better. Demand it.

All of this has taken us into the realm of game theory: how do we consider competitive response in our strategic actions? How do we know the competitive "reaction elasticity"? This is where choice theory comes in. We can combine game theory with choice theory in a creative way to address these issues in practice. While much has been written herein about the "big-picture" view of a firm's strategy, the notion of customer insight is a critical skill that every company (big or small, B2B or B2C, local or international) needs to master.

---

13 Examples of studies that provide detailed estimation of this sort include, but are by no means limited to: Cotterill, Putsis, and Dhar, "Assessing the Comparative Interaction"; Barry L. Bayus and William P. Putsis, Jr, "Product Proliferation: An Empirical Analysis of Product Line Determinants and Market Outcomes," *Marketing Science*, 18 (2) (1999): 137–53; Putsis and Dhar "An Empirical Analysis"; Ronald W. Cotterill and William P. Putsis, Jr, "Do Models of Vertical Strategic Interaction for National and Store Brands Meet the Market Test?," *Journal of Retailing*, 77 (1) (Spring 2001): 83–109; and Ronald W. Cotterill and William P. Putsis, Jr, "Market Share and Price-Setting Behavior for Private Labels and National Brands," *Review of Industrial Organization*, 17 (1) (August 2000): 17–39, reprinted in Harry M. Kaiser and Nobuhiro Suzuki, *New Empirical Industrial Organization and the Food System* (New York: Peter Lang Publishing, 2006).

Some Concluding Thoughts: The World Is Changing. Learn from It. Use It to Your Advantage.

Just think of the pocket computer we carry around with us every day – the smartphone. In 2011, Eric Schmidt, the executive chairman of Alphabet, eloquently described convergences associated with the smartphone in a speech in Germany:

> We have a product that allows you to speak to your phone in English and have it come out in the native language of the person you are talking to. To me this is the stuff of science fiction. Imagine a near future where you never forget anything. [Pocket] computers, with your permission, remember everything – where you've been, what you did, who you took pictures of. I used to love getting lost, wandering about without knowing where I was. You can't get lost anymore. You know your position to the foot, and by the way, so do your friends, with your permission. When you travel, you're never lonely. Your friends travel with you now. There is always someone to speak to or send a picture to. You're never bored. You're never out of ideas because all the world's information is at your fingertips. And this is not just for the elite. Historically, these kinds of technologies have been available only to the elites and not to the common man. If there were a trickle down, it would happen over a generation. This is a vision accessible to every person on the planet. We're going to be amazed at how smart and capable all those people are who did not have access to our standard of living, our universities, and our culture. When they come, they are going to teach us things. And they are coming.
>
> There are about a billion smartphones in the world, and in emerging markets the growth rate is much faster than it is anywhere else. I am very excited about this.[14]

---

14 Source: Fred Vogelstein, *Dogfight: How Apple and Google Went to War and Started a Revolution* (New York: Farrar, Straus and Giroux, 2013), 135.

The book you have just read set out the premise that mobile, ubiquitous, always-on information transforms markets with unprecedented speed; furthermore, successful companies today must compete intensely via the utilization of key *strategic control points* to squeeze margins within their own value chains and across other value chains – something we defined as the *competitive ecosystem*. Firms must also find ways to align incentives throughout these interconnected value chains. Game theory teaches us how to do this by thinking ahead and redefining our rival's strategic opportunity set.

Companies that typify these principles are Amazon, Apple, and Google. For each company, success depends not only on the acceptance of their products and services in the marketplace but also on how they exert control throughout their value chains and how they leverage success in one part of a business to extract margins in other parts. Think of the multidimensional brilliance of Jeff Bezos and Steve Jobs. Their obsessive need to control every aspect of their offerings (i.e., to coordinate, control, extract value, and leverage strengths not only within their supply chains but also away from their core businesses) has been a key strategic focus for both companies (e.g., Apple's ecosystem margins and Amazon's ability to extract margins through its Marketplace). As a result, suppliers, assemblers, manufacturers, and customers alike are often aligned with the interests of Amazon and Apple and provide deep, substantive, sustainable, and profitable competitive advantages for both companies. Thus, market success today depends not only on the products you deliver but also on how you deliver them. This is an important theme throughout this book – the motivation behind much of what we see in the strategic decisions that drive successful companies today, and what successful companies like Amazon, Walmart, Procter & Gamble, and Apple know at their cores.

Google – like Apple with the iPhone before it – has also leveraged its core business strength by utilizing the principles of game theory to its advantage. To illustrate, think for a moment about the obsolescence of mobile phones. What if, someday soon, we don't need phones anymore? "Wearables" may replace our phones sooner than we think (e.g., within glasses, fitted contact lenses, or clothing) – with the potential to display weather forecasts, optimal routes (to get you where you want to go most efficiently), calendars, and/or video conferences. This isn't science fiction but reality – complete with patent applications pending for embedding the technology in our contact lenses (brought to us by Google, Samsung, and Sony).[15] This is what we call a paradigm shift – something that Apple mastered during the era of Steve Jobs.

By contrast, Nokia has seen significant market share declines in many of its major markets – in large part because it thought that it was in a handset (rather than an information and convenience) business. By the time it realized that it wasn't, the smartphone revolution had left it in the dust. Ironically, Nokia had actually developed smartphone technology well ahead of the competition; however, it had decided not to take the technology to market – betting instead on the continued growth it was enjoying in the handset market.[16] Growth can be a dangerous drug; it makes it easy to miss all of the warning signs. Good companies such as Apple and Google are relentlessly looking to displace current growth with new avenues of growth. In the past, Apple led the shift to new growth; Google is leading the shift today; and Nokia missed the paradigm shift.

Think ahead, plan ahead, use strategic control, align incentives.

Use the carrot and the stick to your advantage.

---

15 See, e.g., Heather Kelly, "iPhone Photography Is Cool, Eyeball Photography Is Cooler," *CNN.com*, 12 May 2016: http://money.cnn.com/2016/05/12/technology/eyeball-camera-contact-sony/.

16 See Anton Troianovski and Sven Grundberg, "Nokia's Bad Call on Smartphones," *Wall Street Journal*, 18 July 2012: http://online.wsj.com/article/SB10001424052702304388004577531002591315494.html.

Chapter 8: Key Foundations and Business Principles

- Make information analytics a priority.
- Use information strategically.
- Think ahead rather than react – order matters.
- Think about drawing a decision tree for your business following these guidelines:
    - List the set of options for your business, for the strategic issue at hand. Be complete.
    - Draw one branch of a tree for each available option.
    - One at a time, list the set of options available for each of your competitors for each branch of the tree you just drew.
    - For each of this larger set of branches, assess the outcome for your firm – how good or bad would this be?
    - Pick the best branches for your firm. What are the common elements for a "good" outcome? Is it a common first step? Are some of the outcomes particularly bad outcomes for your firm? If so, can you limit the likelihood of those outcomes by picking the best strategic option for your firm first?
- Traditional demand elasticity only assumes a static market. Companies need to establish competitive assessment based on residual demand elasticity, which can be estimated using empirical analysis.
- Empirical analysis is even more important (and complex) in B2B markets, since both horizontal and vertical (such as "pass through") moves need to be considered.
- Demand estimation of residual elasticities and don't accept simple willingness to pay (WTP) measures and surveys; nor should you accept "Marshallian" elasticities without attention to competitive response.
- Require business-case justification for strategic decisions, and mandate financial justification of strategic choices.
- Most importantly, recognize that order matters – the unconditional does not equal the conditional. Use this knowledge to your advantage.

Index

Page numbers in italics refer to figures and tables.